T0357731

HOMESTAND

ALSO BY WILL BARDENWERPER

The Prisoner in His Palace: Saddam Hussein, His American
Guards, and What History Leaves Unsaid

HOMESTAND

*Small Town Baseball and the Fight
for the Soul of America*

Will Bardenwerper

Doubleday
New York

FIRST DOUBLEDAY HARDCOVER EDITION 2025

Copyright © 2025 by Will Bardenwerper

Penguin Random House values and supports copyright. Copyright fuels creativity, encourages diverse voices, promotes free speech, and creates a vibrant culture. Thank you for buying an authorized edition of this book and for complying with copyright laws by not reproducing, scanning, or distributing any part of it in any form without permission. You are supporting writers and allowing Penguin Random House to continue to publish books for every reader. Please note that no part of this book may be used or reproduced in any manner for the purpose of training artificial intelligence technologies or systems.

Published by Doubleday, a division of Penguin Random House LLC, 1745 Broadway, New York, NY 10019.

DOUBLEDAY and the portrayal of an anchor with a dolphin are registered trademarks of Penguin Random House LLC.

Library of Congress Cataloging-in-Publication Data
Names: Bardenwerper, Will, author.
Title: Homestand : small town baseball and the fight for the soul of America / Will Bardenwerper.
Description: First edition. | New York : Doubleday, [2025]
Identifiers: LCCN 2024025067 (print) | LCCN 2024025068 (ebook) |
ISBN 9780385549653 (hardcover) | ISBN 9780385549660 (ebook)
Subjects: LCSH: Minor league baseball—United States—Clubs—History. |
Community life—United States—History. | Country life—United
States—History. | Small cities—Social aspects—United States. | Small cities—
Economic aspects—United States. | Social values—United States. |
United States—Social life and customs. | Bardenwerper, Will.
Classification: LCC GV875.A1 B334 2025 (print) |
LCC GV875.A1 (ebook) | DDC 796.357/640973—dc23/eng/20241119
LC record available at https://lccn.loc.gov/2024025067
LC ebook record available at https://lccn.loc.gov/2024025068

penguinrandomhouse.com | doubleday.com

PRINTED IN THE UNITED STATES OF AMERICA
1 3 5 7 9 10 8 6 4 2
The authorized representative in the EU for product safety and compliance is Penguin Random House Ireland, Morrison Chambers, 32 Nassau Street, Dublin D02 YH68, Ireland, https://eu-contact.penguin.ie.

To my grandparents Herbert and Helen Bates
and my great-aunt Marie O'Shea

"... No, he's a gambler." Gatsby hesitated, then added cooly: "He's the man who fixed the World's Series back in 1919."

"Fixed the World's Series?" I repeated.

The idea staggered me. I remembered, of course, that the World's Series had been fixed in 1919, but if I had thought of it at all I would have thought of it as a thing that merely *happened,* the end of an inevitable chain. It never occurred to me that one man could start to play with the faith of fifty million people—with the single-mindedness of a burglar blowing a safe.

"How did he happen to do that?" I asked after a minute.

"He just saw the opportunity."

— F. Scott Fitzgerald, *The Great Gatsby*

Contents

Dramatis Personae

Robbie and Nellie Nichols—Owners of the Batavia Muckdogs and
   Elmira Pioneers
Barry Powell—Longtime baseball scout and assistant coach of the
   Jamestown Tarp Skunks
Marc Witt—General manager of the Batavia Muckdogs and
   Elmira Pioneers and son-in-law of Robbie and Nellie

Batavia

Guy Allegretto—Decorated Vietnam combat veteran and devoted
   fan of the Batavia Muckdogs
John Carubba—YouTube "Voice of the Muckdogs"
Dr. Ross Fanara—Octogenarian season ticket holder who, along
   with his wife, Shirley, raises two of his great-grandchildren; close
   friends with Guy Allegretto
Dave Fisher—Gulf War veteran and volunteer security guard at
   Dwyer Stadium
Bill Hume—Owner of Foxprowl Collectables
Bill Kauffman—Local author, former Muckdogs board member,
   and longtime season ticket holder
Joe and Sandra Kauffman—Bill's parents; Joe is a former
   Muckdogs batboy who has been going to games since the 1940s

Ernie Lawrence—Musician, hospice volunteer, rosary maker, and
Muckdogs season ticket holder

Joey "Skip" Martinez—Batavia Muckdogs manager

Erik Moscicki—Batavia Muckdogs clubhouse manager

Julian Pichardo—Batavia Muckdogs pitcher and Tampa native

Cathy Preston—Trivia fanatic and Muckdogs season ticket holder
who keeps score at every game

Jerry Reinhart—Batavia Muckdogs infielder/designated hitter,
Batavia native, and local fan favorite

Russ Salway—Muckdogs season ticket holder who used to host
minor leaguers in his basement as part of the host family
program

Paul Spiotta—Muckdogs public address announcer and Strat-O-
Matic baseball enthusiast

Betsey Higgins and Ginny Wagner—Best friends from Buffalo
who attend every Muckdogs game

Eric Zwieg—Fiftysomething graduate student, author, playwright,
Muckdogs fan, obsessive New York Mets fan, and Dwyer
Stadium's resident contrarian

Elmira

Charles Bennett—Former "carny" and member of a small group of
fans who chase foul balls in the Dunn Field parking lot

"Popcorn Bob" Brinks—Longtime popcorn maker at the Dunn
Field concession stand and talented artisan

Herb Tipton—Ninety-three-year-old Korean War veteran who has
been attending Elmira games in the same seat at Dunn Field
since 1973

HOMESTAND

December 2021

I t was dark and cold. A biting wind was gusting in from beyond the left-field fence as Betsey Higgins and Ginny Wagner took their seats. It was a typical December late afternoon in western New York, so the two women, friends of nearly four decades, knew they would need to sit huddled next to each other for warmth on the metal grandstands along the third-base side of Batavia's Dwyer Stadium. Upon learning of a last-minute pre-Christmas team merchandise sale, they'd made the familiar forty-five-minute drive east from their homes in Buffalo to this small former minor league ballpark tucked into a working-class neighborhood not far off the New York State Thruway. It was an easy decision, one that required little convincing on either's part. They were both equally homesick for the place they'd spent countless nights over many summers.

Alas, the merchandise was unimpressive. Betsey bought a knit cap that didn't even fit, knowing she would have felt bad leaving empty-handed. Before they returned home, though, the women had wanted to make one more stop. They asked the lone employee working there on the grim afternoon if they could check out the bleachers. "He must have thought we'd been drinking," Betsey said with a chuckle as she told the story. He waved them through, leaving them to dodge icy puddles en route to their seats. As Batavia Muckdogs season ticket holders, they didn't need directions to their usual spot on the freezing bleachers.

They grimaced as their bodies made contact with the icy grandstand. They were alone. The ballpark was empty. There were no cheerful shouts from young kids giddy to escape the watchful eyes of their parents beneath the bleachers, no packs of teenagers roaming about just as their parents had decades before. Bill Kauffman's unmistakable laugh couldn't be heard drifting down from a few rows above them. Bill's octogenarian parents, Joe and Sandra, weren't sitting nearby, bundled up to protect from the "chill" of a summer night. Cathy Preston wasn't seated behind the dugout dutifully keeping score in a worn notebook; nor was Ernie Lawrence hunched over a few sections beyond them, quietly working to build a rosary. There were no players digging into the batter's box as a mellifluous introduction by public address announcer Paul Spiotta echoed overhead. Team owners Robbie and Nellie Nichols weren't in their usual spot taking orders at the concession stand. There was no savory waft of popcorn and Italian sausage floating around them. Most noticeably, there was no gorgeous sunset beyond the outfield fence. Instead, an oppressive wall of dark clouds seemed to stretch from the edge of Dwyer Stadium all the way to Lake Erie, forty-five miles to the west.

Aside from the Muckdogs, Betsey and Ginny weren't even sports fans. The afternoon, they agreed, was miserable, and they lasted only about five minutes before retreating to the warmth of their car for the ride back home to Buffalo.

They also agreed that—despite the eerie quiet, the ominous clouds, and the bitter cold—it was, for a brief, transcendent moment, "like we were back in heaven."

Introduction

The memory is always the same. My younger brother and I are in my grandparents' backyard. The grass is freshly cut, because I'd have just finished mowing the lawn under my grandfather's watchful eye before dumping some flour onto the ground to mark baselines and batters' boxes. Once the lines were marked, we would have carefully laid out the set of rubber bases our grandfather had bought for us at the nearby sporting goods store, straightening them out just so.

And then we would play. One-on-one baseball, employing imaginary baserunners and fielders, keeping score in a spiral notebook. It was no longer a modest suburban backyard. It was Fenway Park. The Nerf ball line drives caroming off my grandpa's house were striking the Green Monster with a satisfying thump.

Time moved with the languor unique to childhood, fireflies flickering in the summer dusk, my grandfather watching from under a shade tree with a glass of Scotch in his hand. He would occasionally heckle us good-naturedly, his Bronx accent unchanged, despite being many decades removed from "the old neighborhood" where he'd grown up playing stickball over fifty years earlier.

I am now closer to the age my grandfather was then than I am to my younger self, a kid channeling Roger Clemens, blowing fastballs by his hopelessly overmatched younger brother. These days, even the two years I spent playing baseball in college at Princeton have begun to fade in my mind. Yet this memory of my childhood remains pristine, somehow growing even more vivid with the passage of time.

When I was young, those evenings seemed as if they would stretch on forever, the sun suspended just above the horizon, never setting on our happiness.

Only years after the final pitch was thrown toward the upright green wheelbarrow that served as both catcher and strike zone would I realize that the game was over, and that those magical summer evenings with my brother and grandparents were the happiest I would ever be.

*   *   *

On the morning of September 11, 2001, I was at my desk at a Manhattan financial firm. As the planes struck the World Trade Center, we gathered together to watch our CNBC monitors in disbelief. At the time I was only a few years out of college, busy enjoying life as a twentysomething in New York City. But in the days following the attacks, the Excel spreadsheets I busied myself with suddenly seemed unfulfilling. I quit my job with an unfocused but overwhelming desire to serve my country. I would go on to volunteer to spend the next five years serving as an infantry officer in the Army.

My decision to serve was not a rational one. I didn't have a long-term plan; nor was I narcissistic enough to believe that my service alone would have any impact on US foreign policy. Still, as I watched the FDNY and NYPD working tirelessly in the hours and days following the attacks, I couldn't help but be inspired by their selfless service. I wanted to find a way to make my own contribution, however modest. This sentiment was coupled with an even more abstract desire to defend some sort of imagined Norman Rockwell Americana—the iconic scene of Robert Redford playing catch with his son alongside a cornfield in *The Natural* often came to mind—a vision that had always appealed to the romantic in me. This America had, of course, never really existed, yet suddenly felt endangered.

I returned to America after a violent year deployed to Iraq's Anbar Province, my infantry battalion of roughly 650 soldiers suffering high casualties with 16 killed and nearly 200 wounded. Some were my friends. Although I was fortunate enough not to suffer from any of the typical manifestations of PTSD, still, as years passed, I found myself increasingly adrift from, and demoralized by, a country that seemed to be coming apart at the seams. On the macro level there was much to lament, including corrosive politics, widening income inequality, struggling inner cities, and hollowing small towns. More personally, after those many months living as a member of a small tribe who did everything together, I couldn't wrap my head around what the "real" world looked like when I returned, face-to-face, real human interactions increasingly giving way to soulless virtual contact.

But what troubled me the most was the fracturing of community, an erosion of the societal bonds holding us together. This was the loss that seemed to me most likely to threaten the soul of the country. It felt as if we were experiencing a gradual evaporation of the America where people from all walks of life came together over beer and BBQ at the local ballpark. Which was exactly what I'd told myself, however naively, I had been fighting to preserve. With each election cycle, campaign yard signs gradually began to strike me not as healthy signs of a vibrant democracy, but rather as demoralizing reminders of tribal bifurcation. After fighting alongside fellow young Americans taking on a real enemy that was trying to kill us, it was depressing to see how many Americans back home saw the opposing political party as the existential threat that needed to be vanquished by any means necessary.

The idea of community, or the lack thereof, was at the front of my mind when I first learned of Major League Baseball's rumored elimination of forty-two minor league teams scattered in smaller cities and towns across America. This news felt like another damning piece of evidence that the country was moving ever more quickly in the wrong direction. I came across the story on a brisk fall morning in 2019 in a coffee shop not far from the home in Denver that I shared at the time with my wife, Marcy, and young son, Bates (our only child until his sister, Shea, arrived in 2022). According to *Baseball America,* after the completion of the 2020 season, MLB was considering reducing the number of their minor league affiliates from 160 to 120 following the expiration of the Professional Baseball Agreement (PBA) governing their relationship with minor league baseball. They believed they could do this as they negotiated a new PBA simply by not renewing the Player Development Contracts

(PDCs) that established the individual affiliations between major league organizations and the ownership of the minor league franchises they wanted to drop.

A month later the *New York Times* published a list of forty-two teams slated for elimination (along with two independent-league teams likely to be added to the minor leagues). As I read about some of the towns on MLB's chopping block—working-class communities like Pulaski, Virginia; Elizabethton, Tennessee; Bluefield, West Virginia; Williamsport, Pennsylvania; and Batavia, New York—the decision by billionaire major league owners to extinguish these community ball clubs, some of the few remaining places where people could still find happiness and connection, for affordable prices, as they had for generations, merely to save the equivalent of one major league minimum salary, struck me as emblematic of so much of what was wrong with today's America.

Is *this*, I found myself asking, as I had too many times over the years, the set of values we, as a country, were fighting for?

These rumors of minor league "contraction" became a reality prior to the 2021 season. After the 2020 minor league season was canceled due to COVID-19 worries, MLB officially reduced the number of affiliated minor league teams from 160 to 120 before the summer of 2021, entering into new ten-year Professional Development Licenses (PDLs) with those clubs fortunate enough to be spared elimination.

For over a century, minor league ball clubs had provided these small towns with so much more than just baseball, helping anchor communities that were running adrift, buffeted by powerful socioeconomic forces. Industries and factories may have left, but baseball had not. And now the cities and towns that had been stripped of their teams would never even have an opportunity to say goodbye. Meanwhile, private equity vultures had already begun to circle the teams that had thus far escaped MLB's scythe.

The decision to cut so many minor league teams broadly reflected the philosophy espoused by New York Yankees general manager Brian Cashman, who said: "Bottom line is this is big business . . . This should be run like a Wall Street boardroom where you pursue assets. No different than if you're in the oil industry and you want to buy some oil rigs out in the gulf."

But should that be the case? What is baseball? Is it really our

"National Pastime," an enduring slice of Americana, as the powers-that-be have marketed it for decades? Or is it—as the decisions made by MLB's owners and Commissioner Rob Manfred's front office would suggest—just a business, where efficiency and profits drive all decisions? Does an enterprise that purports to be part of the fabric of America have a responsibility to prevent that fabric from fraying?

This isn't just a story about baseball. This is a story about America, and where we go from here. We have long lamented the closing of the mills and factories in these small and midsize cities all over the country. Now the ballpark, that friendly gathering place where relationships are nourished over the course of summers in the grandstands, is under siege. Are we going down the road where MLB simply snuffs out (or private equity buys up, or market forces destroy) the local purveyors of baseball across the country? Many of these places had been on the ropes for a long time. These closures would inevitably result in one fewer place for people to go to enjoy a sense of fraternity in an otherwise increasingly partisan, digitally connected world, a world accelerating toward physical and psychic isolation, seductive screens replacing lively bleachers. I wondered whether this would be the final knockout punch for many of these small communities, who were already struggling too much.

And if that grim future is not what we want for our smaller cities and towns—places like Lowell, Massachusetts; Billings, Montana; and Charleston, West Virginia—indeed, for America itself, where, then, might we find some hope?

Maybe a cure to some of what ails us can be discovered in the stands of Dwyer Stadium in Batavia, New York. Despite being the place where the New York–Penn League had been established in 1939, Batavia (along with most of the rest of what had been the Class A Short Season League) had been stripped of its minor league affiliate. And yet, for now, baseball survived. There, overlooking a lovingly cared-for diamond in a small town of about fifteen thousand in western New York, Batavia Muckdogs fans, young and old alike, those with money and those without, continue to gather on warm summer nights with smiles on their faces. They are supporting a new homegrown team that had recently been established to fill the void left by MLB's decision to shutter their longtime minor league franchise. This new team (though bearing the same Muckdogs name) was composed of college players as opposed to drafted professionals. They played in the same stadium, fighting under new ownership to carry on the rich history binding baseball to Batavia.

Dwyer Stadium is just the kind of place that reminded me of those idyllic evenings playing baseball in my grandparents' backyard, my brother and I stopping to go inside only when it grew too dark to see the yellow Nerf ball. And now even this new team's survival was by no means guaranteed. Batavia itself was at an inflection point: Would baseball, a last bastion of civic pride, endure, or would its collapse hasten the town's slow and seemingly inexorable slide toward senescence, like so many of its Rust Belt neighbors? Would the life of a vibrant community still course through Dwyer's grandstands, a place where the bleachers bend under modern-day forces, but have yet to break?

We all need something to believe in. I recently bought my son, Bates, his first baseball glove. As I began to gently toss the ball to him, the first thing I thought of were those sunset games in my grandparents' backyard. The memory was so vivid, the mental images so immediate, that it felt like my late grandfather might join us at any moment, glass of Glenlivet in hand, poised to toss us the ball with the smooth three-quarters delivery he had once displayed as a semipro second baseman.

At the same time, though, the daydream felt impossibly far, separated not only by the thirty-five years that have passed but also by the profound changes to the way we live. The game of catch with my son seemed as much a sacrament to the past as a vital part of the present, much less representative of a future we could look forward to sharing.

What America would my children live in? I had a feeling that some answers could be discovered in Batavia, through the lens of baseball, possibly the most American thing we have.

And so I shelled out $99 for my own 2022 Batavia Muckdogs season ticket.

I wanted to find out for myself what we, as a country, risked losing, and whether there was any chance it might be saved.

1

The Localist

Winter, 2022

To live in Pittsburgh in winter is to resign yourself to long stretches when the sun is a mere abstraction, a long-distant memory to fantasize about but rarely experience. My first two years here had marked quite an adjustment from Denver's three-hundred-plus annual days of sunshine, a fact I reminded my wife and friends about so frequently that they began sarcastically referring to me as "the weatherman," rolling their eyes at each unsolicited reference to Pittsburgh's endless gray winter pall. Still, as I headed north to Batavia on yet another gloomy day, I knew that I would find even less sympathy there, as I was on my way to the heart of western New York's "snow belt," a region notorious for long, dark winters and epic dumps of snow.

I was making a preseason trip to meet some of the fans who for years, and sometimes decades, had counted visits to Dwyer Stadium as a fixture of summer life. Though Batavia had recently lost its minor league professional baseball team (which had gone by a number of names before becoming the Muckdogs in 1998), to the devastation of generations of fans, a new team had been welcomed with open arms. Longtimers might have been more skeptical of the collegiate newcomers who had set up shop in their beloved stadium, but luckily there was an interesting spin to the familiar narrative of a hardscrabble, blue-collar town being victimized by greedy outsiders—in this case personified by the MLB Commissioner's Office and powerful ownership groups. Thankfully for local baseball fans, a former minor league hockey player from Canada turned hustling entrepreneur, Robbie Nichols, and his wife, Nellie, had approached the city council in the winter of 2021 with a bid to restore competitive baseball to Batavia. They proposed establishing a collegiate summer league team to replace the old Muckdogs, which had been stocked with drafted professionals as an affiliate (most recently) of the Miami Marlins. The new team would bear the same Muckdogs name and compete in the Perfect Game Collegiate Baseball League (PGCBL).

The Nichols were successful owners of the Elmira franchise, which already played in that league, and thus their proposal was quickly accepted. For Robbie, the purchase marked another step forward on the road of sports ownership. The journey had begun when he was twelve years old, on a long drive with his father to a hockey game in his hometown of Hamilton, Ontario. His dad casually asked him what he wanted to do when he grew up, to which Robbie, like so many little boys in Canada, responded, "I wanna be a pro hockey player." His dad, not one for sugar-coating things, responded, "That's a one-in-a-million chance. What's your backup plan?" Robbie thought for a moment before blurting out, "I'll coach hockey." His dad fired back, "That's even harder. There's only one of them for every team." The young Robbie was not to be denied, though. "That's fine, then I'll just buy my own team," he said.

He would eventually make good on that statement, serving as general manager of the Elmira Jackals of the East Coast Hockey League before expanding to baseball and buying the Elmira Pioneers of the PGCBL and ultimately getting clearance to save baseball in Batavia. After receiving city council approval, Robbie and Nellie successfully resurrected the Muckdogs just before the 2021 season.

Robbie had already demonstrated a knack for drawing a crowd, and his teams in Elmira were always among the league leaders in attendance. In the summer of 2021, the inaugural season of the Batavia Muckdogs, his new team would be no different. Local baseball fans would pack city-owned Dwyer Stadium, which opened in 1996, replacing rickety old MacArthur Park, where Batavia's minor league teams had played since 1939. Though the fans were no longer watching professionals take the field, as the rosters were now largely populated by players from small Division I and Division III schools, attendance numbers from this first season even eclipsed some previous summers when drafted professionals had been playing on the same diamond.

Why? What was going on in Batavia?

* * *

In an effort to get some answers, I had to dodge icy puddles as I made my way to join Batavia native Bill Kauffman for a few pints of Guinness at O'Lacy's, a cozy Irish pub tucked away alongside an alley a few blocks off Main Street, about a mile from the ballpark. I would soon discover that Bill is a character in a town full of them, which said a lot. He was also something of a local literary celebrity, having authored several nonfiction books that were prominently displayed in the town's Holland Land Office Museum.

Bill grew up a few blocks from Dwyer Stadium's predecessor, MacArthur Park, and had been a devoted second-generation fan of minor league baseball in Batavia. Bill's father, Joe, was born in 1936 and had grown up in the 1940s and '50s with the stadium as his playground. As a child, Joe had served as a batboy, foul ball shagger, and vendor for the team, selling peanuts, popcorn, and Cracker Jacks for 10 cents, of which he would give 7 cents to the owner and keep 3 cents per sale for himself. More recently, Bill had served on the board of the community-owned minor league franchise. I sipped my Guinness and allowed Bill's contagious enthusiasm, for both Batavia and the importance of the Muckdogs to the local community, to wash over me. The extent of his affection for Batavia and baseball was perhaps offset only by his antipathy toward MLB leadership.

"My contempt for MLB," Bill said, "knows no bounds." He rebelled against what he saw as a small cartel of billionaires paying multi-millionaires to play longer games featuring less action in competitively imbalanced leagues dominated by a few big-market teams. Even as we met, MLB and the Players Association remained locked in an ugly lockout imposed by Commissioner Rob Manfred that threatened the 2022 season. The sight of these two powerful groups bickering over which group might grow relatively more rich than the other, while ordinary Americans struggled to rebound from the economic devastation wrought by COVID, provided ample ammunition for Bill's argument.

Bill believed towns like Batavia had been neutered by a political system and economic forces that left them with little real power, and at the mercy of decisions made in distant cities. He would romanticize "that little egalitarian village where the shopkeeper and jazz musician and the carpenter might live in liberty and fraternity," and saw this idealized place as under siege by predatory outside powers. The decision by MLB to slash 25 percent of the minor league teams in places like Batavia and similar small towns across America was just the latest such indignity.

It is worth noting that the loss of minor league baseball in Batavia was special in part because of what had been (on paper, at least) its very ordinariness. It hadn't enjoyed the highest attendance of the clubs that had been eliminated; nor had it been on the cutting edge of wacky baseball promotions like the Savannah Bananas. Dwyer Stadium, though a pleasant and well-cared-for place to take in a game, had by no means been among the most impressive minor league ballparks. But it had possessed that mysterious alchemy found in small town ballparks, the magic that led to relationships being created and strengthened over years and decades, and moments of joy shared across generations. And in this Batavia risked losing what all the towns that had been stripped of minor league baseball risked losing.

Though initially upset to learn of the contraction of the minor leagues, and the possible permanent loss of baseball in his hometown, Bill, a lifelong Batavia season ticket holder, considered the eventual outcome—this locally owned collegiate summer team with no affiliation to Major League Baseball—to be a possible blessing in disguise. He had felt like a "collaborator" rooting for a team that was connected to what he viewed as Rob Manfred's toxic leadership. He much preferred supporting a locally owned venture that had a decentralized "Wild West" feel to it. In his eyes, the new product was a welcome step back to the rich tradition of old industrial league mill teams that dotted the rural American landscape in the early 1900s. He encouraged me to spend the summer at Dwyer Stadium if I wanted to discover what made small town baseball so special.

*   *   *

Batavia is an old railroad town in western New York. It was once full of heavy industry and has always been surrounded by fertile farmland, the local "mucklands" that inspired the team's name. Once prosperous in the first half of the twentieth century, Batavia began to struggle economically when the New York State Thruway bypassed Main Street, leading to the gradual death of many local businesses as passing travelers no longer knew they were even there. "Urban renewal" projects, in which many of the historic old buildings along Main Street were bulldozed to make room for modern, brutalist-style constructions, ravaged the once stately downtown, with older businesses wiped out in favor of sterile strip malls and chain stores alongside the interstate. This was followed by the exit of much of its remaining industry in the 1980s.

On summer weekends today, thousands of vacationers pass exit 48 of the New York State Thruway in a hurry to get back to their suburban New York or Boston homes. Some, tired from hours behind the wheel, may pull off the interstate and check into one of the chain hotels located alongside the highway, not far from the usual assortment of Applebee's, McDonald's, Subways, and Taco Bells. They may never even notice, or will soon forget, the name of the town where they stayed. Not many will venture an extra few miles into its downtown, where only a few relics of old Batavia remain, such as the Adam Miller toy store and Oliver's Candies, both of which have been delivering smiles to generations of Batavia children. These beloved establishments have been joined in recent years by a handful of newer restaurants and coffee shops that have sprung up alongside abandoned storefronts, but they too struggle to attract passing travelers.

Batavia has been hit hard by the successive punches of the interstate's bypass of the downtown, urban renewal, deindustrialization, and then the opioid epidemic. Still, although the town counts few of the economically privileged "1 percent" among its inhabitants, Batavia is lucky enough not to be beset by extreme poverty. It is a working-class place with little evidence of the extremes of wealth that can be found near larger cities. The nicest Victorian homes on stately Ellicott Avenue may be valued at $300,000, and perfectly comfortable family homes on the welcoming tree-lined streets north of Main Street near Dwyer Stadium can be had for under $200,000. Houses in the grittier area south of Main, where the predominance of any crime Batavia experiences takes place, are closer to $100,000. Just as there are no million-dollar homes, there are also few signs of homelessness. The residential architecture reveals the evolution of Batavia from a walking community to a car-centric commuter one, as most homes constructed before the 1950s featured large front porches while most built in the 1960s and later have flat fronts, an impediment to any sort of informal neighborhood socializing.

Batavia is a small town on the rural periphery of the Rust Belt, on the surface anonymous and indistinguishable from hundreds of others like it. Yet, over the course of the following year, with the help of friendships nurtured in the bleachers of Dwyer Stadium, I would slowly discover how many strands of stories ran beneath this surface, and the role baseball played in stitching them all together.

*   *   *

Minor league professional baseball in Batavia dates back to the establishment of the Batavia Giants in 1897, a team that joined four other towns along the New York Central Railroad to comprise the New York State League. The Batavia squad had a dismal season, finishing with eight wins to go with thirty losses, and ultimately relocated to Geneva, New York. It would be forty-two years before professional baseball would return to Batavia, in 1939. In the meantime, less competitive semipro teams—those unaffiliated with a major league organization—continued to play, with the Batavia Bees and Polish Falcons entertaining townspeople. Exhibition games against legendary barnstorming Black teams like the Ethiopian Clowns and New York Colored Giants drew especially well.

Led by Branch Rickey's St. Louis Cardinals (and, later, Brooklyn Dodgers), the system of identifying and developing talent for major league clubs would change dramatically in the 1930s. Earlier in the century, minor league teams had been independent entities that made money selling players to big-league clubs at a profit. Babe Ruth may be the most famous example of this, as he began his playing career with the then minor league Baltimore Orioles before being "sold" to the Boston Red Sox for $16,000. Rickey, though, built the Cardinals into a dominant club in the 1930s by purchasing entire minor league teams and stocking them with players. Thus, what became known as the "farm system" was born, with major league franchises either owning or signing affiliation agreements with minor league clubs. In 1949, the peak of the postwar minor league baseball boom, the National Association of Professional Baseball Leagues included 448 teams in 59 leagues.

It was during this era that baseball looked to western New York for the establishment of a low-level Class D league. On January 9, 1939, seventy-five baseball officials convened at Batavia's Hotel Richmond and developed plans for a new PONY (Pennsylvania, Ontario, and New York) League, whose original six teams would be located in Batavia, Jamestown, Niagara Falls, Olean, Bradford (Pennsylvania), and Hamilton (Ontario). Its first pitch would be that summer, and, with the exceptions of 1954–56 and 1960, affiliated minor league baseball would be a defining part of Batavia summers.

In the words of Rich Schauf, a retired Batavia cop and Muckdogs season ticket holder for twenty years, Dwyer Stadium served as a "front porch" of sorts for the entire community, the place where locals came together to catch up. "Where else are you gonna sit outside until ten p.m. with your friends and neighbors?" Schauf asked. Where else would Batavians go to develop relationships that, when it came time to say goodbye at season's end, Schauf told me, it sometimes felt as if you were "losing a friend"?

Then, on June 30, 2020, due to concerns over COVID, the minor league baseball season was canceled for the first time since the minor leagues had been founded in 1901, followed months later by confirmation that professional baseball would not return to Batavia, as it was one of the cities that would lose its team to MLB's contraction of the minor leagues.

It wouldn't be until June 2021, nearly twenty-one months after the final pitch of the 2019 season had been thrown, that the gates of Dwyer would reopen to the Muckdogs faithful. Although Robbie and Nellie Nichols's college players had replaced drafted professionals, the crack of the bat again marking the beginning of summer, as it had for over a century, came as a desperately welcome relief to local fans.

2

The Boys Are Back in Town

May 30

The collegiate Muckdogs had, by all accounts, a tremendously successful opening season in 2021, with an average attendance of nearly two thousand. For a town of just over fifteen thousand, that meant that on many summer nights more than 10 percent of the population could be found inside Dwyer Stadium. Would it endure, though, or was it just a brief honeymoon period as locals were desperate for the return of *any* form of baseball, and an opportunity to socialize, after having a season canceled by COVID?

I arrived in town on Memorial Day weekend of 2022, having been told that the annual Memorial Day Parade in Batavia was a big deal. The town struck me as an overtly patriotic place, one that took great pride in the numbers of native sons and daughters who'd served in the military, and in honoring those lost to war. Muckdogs owner Robbie Nichols thought having the team march in the parade would engender goodwill in the community. When I arrived in the parking lot of a strip mall on the eastern flank of Batavia's Main Street, where the parade participants were assembling, I met the team and its manager, Joey "Skip" Martinez, for the first time. Shortly after I arrived, the players and the Muckdogs dance team, composed of local high school girls and coached by the mother of one of the players, assembled in front of the Herb City Vape Shop for a team photo.

The day was gorgeous, eighty-five degrees with a light breeze, not a cloud in the blue sky. The players wore red and black Muckdogs jerseys and caps along with shorts, making small talk as they got to know each other in the parking lot that was beginning to fill with marchers from other local organizations like the Boy Scouts and various church groups.

It was easy to spot Robbie Nichols, the Muckdogs owner. Mustachioed and burly, he looked the part of the longtime minor league professional hockey player he had been, his career having flamed out just shy of the National Hockey League (NHL). He pointed out a few returning players, many of whom were looking for their last chance to showcase their talents in the hope of getting drafted, hopes that would now be significantly harder to achieve since the Major League Baseball draft had been reduced from forty rounds to twenty. This was partly due to the increasingly common belief that, in the words of Sig Mejdal, assistant general manager of the Baltimore Orioles, "the days of finding an undiscovered talent in the fortieth round are gone" due to advances in technology and analytics.

As the participants got ready for the parade to begin, the players gathered behind the tricked-out Jeep driven by Dave Fisher, a bearded and heavily tattooed Desert Storm veteran. Fisher said Robbie asked him to work security at the games, telling him, "I have the perfect job for you. You're a scary-looking combat vet, people won't give you shit." Whereas in days gone by he'd battled T-72 tanks from Saddam Hussein's old army, Fisher now focused on "the same young teenagers who always cause me trouble, whose parents drop them off and expect me to babysit them while they hang out behind the first-base bleachers standing on tables and making messes with their food."

As the parade slowly made its way down Main Street, "The Boys Are Back in Town" blasted from the speakers of Fisher's Jeep. The manager, Skip Martinez, a natural showman, stood on the Jeep's running boards, waving to those lining the sidewalks. Martinez's circuitous route to coaching in the PGCBL was emblematic of the strange paths followed by the men who populate the back roads of baseball. He grew up in the rough neighborhood of East New York in Brooklyn, and baseball was what kept him out of the trouble that found so many other young men he knew. The smooth-fielding shortstop played for Manhattan Community College and had hoped to get drafted, before a broken ankle shattered that dream. He was able to sign a free agent contract with the Detroit Tigers organization, though, where he briefly played rookie ball. After this and his stints playing in Puerto Rico and in the Dominican Republic failed to get him any closer to the big leagues, Martinez ultimately hung up his cleats and quit playing.

Like so many baseball nomads, Martinez would settle in Florida, where he hung out a shingle to start coaching baseball, which he had now been doing for the better part of twenty years. Robbie had hired him the previous spring to coach Batavia's first summer in the PGCBL, and the big-city native quickly grew to love the small town on the edge of the Rust Belt, where he and the players were treated like celebrities when they went out to grab a bite to eat at the Miss Batavia Diner or some wings and a beer at Tully's. After finishing the inaugural campaign at 21-19 and narrowly missing the playoffs by one game, Martinez was awarded a two-year contract extension by Robbie on the field during the last home game. Muckdogs fans, who had grown to love the charismatic New Yorker now known to all as Skip, gave him a rousing ovation. Martinez was overwhelmed by the crowd's embrace, saying, "This passion, this recognition, is what you're in it for, since you're not gonna get rich doing this."

The parade route was lined with people of all ages, from little kids shouting "Dewey! Dewey!" trying to get the attention of the Muckdogs mascot, to their parents and grandparents watching over them. The adjoining neighborhood featured modest homes with neatly kept yards, many with American flags, some Marine Corps flags, Buffalo Bills flags, and a smattering of Trump flags (Genesee County, like most of western New York, has voted solidly Republican in recent elections). Everyone was smiling. There was an almost palpable lightness in the air, a collective exhalation after what had seemed like a relentless onslaught of bad news and divisiveness, from COVID and ensuing lockdowns, war in Ukraine, inflation, and, most recently and closest to Batavia, a horrific, racially motivated mass shooting just a few weeks prior that left ten people, all of whom were Black, dead in a supermarket in nearby Buffalo.

The parade wrapped up at a monument to honor the Batavia men and women who had died in overseas wars, shortly before a Memorial Day ceremony was to begin. Memorial Day had assumed more significance for me following my Iraq deployment. I had lost not one but two good friends, and had spent my thirtieth birthday convoying across the Anbar desert to a neighboring army base to let one of my best friends know that our mutual friend had been killed by a rocket-propelled grenade attack on his Humvee in Ramadi.

During the ceremony, each name that was etched in the monument was read aloud and accompanied by the ring of a bell. The solemn event then concluded with the playing of "Taps" and "God Bless America." It heartened me to think that my friends who never made it back from Iraq and Afghanistan might be similarly remembered.

3

Eli Fish Season Ticket Holder Party

May 31

On a warm May Tuesday night following Memorial Day weekend, local baseball fans assembled at the Eli Fish Brewing Company for the "season ticket holder party" to welcome that summer's Batavia Muckdogs. The evening had an air of promise, the setting sunlight streaming through the brewery's front windows marking the end of a winter's hibernation.

Whereas one can't go a few blocks in trendy urban neighborhoods without stumbling across an old warehouse now occupied by tattooed and bearded hipsters serving IPAs, Eli Fish was still unique in this region, where local watering holes adorned with fading Bills and Sabres posters remain the norm and where you half expect to see long-retired Bills great Jim Kelly handing off to Thurman Thomas on the TV over the bar. Eli Fish, housed in the former home of the J.J. Newberry five-and-dime store, one of the few remaining historic buildings on Main Street to escape demolition during "urban renewal," embraced the new brewery aesthetic. A large space, yet still featuring a welcoming vibe, it had high ceilings, exposed brick on some walls, hardwood floors, and chalkboards above the bar listing craft beers with clever names.

The collegiate Muckdogs sat smiling in their uniform tops and casual shorts, arrayed in folding chairs in front of the assembled fans. Though some of them were returning from last summer, others had just met a day earlier at the parade and, later in the afternoon, in the dorms they would be sharing at a nearby community college. When infielder Caleb Rodriguez from Division III Kean University in New Jersey had arrived at the dorms and looked around at teammates from as far away as Texas, Florida, and California, he couldn't help but feel a little anxious. His initial nervousness had been compounded when the players were instructed to quickly choose roommates for the summer, leading to an uncomfortable *Real World* sort of encounter where they had to quickly and awkwardly size each other up before determining who would live together. Caleb would make the initial overture to Dallas Young, an outfielder from Detroit, engaging in some small talk before asking, "Will you room with me?" He was relieved to get a "Sure," at which point they snagged a room. The two would go on to become close friends over the course of the summer, enjoying excursions like heading to the Rochester Zoo together on rare off days.

As a standing-room-only crowd ranging from grandparents toting walkers to toddlers crashing around the aisles looked on, team owner Robbie Nichols stood before his players, microphone in hand, and thanked the attendees for purchasing the $99 season tickets.

Robbie was a former hockey brawler who led most of his teams in penalty minutes—though not a player without some skill, as evidenced by his respectable goal totals—and he walked with a noticeable limp. He didn't strike me as someone given to embellishing injuries. It turns out the limp wasn't left over from a long-ago hockey injury. Though reluctant to discuss it, over the winter Robbie had been diagnosed with a rare and sometimes debilitating condition called complex regional pain syndrome. The ailment's origins were often mysterious, but it could result in excruciating pain with no known permanent medical remedy, leading it to sometimes be called "the suicide disease." Robbie had arrived at the brewery that evening directly from medical appointments in Buffalo, where a specialist had suggested an elaborate surgical procedure that would have cost upwards of $150,000. And so, for now, he vowed to soldier on.

Robbie invited the guests to pick up "goodie bags" containing their tickets at a folding table to his left, manned by the summer's crop of interns, eager college students who worked for free in exchange for what they hoped would be marketable experience at this, the lowest rung of sports management. Their enthusiastic smiles and palpable energy were evidence that they hadn't yet endured the grueling summer schedule that led to Robbie's admonition that "if you aren't willing to put in eighteen-hour days, the business of sports isn't for you."

Robbie shared the duties of owning and running two teams (Batavia and Elmira) in the PGCBL with his wife, Nellie, a vivacious Mexican American woman who had grown up in the Los Angeles foster care system, a very long way from the small town in western New York she now found herself in. Nellie had put together brown paper "goodie bags," each containing boxes of Cracker Jacks along with twenty-four old-school hard tickets wrapped in a rubber band, with the purchaser's name carefully written in marker on the outside of the bag. I thumbed my thick wad of tickets with satisfaction, imagining the games I was already looking forward to attending.

Despite Robbie and Nellie's genuine loyalty toward—and affection for—their local customers (it was not uncommon for them to help shovel out some of their older fans following ferocious western New York snowstorms), the husband-wife team were known for being tough businesspeople. And in a sense, they didn't have much of a choice. Unlike some of the league's owners, who treated their teams as more of a summer hobby or side hustle, for Robbie and Nellie, this was their primary business, and one with notoriously thin margins. Teams were purchased for anywhere from $200,000 to $1 million, and the hope was that they would appreciate in value, though the history of sports franchises in smaller communities is littered with the carcasses of failed teams. Robbie and Nellie's eye toward the bottom line was evident this evening; the Cracker Jack boxes were the only free items on offer, and the attendees were required to pay for their own food and beer.

Robbie may have never been able to return baseball to Batavia without the devoted efforts of another longtime Muckdogs fan, Russ Salway, who helped generate support for the launch of Robbie's collegiate team in the local baseball community. Salway, like Bill Kauffman, had served on the board of the Genesee County Baseball Club, which for decades had run the old minor league Muckdogs. Batavia baseball's relationship with the Salway family went back generations to when they owned and managed Salway's, "The Big Store on a Little Street." Salway's opened nearly one hundred years ago, selling everything from sporting goods to guns, from clothing to feed for livestock. An ad for Salway's had been on Batavia's left-field fence during the New York–Penn League's inaugural season of 1939, when they were known as the Clippers.

When then owner Fred Salway sold the longtime store to the Urban Renewal Agency in 1965, the popular shop became one of the first of the local mom-and-pops to leave their downtown homes. This move helped accelerate the process that transformed what had been a bustling marketplace lined with turn-of-the-century buildings into a wasteland of sterile concrete constructions, a neighborhood stripped of its vitality. Bill Kauffman, writing in his ode to his hometown *Dispatches from the Muckdog Gazette*, was scathing in his indictment of this process:

> The city fathers rushed headlong into urban renewal, whereby the federal government paid Batavia to knock down its past: the mansions of the founders, the sandstone churches, the brick shops, all of it. Batavia tore out—literally—its five-block heart and filled the cavity with a ghastly mall, a dull gray sprawling oasis in a desert of parking spaces. The mall was a colossal failure, but it succeeded in destroying the last vestiges of our home-run economy. JC Penney and Wendy's were in; the Dipson Theater and the Dagwood Restaurant were out.

In the wake of Batavia's losing its minor league franchise, Robbie first reached out to Salway in 2020 as he explored the feasibility of launching a college summer team with the same name in the same city-owned stadium. Salway, who would walk his children the few blocks from his home to Dwyer Stadium in a stroller when they were babies, had lived and breathed Muckdogs baseball for decades. He waxed poetic when describing the allure, explaining that for him going to Muckdogs games was "like going to church—my kind of church . . . a community gathering place where there are no social distinctions, that feels like a large family you see every day, outside, with a few beers and a beautiful sunset."

*   *   *

As the Muckdogs players circulated through the brewery to meet the assembled fans, two smiling young Black kids darted past me to press an older white man for the answer to a burning question: "Where's Dewey?" they asked, referring to the Muckdogs mascot. I soon learned that the two kids were the great-grandchildren of the man, eighty-year-old Dr. Ross Fanara, who had been raising them along with his wife, Shirley, since they were a few months old. Their grandmother was a nurse who worked long shifts at the Veterans Administration and therefore wasn't in a position to offer much help, their father had left, and their young mother "wasn't equipped" to care for them for reasons Fanara never shared with me. At six, Kartier was the older of the two. He bragged that he was a red belt in karate, and went to all the Muckdogs games, which was why he was so eager to see Dewey.

The Fanaras were lifelong Batavia baseball fans. In years past they also regularly hosted players in their home when that had been the preferred source of player housing, with Shirley earning the nickname of "Muckdogs Mom" for her efforts in helping all players secure housing in the community. Ross had a slight build, partially the result of a childhood bout with polio that he discovered only when he began to fall while playing shortstop for the Moose Dodgers in the Batavia Little League. He was struck two years before the vaccine was developed. A practicing Catholic, he recalled lying "crippled in bed and making a deal" with God, vowing to spend his life helping people if he recovered. He did recover and was even able to play baseball again in the local Babe Ruth League at MacArthur Park. He would go on to fulfill his side of his bargain with God by spending a long career serving veterans as a podiatrist for the Veterans Administration.

As his great-grandkids scampered around the brewery, Dr. Fanara displayed a wry, self-deprecating sense of humor, recalling how the previous summer for his eightieth birthday he'd thrown out the first pitch, deciding to wind up and really let one go, only to miss the catcher by ten feet, the ball sailing "somewhere onto Bank Street." Despite the wild pitch, it was clear from the glint in his eyes that it remained a treasured memory. When asked what baseball meant to Batavia, Dr. Fanara, without hesitation, answered, "Everything."

Next up, the manager, Skip Martinez, took the microphone to

introduce the team. Martinez was at ease with the mike and seemed like a born raconteur. A big man with a few extra pounds around his midsection, he reveled in the attention, telling me later, "You want to feel like a rock star, become the Muckdogs manager." The players were all over the spectrum physically, from a few filled-out muscular "men," who wouldn't appear out of place on a minor league field, to gangly "boys," who looked more like the high schoolers they recently had been than the drafted professionals some still dreamed of becoming.

Skip explained how he had spent the off-season recruiting them from as far afield as Texas and the Tampa area he now called home. The recruiting process was somewhat haphazard, depending a lot on Skip's relationships with various college coaches, word of mouth between former players and their teammates and friends, and scouting college teams closer to his Florida home. This summer the Muckdogs added a healthy dose of "hometown" kids from western New York, which Robbie and Nellie especially valued, as they could be counted on to draw local friends and family.

The players would pay around $1,500 to be on the team for the summer—common practice in the league—which included shared dorm rooms at a nearby community college, postgame meals, uniforms, bus travel to away games (the longest ride around three and a half hours), and, most importantly, the opportunity to play in front of adoring crowds in Batavia while hopefully improving as ballplayers. By now word had begun to get out that Batavia was a great place to play, featuring pregame pageantry and in-game promotions that would put some minor league clubs to shame. These efforts resulted in crowds that averaged almost two thousand fans, while some other collegiate summer league teams were lucky to pull in a few hundred. Some of the players still hoped to get drafted or land an independent-league contract while others just wanted to work on their game so they could excel at the college level. Skip nodded approvingly as he surveyed his new squad and said they were "locked and loaded" for a championship run.

The loudest cheers were reserved for a handful of homegrown players, most notably Jerry Reinhart, a former Batavia High School star quarterback and baseball player who had just completed his college career at Division I University of Akron. Reinhart had grown up playing Little League baseball on the fields just beyond the left-field fence at Dwyer, posting up along the third-base fence line to try to snag autographs from minor leaguers much like today's Batavia kids now hounded him. The square-jawed twenty-two-year-old, with All-American good looks and a neatly trimmed beard, said he couldn't "lollygag" on the field or his grandparents would give him grief from their regular seats above the third base dugout. This summer might mark the final chapter of his baseball dream—a dream dating back to a childhood visit to the old Yankee Stadium, where his father got him into the dugout to meet Derek Jeter. If his performance this season didn't land him a professional contract, he would likely join his father's business renting construction equipment.

One young man onstage clad in red Muckdogs gear stood out from the rest. It was the clubhouse manager, Erik Moscicki. He couldn't have weighed more than 140 pounds soaking wet, wore thick glasses, and walked with a noticeable limp, the result of the cerebral palsy he was born with in his right leg. Still, he seemed to enjoy an easy chemistry with, and degree of respect from, the returning players and some of the fans.

While most of the guests were from nearby, a few had arrived from farther afield, including best friends Betsey Higgins and Ginny Wagner. Friends for nearly four decades after first meeting while working the same shift at Buffalo's Video Factory movie-rental store in their early twenties, the two had now been making the forty-five-minute trek east from their homes in Buffalo for four summers, ever since a friend "dragged" Betsey to a game, where, she said, it was love at first sight. Neither was a big sports fan. Betsey, one of seven kids—"an Irish Catholic thing," she joked—had family roots in Buffalo's "Old First Ward," a traditionally Irish neighborhood on Buffalo's south side and was a librarian and self-professed bibliophile. Her childhood had been marked by season tickets to the opera that her mother insisted they attend, while one of her brothers boasted of never having attended a professional sports event. Ginny, meanwhile, was an administrator at the University of Buffalo who "hates the NFL," blasphemous words in a region where Bills flags are displayed year-round.

The twosome had been crestfallen when they learned that their minor league Muckdogs had fallen victim to MLB's contraction two summers ago. When Betsey got the news, she knew she wasn't the only one who would be crushed. "These are my people, and I just wanted to hold everyone," she recalled.

On this night, though, their mood mirrored the cloudless blue skies over Batavia. Ginny said she felt as if she was "getting ready to go on a date" all afternoon, a sense of delightful anticipation building as the hour drew near for her to get behind the wheel of her Kia to go pick up Betsey from her snug, book-lined home in Buffalo's charming Elmwood Village neighborhood. When Ginny got to her house, Betsey teased her for having "pressed her shorts," the two all smiles anticipating the arrival of summer following Buffalo's seemingly interminable gray winter. Sometimes during the cold and dark winter months, the two women would simply call each other to leave voicemails of the song "Sweet Caroline" playing. It was an effort to deliver encouragement by evoking the late-inning feel of summer nights at Dwyer, when the song was always played. Just a few notes of the song could make Betsey "almost feel the breeze and imagine the beautiful sunsets and lights coming on."

They would end their messages with the comforting refrain "Just wait till June," reminding each other that Opening Day was on the horizon, however distant it may have sometimes appeared.

Now June was only hours away.

4

Elmira Pioneers Home Opener
vs. Batavia Muckdogs

June 3

The rolling farmland of western New York between Erie, Pennsylvania, and Elmira was bathed in sunlight, with temperatures hovering in the high seventies. Robbie and Nellie Nichols must have been thrilled with the weather, as home openers are always relied on to be one of the larger gates of the summer, and both of the teams they owned in the PGCBL had one this weekend. Their Elmira Pioneers were slated to kick off their season this Friday night, followed by the same two teams squaring off at Batavia's home opener about a hundred miles to the northwest on Saturday night. As owners of both teams, they were less concerned with "rooting" for either one when they played each other as they were with drawing strong crowds and making money. With only thirty-something home games for each team to work with, and attendance, concessions, and merchandise sales comprising a large chunk of their annual revenue, every home date counted.

Elmira had been hit hard by Rust Belt deindustrialization. There were boarded-up storefronts, the streets largely devoid of people despite the fact it was a beautiful summer Friday afternoon. The contrast with nearby Corning—whose economy had been bolstered by the headquarters of the multinational corporation of the same name—was stark. Corning featured a Main Street where coffee shops, breweries, and boutique restaurants gave the town a feel of a Boulder, Colorado, or Burlington, Vermont. In Elmira, shirtless grown men pedaled by on children's bikes, the tattoos on their bodies faded like the desiccated businesses they passed by. The residential boulevard leading toward the stadium was lined with once proud old Victorian homes, some with owners still fighting to maintain appearances with fresh paint and neatly maintained yards, while others had let their properties fall into disrepair. Several of these homes displayed enormous Trump flags, with the occasional derogatory "Let's Go Brandon" banner thrown in for good measure. The ubiquitous Trump signage served as a constant reminder that while I was in perennially blue New York State, this western swath of struggling industrial pockets surrounded by rural farmland (and featuring a remarkable number of prisons) remained overwhelmingly red. And as someone who—like so many Americans—would desperately prefer less division and a renewed sense of national unity, I found them just as tiresome as the ubiquitous left-leaning signs adorning the suburban yards of my neighbors back home outside Pittsburgh.

Dunn Field had first opened its doors in 1939 but resided on a site where there had been a stadium dating all the way back to the late 1800s. The grandstand was fully covered by a blue roof resting on steel support columns, somewhat reminiscent of old Tiger Stadium in both color and design. It was, quite literally, crumbling, blue paint chipping off the ancient wooden seats, chunks of concrete missing from its walls. At the risk of romanticizing disrepair, you couldn't help but feel tangibly connected to the rich history of baseball in Elmira as you walked through the old ballpark, which possessed a raw authenticity you don't see much anymore.

An enormous poster affixed to the exterior facade of the stadium featured a picture of Babe Ruth and Lou Gehrig in the Larrupin' Lou's and Bustin' Babes uniforms they wore during their famous barnstorming tour of 1928, when they made a stop in Elmira. Those were the days when even the icons of the sport had side hustles in the offseason. Ruth's highest salary in 1931 was $80,000, or just over $1 million in today's dollars, a far cry from Major League Baseball today, when unknown journeymen can make that much and superstars are now closing in on long-term contracts approaching a billion dollars.

The legendary Yankees squad of 1928 had just swept the Cardinals, with Ruth batting .625 and Gehrig .545, when the two greats arrived in Elmira to much fanfare. Schools were closed early so kids could attend, with a local promoter shuttling hundreds of "crippled children" to the ballpark to see their heroes.

And did they deliver . . . The offensive fireworks were punctuated by a home run walloped by Ruth that traveled an estimated five hundred feet, which he maintained was one of the longest he ever hit. According to the local paper, "The sphere ascended skyward with the speed of a bullet after its collision with the Ruthian war club and was still traveling upward as it went over the fence."

Hours before the first pitch of the season opener was thrown, owner Robbie Nichols gave me a quick tour of the concourse, which had framed pictures showcasing the stadium's history, including a photograph of one of baseball's iconic "lifers," Don Zimmer. The picture was of Zimmer, who spent sixty-six years in professional baseball, getting married at home plate before a game in Elmira, escorting his bride-to-be to the altar under a canopy of bats held aloft by his teammates.

"I should've cleaned this off," Robbie said as he used his shirt to wipe a smudge off the photo's glass case.

Robbie and his crew hustled about, ensuring that everything was ready to go for the opener, at one point Robbie asking an intern to go find three screws to repair a ticket stand near the front entrance. A nearby sign listed ticket prices: "Students $5, Adults $10, VIP $15."

The press box was perched atop the grandstand, reachable only via a crumbling staircase, the paint slowly peeling off its cinder-block walls. Robbie told me it was "the best view in baseball," a 360-degree panorama revealing the baseball diamond directly below, sandwiched between verdant foothills overlooking the Chemung River to the east and tree-lined residential streets ringed by more rolling hills to the south and west. The sun cast a few final golden rays over the grassy parking area behind us, adding to the enchanted feel.

I noticed a sign reading "VIP Suite" with the Elmira Pioneers logo emblazoned on it next to the concession stand atop the grandstands. Curious as to what lay behind the modest-looking doors, I ducked inside. I discovered a room featuring some mismatched furniture, an old DVD player, and children's toys strewn about, more unfinished basement rec room than luxury box. Robbie told me that was where his grandkids usually played while their parents—who had followed Robbie and Nellie into the family business—worked the games (though he would sometimes rent it out).

As game time approached, the gates opened and excited fans who had been queued up outside streamed into the old ballpark for the first time in nine months. Three young teenagers from the Twin Tiers Cadet Squadron dressed in Air Force uniforms gathered near the first-base line with Stitches the mascot for a last-minute pregame huddle before taking the field to help present the colors. Stitches was a diminutive seam-headed baseball with a smiley face and coonskin Pioneers cap. His outfit had a weathered look that suggested it hadn't been upgraded in quite some time. The evening's "Baseball Buddies," children wearing the uniforms of their area youth league, paired up with players from the Pioneers for a pregame catch, radiating happiness the way only young kids can.

*   *   *

The scene at Dunn Field was a genuine slice of Americana out of a Norman Rockwell painting—but unself-consciously so. In this respect it was the antithesis of MLB's recent *Field of Dreams* games played in tiny Dyersville, Iowa, near the location where the 1989 movie was filmed. The inaugural game in 2021 borrowed from the film's iconic imagery, with Kevin Costner leading players onto the field from the cornstalks ringing the outfield while the national anthem was sung, playing up the sport's rural nostalgia to a credulous national sports media.

The 2022 sequel was even more brazen in its efforts to tug on the heartstrings of sentimental fans, beginning with Ken Griffey Jr. emerging from the same cornfield and striding into the outfield with his father, Ken Griffey Sr. As they walked, Junior earnestly asked, "Dad, wanna have a catch?" before they started gently tossing a ball back and forth. Soon dozens of other kids and parents came jogging through the cornfield to share the outfield with the two MLB greats and play catch. All the while an elegiac classical music score was trumpeted over the PA system.

Somehow few, if any, from the national media called attention to the glaring hypocrisy that all this pageantry was dreamed up in the same MLB headquarters in New York that had just conceived the plan to snuff out minor league baseball teams just down the road when they eliminated the Burlington Bees and Clinton Lumber-Kings in the 2021 contraction of the minor leagues. Burlington and Clinton, small Iowa communities tucked alongside the Mississippi River just a few hours away, had hosted low-level minor league teams for well over a century.

There were eight thousand seats in the stadium MLB spent roughly $6 million constructing for the special game—or approximately the same amount MLB clubs would have spent supporting an entire season of the old New York–Penn League before they extinguished it. Some tickets to the game were made available to Iowa residents via a lottery for between $375 and $450, before many landed on the secondary market, where they fetched a starting price of $750, with the best seats commanding as much as $5,000. This all but ensured that the Dyersville grandstands would be filled not with local baseball fans, but with big spenders and corporate patrons, flying in from the coasts to celebrate "grassroots" baseball in an Iowa cornfield.

Nonetheless, by MLB's metrics, the inaugural game was surely considered a roaring success, earning media acclaim and nearly six million television viewers on FOX, the sport's largest regular-season audience in over fifteen years. I couldn't escape the thought of my five-year-old son Bates, though, and the sports paraphernalia cluttering his bedroom. Despite its success, this *Field of Dreams* game would do little to help any of the five-year-olds in Burlington, Iowa, who slept beneath posters of their MLB heroes. After all, their dreams of seeing future major leaguers at their local ballpark had already been shattered.

*   *   *

As the first pitch in Elmira drew closer, the grandstands were already nearly full. It appeared likely that there would be a sellout crowd of over four thousand, remarkable in the collegiate summer league world, where crowds often numbered in the hundreds and two thousand fans would be a great night for most teams. I spotted Robbie and Nellie weaving their way through the excited throngs toward the field for the pregame ceremonies, Robbie in a red Pioneers golf shirt and Nellie wrapped in an American flag shawl. I asked Robbie how his foot was feeling, and he grimaced, telling me he was in pain, but nonetheless forced a smile. I'd googled the disease that had struck him—complex regional pain syndrome—since we'd last spoken and was now familiar with just how serious the diagnosis was.

General manager Marc Witt, thirty-five, beginning to bald, quick to smile, and always hustling, had arranged for an old Chrysler LeBaron to shuttle employees from a nearby axe-throwing business to home plate to toss axes at the logo of the visiting Muckdogs. Only the old jalopy wouldn't start. Marc scrambled to round up some interns to help the visiting axe throwers push the broken-down car toward home plate, leaving the confused crowd to wonder whether this was part of the skit or not. Having worked up a sweat from his unexpected pregame exertions, Marc came off the field shaking his head, muttering, "Everything that could go wrong went wrong."

The one thing that went right—and the most important thing from an attendance standpoint—was the weather, as it was nearly eighty degrees without a cloud in the sky.

Nolan Sparks, a rising junior at the University of Rochester, took the mound for Batavia. The short and stocky right-hander's fastball had topped out at 83 miles per hour during his high school years outside Denver, Colorado, and as a result he had been passed over by big-time college programs. Rochester took a chance on him, though, and must have been thrilled when he arrived throwing in the low 90s, attributing his dramatic increase in velocity to hard work in the weight room. Tonight Sparks was bringing the heat for the visiting Muckdogs, his fastballs bursting into the catcher's mitt with loud pops.

Batavia's Jerry Reinhart got the scoring started in the top of the fourth when he sent a seeing-eye base hit to right with runners on first and third, giving the Muckdogs an early 1–0 lead. In the dugout the players were still getting to know each other, making small talk about where they were from, what leagues they'd played in, and how hard they threw. It would be Skip Martinez's job to ensure that the group came together as one despite the hasty assemblage of disparate parts.

An error, followed by the only hit Sparks would surrender, an Elmira triple in the bottom of the fourth, tied the score, bringing the crowd to its feet. It would be the only blemish on an otherwise dominant four innings for the Batavia hurler, in which Sparks struck out five and didn't surrender an earned run.

As Sparks exited the mound to the cheers of his teammates, and right-hander Joe Tobia from the University of Albany began his warm-up tosses, I eyed the crowd around me. Young kids tugging at their parents' arms to go get cotton candy, packs of teenagers roaming the concourse, seniors pushing walkers toward their seats. A number of men wore Vietnam veteran ball caps, but the longest-tenured fan was surely ninety-three-year-old Korean War veteran Herb Tipton. Herb had occupied the same seat in Elmira since 1973, about ten rows from the field, right between home plate and first base. He still drove himself to every game from the downtown assisted-living community where he lived in a small apartment decorated with Elmira Pioneers mementos, religious missals and biblical quotes, and a framed photo of him and his late wife from their wedding day in 1955. Though his body had aged since the photo, his smile was unchanged. Only when the Pioneers were "playing lousy" would his native good humor sometimes give way to brief flashes of frustration.

Herb was usually the first fan to arrive, an hour before the gates even opened to everyone else. After Nellie or Marc let him in, he would count out exact change for a Coke and popcorn from Nellie before the concession stand had officially opened. For decades his summer evenings had revolved around Elmira baseball, and he could almost always be found quietly taking it all in, a serene smile on his face. The game had assumed an even greater importance in his life following the death of his wife of sixty-one years, whom he called "a helluva woman who kept me straight." When people marveled at his longevity, Herb attributed his health to the fact he didn't drink or smoke or mess around with women, prompting his daughter to laugh and tease him, "What do you mean, I've seen you with tons of women at those ball games."

I'd heard a lot about a guy who went by "Popcorn Bob" and had assumed what sounded like an almost mythic status making pop-corn at Dunn Field for longer than many fans could remember. If one were to close one's eyes and imagine what someone who had been making popcorn in a hot and crowded minor league conces-sion stand for the better part of forty summers might look like, one would envision someone who looks a lot like Bob. He wore a white

T-shirt that read "Popcorn Bob" in small letters across his chest and a white Elmira ballcap with a shock of graying hair shooting out from under it. He had a neatly trimmed mustache and was sweating as he hustled to fill orders in the claustrophobic corner of the concession stand where his popcorn machine was located. Bob said there was a secret recipe to his popcorn but "I'm not telling . . . Nellie watched over my shoulder one time, and I purposely messed up so she couldn't copy me."

Orders for popcorn came in fast and furious from Nellie, and Bob rarely got a chance to sneak a peek at the game. It wouldn't be until he got home late at night that he said he could finally "peel the salt and butter off myself." His wife, Stephanie, worked in the concession stand with him, where she specialized in pretzels, though sometimes she left a little earlier so she could catch a few hours' sleep before her alarm went off at 3:30 a.m. for her 5:00 a.m. shift filling online orders at Walmart. She'd work there until 2:00 p.m., take a midafternoon break, and then report to Dunn Field at 5:00 p.m. to begin her five hours at the concession stand.

Despite the grueling schedule, both seemed to enjoy their work, especially Bob. The fact he'd been doing it for the better part of four decades suggested as much. "It feels like home," he said. "I know everybody, and everybody knows me. They'll even shout out 'Hey, Popcorn Bob!' to me at the mall."

As I watched Bob work, I noticed his warm interactions with the regulars, some of whom he'd known for over thirty years. I couldn't help but think about how more MLB ballparks are now promoting self-checkout options where the customer can order from an iPhone app and then grab and pay for the food without ever having to interact with a human. It is another move toward "efficiency," the value that reigns supreme on the business school campuses and management consultancies where many of today's baseball leaders learned their craft. More and more locally owned minor league teams are being bought out by private equity—Diamond Baseball Holdings, an ownership group backed by private equity giant Silver Lake, with over $100 billion in assets under management, has already gobbled up thirty-five affiliates (or nearly 30 percent of all minor league teams), and its appetite shows no signs of waning. One can't help but wonder what will become of the "Popcorn Bobs," laboring with a smile in small ballparks across America, in this new world where return on investment (ROI) is the sole operating principle. As one former minor league owner who had bought a team "100 percent for fun and 0 percent for money" put it, "Private equity is, by definition, about money. There's no way to dress it up as something else." Given this reality, he and others associated with the minor league game can't help but be concerned for minor league towns where private equity ownership may confront decisions pitting the good of the community against a dent in their ROI.

*　　*　　*

Private equity's recent move into the world of minor league baseball has not been without controversy. The CEO of Diamond Baseball Holdings, the firm that has led the charge, is Peter Freund, who was a minor league owner and a director of the New York–Penn League (in which Batavia played) when, in October 2020, he was hired by MLB to advise on the contraction of the minor leagues. There was a degree of irony in Freund's decision to assist MLB in this effort, as he had until then been a critic of contraction, at one point earlier that year saying, "The reality is this [contraction] has nothing to do with facilities and it has nothing to do with travel. It has to do with saving money on Major League Baseball's side . . . The only thing this has to do with is if they eliminate 40 clubs, that's that many fewer players they have to pay. It's that basic."

When Freund was hired by MLB, his role, according to Dan Halem, MLB's deputy commissioner and chief legal officer, was to "assist us in transitioning to a Minor League system that will better serve Minor League fans, Minor League players, Minor League owners, and our Major League Clubs."

Several months later MLB released the results of the work Freund helped orchestrate. They had eliminated forty minor league affiliates in what constituted the most dramatic overhaul of the minor leagues in over fifty years. It was unclear how this new system would "better serve Minor League fans and owners"—as Halem had claimed—in the forty communities that were being stripped of their minor league teams.

A year later, in 2021, sports and entertainment giant Endeavor (which at the time was partly and is now fully owned by Silver Lake) announced the creation of Diamond Baseball Holdings (DBH), with Peter Freund as its CEO. The new firm boasted of a "strategic partnership with MLB" and, in December of 2021, announced the purchase of its first ten minor league teams.

As Diamond Baseball began buying up the minor league clubs that remained, there was reason to be skeptical of the impact private equity-backed ownership would have on the minor league landscape, given its well-known playbook of cutting costs, raising prices, and overall zeal for unlocking "efficiencies." One person who would benefit, though, would be Freund himself, as CEO of the firm that was amassing a substantial portfolio of the teams that had escaped the cuts he'd helped oversee. His partner, Pat Battle, Diamond Baseball's executive chairman, would tell *The Athletic,* "Whether you're a DBH team or not, we're all in this together. And we do believe a rising tide lifts all boats." Left unsaid was the fact that his partner, Freund, had helped advise MLB on the sinking of forty of those boats.

This raises some troubling questions. As a professor of sports business noted, "These properties [the minor league clubs acquired by DBH] were distressed because of the decision he [Freund] helped advise, then he purchased those distressed assets . . . He helped dismantle the National Association and then scooped up the remains." While Diamond Baseball has reportedly been paying reasonable market prices for the teams they are buying, there is no doubt that some longtime owners have been more inclined to sell franchises given the sudden transformation of the business landscape. Minor league clubs that had for decades seemed likely to endure indefinitely suddenly seemed on less secure footing following the elimination of 25 percent of minor league teams and rumors of more cuts to follow when the new professional development licenses (PDLs) between minor league franchises and their major league parents expire in 2030. In the words of a sports business professor, "If I owned a minor league team now, I'd get the hell out, as I wouldn't want to run the risk of being left holding a bag of sand." He would add that the clubs owned by Diamond Baseball, by virtue of the firm's enormous stake in the minor leagues, as well as Freund's connection to the commissioner's office, will enjoy a stronger negotiating position should MLB decide to cut more minor league teams.

It is also important to remember that ten years ago a firm like Diamond Baseball would never have been able to purchase so many minor league teams, since there had been a long-standing prohibition against one person (or entity) owning multiple teams in the same league. This rule fell by the wayside as a result of minor league contraction and MLB's takeover of minor league governance.

The bitter taste the entire saga has left in the mouths of many impacted by it is unlikely to soon go away. In the eyes of many of those burned by minor league contraction, Freund's involvement was the ultimate betrayal. Here was a minor league owner jumping to the MLB commissioner's office to help them tear down minor league baseball, and then just as quickly moving to buy up a significant portion of what remained.

One may ask why Silver Lake, known as one of the biggest technology investors in the world, would be so keen on taking over an enormous chunk of minor league baseball. One possible explanation is that they also own a stake (as does MLB) in Fanatics, the sports merchandise firm that has morphed into something of a data company, claiming over eighty million users. According to a 2022 article published by *CNBC Sport*, Fanatics CEO Michael Rubin has boasted that Fanatics has up to "16 data attributes per consumer," a wonky way of highlighting how well the company knows the purchasing habits of millions of people, the kind of data that is a gold mine for retailers and, increasingly, online gambling sites, another market Fanatics is aggressively moving into. Rubin dreams of Fanatics developing into a $100 billion company based in part on its unique ability to harvest the information gained from visitors to its e-commerce sites to sell advertisers and lure millions of new users to its growing online betting ventures. It projects it can do this for a fraction of the "customer acquisition cost"—or the cost of money spent to acquire new customers through methods such as marketing and promotion—of existing online sports books.

How does owning dozens of minor league baseball teams contribute to this business model? Well, apart from the obvious opportunities for the teams themselves to make money and appreciate in value, the data Fanatics gathers from millions of minor league fans can be injected into this proprietary ecosystem. This will enable e-commerce sites to develop targeted approaches "to buy more crap from them," in the words of the sports economics professor, as well as generate hundreds of thousands of new sports gamblers. As this professor put it, each new Diamond Baseball acquisition unlocks a new community composed of tens of thousands of new targets "they can wring money out of."

Fanatics is even cited as a "Case Study" on the Amazon Web Services website, which spells out the playbook—though in deceptively innocuous terms—in surprisingly clear language:

> In addition, more than 250 million people visit the company's 300-plus websites every year. With a massive number of product searches and transactions taking place in a huge online warehouse, Fanatics constantly generates enormous amounts of data . . .
>
> . . . Fanatics is now able to analyze the huge volumes of data from its transactional, e-commerce, and back-office systems, and make this data available to its data scientists immediately for analytics.
>
> As a result of its new business intelligence capabilities, the organization will be able to more easily discover new ways to serve its customers . . . Fanatics can now get actionable, real-time insights into key customer behavior and purchasing patterns—information that can be shared with employees globally.

Of course, describing these efforts as being focused on "serving customers," when in fact they are predicated on harvesting people's personal information to better coax them into spending money and gambling, is rather shameless even by the standards of Orwellian corporate doublespeak.

Some Batavia fans, like Bill Kauffman, saw through the charade. When he and I spoke about contraction and the subsequent private equity feeding frenzy, he made his disdain for the entire process clear: "In the minors, they have performed a disgusting and heartbreaking act of extirpation: a literal uprooting. They wiped out entire leagues, defoliating professional baseball at its grass roots. The mom-and-pop operations; the community-owned clubs; the teams whose management and administration had been the responsibility of local people, and which therefore assumed local personalities and accents, are giving way to private equity–owned teams that have all the character of a spreadsheet."

To its credit, so far Diamond Baseball has retained existing management of the teams it has acquired, and is saying all the right things about continuing with local management and avoiding layoffs. But it's a lot easier to begin "cutting costs" in the form of anonymous employees working hundreds of miles away than to fire the guy you've sweated alongside in a concession stand every summer, who has been making popcorn with the same recipe for forty years. Why would you employ a gaggle of local teenagers, for example, to call season ticket holders and ask them to renew their tickets, or to man a ticket box office, when the tickets could be marketed and sold online, and the subsequent data gathered and sold to the highest bidder?

Of course, with each local fixture like Popcorn Bob who gets eliminated, or high school kid left without a summer job at the ballpark, more of the money generated by the team will be sucked out of the community and funneled to distant corporations and investors, as opposed to compensating local employees who, along with the fans, had comprised a symbiotic ecosystem.

"We're thinking about how to build a company that's beloved by billions of sports fans globally," Fanatics' CEO, Michael Rubin, said at a 2022 sports analytics conference hosted by MIT's Sloan School of Management, according to CNBC. But to be "beloved by billions" will almost certainly sever the personal connections local teams used to have with their fans and employees, with call centers and chatbots gradually replacing the smiling face of one of your neighbors at the ticket window.

A current minor league owner acknowledged that selfishly he may benefit from his team's value being driven up by private equity interest. Nonetheless, he noted the corrosive impact absentee and private equity ownership was likely to have on minor league towns, citing newspapers as an analogy, explaining how old newspaper owners saw the paper as a civic good and interacted with the community at church and local social events. Private equity, on the other hand, will be focused on shareholders in New York and London and providing return on their investment by driving costs down and prices up. "The only Princeton they know is the university, not the town in West Virginia," he said, referring to a place that for decades had hosted a minor league team in the Appalachian League before the league fell victim to contraction in 2020.

Baseball has already begun to resemble yet another extractive industry where dollars are transferred from small towns to big-city owners and investors. That's just how capitalism works, some contend. But if one views this as the inevitable evolution of the business, believing that baseball should aggressively pursue the same sort of efficiencies that any profitable business would, it can no longer simultaneously pitch itself as "America's pastime," an institution that transcends the raw pursuit of money. When the days tolerating "inefficiencies" like Popcorn Bob are numbered, perhaps so too should be the days of MLB taking advantage of its antitrust exemption that is rooted in part on this romantic identity it has carefully cultivated.

*   *   *

Popcorn Bob suggested I meet someone he said was a "real character." High praise, I thought, coming from someone like Popcorn Bob, so I took him up on his offer to walk me outside and introduce me to Charles Bennett, a prominent member of a small sub-tribe of Pioneers fans who hung around outside Dunn Field waiting for foul balls to chase down. We found Charles, forty-eight, outside leaning on his parked car, clad in jean shorts and an Elmira jersey and wearing a baseball mitt. Charles was a former "carny" who'd spent fifteen years splitting time between the back roads of the Northeast, where he traveled as a carnival cook, and Gibsonton, Florida, famed "winter quarters" for carnies that was home to characters like the "Lobster Boy" and sometimes featured elephants roaming backyards. Charles had been born and raised in Elmira, and as a kid had served as a batboy at minor league games at Dunn Field. He told me he hadn't watched a game inside the park since the Marlins affiliate left in 1995, preferring to remain outside with a handful of fellow ball shaggers. His haul varied; his worst night was one ball, and his best was thirty-five. He would periodically gather them together and trade them in to Nellie in exchange for some food or perhaps a jersey.

Charles said he embraced the amateurs playing in Elmira, since they weren't getting paid but instead played because they "loved the game." He'd "given up on the pros who cried that sixty thousand dollars wasn't enough" to earn for a single game, he said, continuing, "To hell with that, I'm done . . . My brother-in-law is a sheriff and won't see that kind of money in his entire life, and he puts his life on the line every day." I didn't have the heart to relay to Charles the news that had just broken hours before that Juan Soto of the Washington Nationals was now on the trade market after turning down a fifteen-year, $440 million offer that would have made him the highest-paid player in baseball history. After a short stint in San Diego, he would go on to sign with the Yankees—a one-year deal worth a staggering $31 million, or nearly $200,000 a game for the 162-game season, with a future mega-contract on the horizon.

A cook by trade, Charles had seen his hours baking at Light's Coffee Shop slashed due to COVID restrictions to the point where the job had no longer been tenable. He now stocked shelves at Dollar Tree for about $13 an hour, which hardly provided enough for him to take care of his mother, who was dying of cancer, and the six-year-old boy he'd been raising since birth. For years Charles had brought the boy, Thomas, to Pioneers games, where he loved to play in a bouncy house. Charles had stepped up to raise Thomas after he'd been born to the sister of a woman Charles had been dating who was "incapable of raising him," Charles said. I was beginning to grow accustomed to this intentionally vague terminology—Dr. Fanara had provided a similar description of why he and Shirley had assumed responsibility for raising their great-grandsons—when people would reference the myriad unnamed problems that impacted the raising of children.

As we spoke, Charles kept a sharp eye out for incoming balls. A compatriot in a Mets jersey positioned inside the ballpark standing along the concourse would signal to him whether there was a right- or left-handed hitter up so he could position himself on the side of the stadium most likely to get a foul ball. Sure enough, I soon heard the crack of the bat and saw a ball gently floating in our direction. Charles took off at a sprint toward its likely landing spot, where he arrived at the same time as a running teenager who emerged with the ball after a bit of jostling. Charles wasn't happy when he returned empty-handed, telling me that that kid always "played dirty," whereas most others in his small fraternity of a half-dozen or so ball shaggers tried to "keep it civil." He told me when there'd been an older man in his seventies in the gang they'd allow him his own little area where he could retrieve balls uncontested, since he "didn't move too well at that age."

Not wanting to miss too much of the game, and hungry for a snack, I reentered Dunn Field, where I discovered that the lines at the concession stand were running over twenty deep. I wasn't thrilled, but it must have been a welcome sight to Robbie and Nellie, not to mention a sight they couldn't miss, as they were likely among the few team owners in sports who spent much of every game working the register to interact with their fans, motivate their employees, and keep an eye on the cash. "One root beer, one Dr Pepper, two cheese-burgers, one Nellie's nachos," Robbie shouted, the long line of cus-tomers digging into their wallets putting a bounce in his otherwise pained steps. When someone left a tip, Nellie would ring a bell and the entire kitchen staff would shout "Thank you" in unison.

A cute young girl, maybe eight, came up to Nellie with a huge smile on her face and proudly explained how sweaty she was, hav-ing just run the bases, which kids were invited to do every game between the fifth and sixth innings. This was the sort of moment that Nellie, a product of the Los Angeles foster care system who had lived in thirteen different homes—"some good and some not so good"—from the ages of two to seventeen, clearly treasured. She would never forget those times during her own childhood when she didn't "have anyone to help, anyone to brush my hair . . . I probably looked pretty scruffy, so I developed an appreciation for people who were kind. They made me want to be a kind person—spicy too—but kind." Nellie's childhood had left her with an understanding of what it was like to have a hunger for acceptance sometimes go unsatisfied. "I understand the look in someone's eyes who is hurting," she said, "and I know they don't need another person looking at them in fear. I want to provide a happy face to everyone."

By the latter innings my own feet had begun to swell and become sore after my having been up on them for the better part of the day; I could only imagine how Robbie's must have felt. Perhaps the work was a distraction from the pain that, during a rare, more introspective moment, Robbie said had made him wonder how much more he could take. He said Nellie's love and support helped him to get through those toughest times.

Nellie marveled at her husband's pain tolerance, and his refusal—so far at least—to allow it to impact his ability to put in eighteen-hour days. When they woke up in the morning, she always asked him how he was feeling, and, without fail, he'd respond, "A little better," even on days she knew that couldn't possibly be the case.

Once the sun set beyond the first-base bleachers, the lines at the concession stand finally dissipated and the temperature dropped quickly. The regulars among the fans pulled out their blankets. The crowd had thinned somewhat, though the promise of postgame fireworks kept many in their seats well after Batavia's six-foot-five, 225-pound cleanup hitter Daniel Burroway's two hits and three RBIs put the game out of reach for the Pioneers.

"Tonight was crazier than I expected," Nellie said with an exhausted exhalation, before adding "in a good way." In addition to the small home Robbie and Nellie owned just beyond the outfield fence of Dunn Field, they also had one a few blocks from Dwyer Stadium in Batavia. While they would commute on the rare day one of the teams was off, or to help each other out when there was a special promotion that promised to deliver more fans than usual, the rough division of labor had Robbie spending most of his summer in Batavia while Nellie ran the show in Elmira.

Despite the challenges of spending so much time apart and working such long hours, Nellie said, "We make it work . . . Your spouse needs to be your best friend and soul mate." Though Nellie's language could sometimes sound as if it was lifted from a well-worn self-help book, I reminded myself that there must be something to it, as she had by all accounts been happily married for twenty-four years despite the stresses that came with their lives. Being married to a minor league professional athlete—basically all the downsides of professional sports' frequent travel and familial dislocation without the upside of massive paychecks—let alone working their current job, owning and managing small businesses located hours apart in an economically distressed region, didn't make maintaining a strong, healthy marriage any easier.

Shortly after the final out of Batavia's 8–2 win was recorded, fireworks began to crackle beyond the left-field fence. The music was overtly patriotic, with "Proud to Be an American" followed by Toby Keith's "Courtesy of the Red, White and Blue" and "American Soldier."

As soon as the fireworks dissipated into the night sky, the Muck-dogs players quickly gathered up their equipment from the cinder-block-walled clubhouse and—still in uniform—made their way out of the stadium. Their warm bus sat idling in the dark parking lot, gentle reading lights glowing inside, a little cocoon of comfort in which they could surrender to sleep as the driver delivered them home.

As midnight approached, and the players slept on their ride back to Batavia, there was no rest on the horizon for Robbie Nichols. He needed to finish settling the day's sales—which were considerable, as there had been a sellout crowd of 4,639, one of the largest crowds in the nearly hundred-year history of the ballpark —and supervising the stadium cleanup before he could head home to catch a few hours' sleep. Then it would be up Interstate 390 to Batavia first thing the next morning to prepare for Opening Day at his other ballpark.

Robbie said the summer would be a long grind, a word he loved, and which no doubt stemmed from his hockey days. Though every team celebrates its stars, it is the grinders who are a hockey team's soul, the guys who—day in and day out—sacrifice their bodies for the greater good of the team. Though not without talent—Robbie was drafted by the Philadelphia Flyers in the ninth round of the 1983 draft and put up respectable goal totals during his decade-long minor league hockey career—Robbie was also tough. He once accumulated 406 penalty minutes in 73 games while playing for the Kalamazoo Wings, which meant he was fighting nearly every night.

The same sort of resolve he displayed icing his bloodied fists in hotel rooms in places like Kitchener, Ontario, and Glens Falls, New York, would be required to endure a summer of eighteen-hour days hobbling around on a foot ravaged by a rare illness.

"I'm gonna kill myself for the next sixty days, but it's worth it," he said, perhaps as much to convince himself as anyone else.

5

Batavia Muckdogs Home Opener vs. Elmira Pioneers

June 4

Batavia's home opener on Saturday afternoon proved to be every bit as glorious as Friday evening had been in Elmira. Seventy degrees, with a few white clouds passing by as a gentle breeze came in from left field. Cracks of the bat accompanied the pregame mix tape that was piped in over the PA system, an eclectic mix of classic rock like "Manic Monday," age-old pregame anthems like "Eye of the Tiger" and "Centerfield," and some more contemporary hits. The dance team, comprised of over a dozen local high school girls, was warming up along the foul line as the grandstands remained empty, the gates not yet opened to the excited crowd massing outside, the line of fans snaking down Denio Street. The field looked wonderful, a testament to the efforts of groundskeeper Larry Hale, a retired corrections officer from the nearby maximum security Attica Correctional Facility, site of the infamous 1971 uprising that resulted in forty-three deaths. Larry looked the part, sporting a bald head and muscular physique, though he was quick to laugh and had an easygoing demeanor. He seemed to take pleasure in his retirement routine of watering the infield dirt and mowing the grass. His son, Alex, a right-handed pitcher and another Batavia High grad, was a late addition to this summer's squad.

Dave Fisher, the tattooed, burly Desert Storm veteran, helped the gameday staff make last-minute preparations before turning his attention to his duties as the sole roving security guard. I would grow to enjoy trading Army stories with Dave, though as a onetime second lieutenant I felt compelled to push back against some of his tales of clueless "butterbars," the Army's not-so-flattering nickname for newly minted officers.

As the evening's color guard, composed of two Vietnam veterans and one Iraqi Freedom veteran from Batavia's American Legion Post 332, assembled alongside a red pickup truck in the parking lot, I made my way to Skip Martinez's office adjacent to the team's locker room. It was a big office, with some lockers for the coaches, a large desk that Skip sat behind—a nametag-style sign saying "Fucker in charge of you fucking fucks" displayed on it—and a leather couch. Skip said he expected returning local players Jerry Reinhart and Tyler Prospero to shepherd the new Muckdogs into the fold and, most importantly, to instill in them a sense of professionalism and personal accountability—playing by "big boy rules," as Skip was fond of saying. One of the bigger challenges he and Assistant Coach Thomas Eaton needed to manage was the workload for the pitchers, carefully calibrating getting them enough innings to make the summer worth their while without overusing them, as was always a temptation with the most successful ones. Veering too far in either direction could damage the coaches' relationships with the schools their pitchers came from and cost them the ability to recruit there for future summers.

Players began to amble into the clubhouse following batting practice. The locker room was a nice one—which made sense, as until a few summers ago it had housed minor league professional ballplayers—with about ten large leather recliners in the middle and gray lockers fronted by folding chairs. The cinder-block walls were painted Muckdogs red, and clubhouse manager Erik Moscicki had carefully hung everyone's uniforms in lockers bearing their name and number. A large vanilla sheet cake reading "Welcome Back Muckdogs" in red icing was on a folding table in the front of the room, courtesy of superfans Hal Mitchell and Theresa Rumble. Mitchell had served as president of the Booster Club for the minor league Muckdogs for nearly twenty years. His memory of games dates back even further, to 1982, when he was working the night shift at the hospital and listening on the radio when a young John Elway, who was playing for the visiting Yankees affiliate from Oneonta, hit a home run in his one summer of professional baseball before embarking on his Hall of Fame football career. More recently Mitchell told of the time he was helping cover the infield with tarp by second base with a young Chase Utley, who would go on to fame with the Philadelphia Phillies, when lightning struck near center field and the two "proved you could jump from second base over the fence by the first-base dugout without hitting the ground."

The front gate to Dwyer officially opened at 6:07 p.m., Journey's "Don't Stop Believin'" blasting from speakers near the entrance, the perfect accompaniment to the happy anticipation of the hundreds of fans already queued up and ready to enter the stadium. Nellie Nichols helped collect tickets and welcome the returning fans, many of them by name. Her enthusiasm seemed undampened by the fatigue she must have felt after working until 2:00 a.m. the previous night in Elmira, as she'd worked alongside Robbie to close out the sales from the overflow sellout crowd, as well as making sure that the kitchen, grandstands, and bathrooms were cleaned up.

Nellie's work ethic likely stemmed at least in part from her challenging childhood and the unforgiving world from which she came. Of her four brothers, two had been shot to death, while a third was serving a twenty-six-year prison sentence. While she and her sister had been placed in the foster system, her brothers were forced to endure a nightmarish home life resulting from their mother's destructive alcoholism. As a child, Nellie would sometimes go home to visit and see her mom's boyfriend "throwing her around like a rag doll." She couldn't help but contrast the violent chaos defining her brothers' home lives with some of the more stable foster homes she had been part of. Nellie was angry with the choices that had landed one of her brothers in jail, but she believed he was fundamentally a "good kid who had to do things to survive." She says her mom was the "best role model I ever had, for what not to be." Recognizing the value of the foster system in delivering her from some of the worst of what her brothers experienced, Nellie had prayed and "promised God that one day when I got my act together I'd be a foster mom." She found a willing partner in Robbie, and together they would serve as long-term foster parents for roughly twenty-five kids over nearly twenty years.

On the field, players had now begun to play catch with boys and girls from the Tri-Town Little League from nearby Alexander, New York. One of the players who seemed especially popular with the youngsters, and enthused to be interacting with them, was the six-foot-five, 235-pound right-hander from Tampa, Julian Pichardo. With a goatee and long black hair flowing from his black and white Muckdogs cap, Pichardo was soon surrounded by kids who looked as if they could have been extras in *The Sandlot,* clad in their green Little League jerseys mismatched with a smattering of jeans, baseball uniform pants, and shorts. Though some initially approached the imposing pitcher with trepidation, they were soon all smiles as he signed their balls and made small talk.

Julian had been a fan favorite the previous summer, serving as an ace of the pitching staff, which he led in starts and innings pitched. He knew that a labor-intensive college season, in which he'd thrown nearly 100 innings at the University of Fort Lauderdale, meant he would need to rest his arm and embrace a more limited role this summer. Still, he remained drawn to the enthusiasm of the Batavia fans and so had returned for another season.

Julian hadn't had the easiest start to childhood either. He'd lost his mother shortly after she delivered him and had been raised by his grandparents. His grandfather Miguel "Mike" Baluja, sixty-five, ran a courier service in Tampa. He and Julian's grandmother Cindy made sure never to miss a Muckdogs game, connecting the You-Tube livestream to a big-screen TV in their living room. Mike said that from 7:00 p.m. to 10:00 p.m. on summer nights, "no one better bother us when we tune in," with occasional friction resulting from times when Cindy's stream on her iPad came through more quickly than the one on the big screen. And so it was that they found themselves tuning in with much anticipation on this evening from Florida's Gulf Coast as baseball returned to western New York's Dwyer Stadium.

The opening of the gates at Dwyer was also a moment long awaited by Buffalo friends Betsey Higgins and Ginny Wagner, whose midwinter phone calls to each other were filled with encouragement to remain upbeat while they counted down the days until the return of pleasant summer nights at Dwyer. Tonight it was finally coming to fruition. Before she'd left home that evening, Ginny had prepared a dinner for her two sons, Thomas and James, ages twenty and eighteen, and husband, Charlie, to enjoy when he got off from his shift driving a Buffalo city bus at 1:00 a.m., later than his usual 9:00 p.m. finish, as he wanted to log some overtime hours. After this, she was free to again resume the game-day rituals she and Betsey had been looking forward to for months, eagerly anticipating their first hot dogs of the summer, always accompanied by Vidalia onions Ginny made sure to bring from home, perhaps washed down with a beer from Batavia's Eli Fish brewery concession stand.

One fan who was not there, missing his first Home Opener in years, was Bill Kauffman, who was stuck quarantining at home with a case of asymptomatic COVID. He would tune in to the broadcast on the Muckdogs YouTube channel from the comfort of home in nearby Elba, describing the experience as "kinda disembodied and strange, given my aversion to the computer and all its works, but I liked the enthusiasm of the young fellow announcing the game, and hey, it was a link to, if in no way a substitute for, the communal aspect of the game." His parents, Joe and Sandra, had made the short two-block walk from their nearby home to be there, though, continuing a lifelong tradition that began for Joe when he attended the 1945 Home Opener of the then Batavia Clippers.

Tyler Prospero, a Batavia native and hometown favorite like Jerry Reinhart, took the mound for the Muckdogs. The bearded six-foot-two, 215-pound right-hander with a sports management degree from nearby Niagara University had come a long way since serving as a batboy for the professional Muckdogs a decade ago. Prospero would cruise through the first, allowing one hit and no runs.

Following the end of the first inning, the in-game "DJ" hosted the "Eli Fish Beer Drinking Competition" atop the third-base dugout, sponsored by Batavia's only craft brewery and featuring two teams composed of father-son pairs matched up, with the father chugging a beer while the son gulped down a glass of water. It looked like fun and, as I thought back to my beer-soaked college days, made me imagine that I might've fared pretty well.

*   *   *

The beer drinking contest was the sort of in-game promotion that independently run small town teams are willing to take a chance on but that centrally managed larger corporate entities often shy away from, lest they offend someone and invite a lawsuit or negative media attention. The goofy but fun promotion reminded me of a discussion I'd had with Mark Cryan, a professor of sport management at Elon University. Cryan had fallen in love with the minor leagues as a child growing up in a tiny town in upstate New York, where the idea of even a minor league team seemed glamorous and "big-time." He would devour legendary baseball owner and promoter Bill Veeck's books *Veeck as in Wreck* and *The Hustler's Handbook,* and later pitcher Jim Bouton's tell-all baseball memoir *Ball Four* and the movie *Bull Durham,* setting him on course to break into the business of minor league baseball. Cryan landed a job as general manager of the Cleveland Indians affiliate in Burlington, North Carolina (which would fall victim to MLB's recent contraction of the minor leagues), where he worked for four seasons as a young man. He said:

> The minor league history is one of pirates, hustlers, and wheeler-dealers. I fear that if MLB seizes more control of the minors, they will snuff this out and turn it into a Home Depot model with regional managers and corporate policies. What had been a laboratory of promotion and entrepreneurialism will become sterilized. The lab will be shut down and turned into a production facility. The business will become more buttoned-down with fewer swashbucklers. The minor leagues will be like every other part of America with a Starbucks on every corner, less community based and with more of a focus on big facilities with good lights and playing surfaces to nurture future major leaguers, while local operators get squeezed out.

Indeed, there were already indications that this was happening. As *Baseball America*'s J. J. Cooper wrote, "[Minor league] GMs have noted that some of the spontaneity and fun of the job has been reduced by MLB-imposed restrictions. Now, all promotions must be approved by MLB, which means there's no longer the chance to come up with a quickie promotion to take advantage of whatever has caught the public's fancy at this moment." Longtime minor league observer Kevin Reichard alluded to this in Ballpark Digest, noting how there was the "widespread belief that the MiLB [Minor League Baseball] overseers are taking the fun out of promotions. There's no way MLB overlords sign off today on legendary promotions like Prostate Cancer Awareness Night, where Myrtle Beach Pelicans GM Andy Milovich received an in-game prostate exam while singing 'Take Me Out to the Ballgame.'"

Batavia, at least for the moment, had managed to preserve the Wild West feel that had historically characterized baseball in smaller cities and towns, avoiding the slick corporate approach that, by sanitizing and homogenizing the minor league experience, threatens to destroy what once made it special.

*   *   *

The Muckdogs began the second inning against the visiting Pioneers in promising fashion when Levis Aguila Jr. was hit by a pitch and then advanced to second on a wild pitch. I would soon discover that this sort of erratic pitching was fairly common. As Jerry Reinhart grounded out to short, nearby fans commented on his football prowess as star quarterback at Batavia High, noting that he once scored five touchdowns in a game.

I joined Betsey Higgins and asked where Ginny had gone. "She's been at the concession stand so long maybe she just took my hot dog money and drove away," Betsey said. Their affectionate jokes and easy repartee date all the way back to 1985, when fate (or Buffalo's Video Factory store manager) brought them together on the same shift. They still laugh at the absurd uniform of black pants, tuxedo shirt, cummerbund, and "the only clip-on bow tie I've ever worn," as Ginny recalls. Betsey was immediately drawn to the "cool cats" who worked there, the "Black city girl" Ginny among them, thinking they were a "breath of fresh air" after "the cliques of preppy girls in their Izod clothing" she'd known in high school. Ginny, for her part, was charmed by Betsey's shy kindness and good humor. She was shocked to arrive home one afternoon and discover Betsey in her front yard helping her dad with yard work.

Ginny still remembered one of their first Friday night shifts when she noticed Betsey stealing glances at a "handsome, tall guy with blond hair." Spotting the man approaching the checkout aisle, Ginny quickly retreated to a back room to provide Betsey an opportunity to interact with him. Returning a few minutes later, after the man had left, new rental in hand, Ginny asked her friend how the interaction had gone. Not well, Betsey replied. She'd clammed up and not said a word. Looking back on those first nights getting to know each other now, Betsey laughed and said, "I guess there's a reason I'm still single. Who knows what would've happened if I'd just said something to him that night." While Ginny's efforts at matchmaking may not have helped Betsey land "the one," they did quickly become fast friends, going out for ice cream, drinks, and double dates together.

As their fifth summer in the Dwyer grandstands commenced, the Muckdogs having introduced a new dimension to their friendship, Betsey marveled at the proximity to the field her general admission season tickets afforded. While these seats were not assigned, most of the regulars would sit in the same area every night nonetheless. Betsey contrasted the wonderful view in front of us with a rare visit to a major league game in Toronto, where she could barely make out the players on the field. Aware that my son Bates was a LEGO fanatic, Betsey told me that she ran a Saturday morning LEGO Club for children at the library where she worked outside Buffalo, and that she would choose a weekly theme tied to that day in history. She proudly told me how well the kids had done that morning constructing scenes based on the "First Public Hot Air Balloon Flight," which had taken place on that day in 1783.

The game remained scoreless, with Prospero pitching three strong innings and giving up no runs on three hits before being pulled. I decided to head over to the Eli Fish beer stand and try out their None Shall Pass IPA. I'd met the brewery's owner, Matt Gray, a Batavia native who, at forty-seven, was just about my age and had impressed me as the sort of local entrepreneur vital to any sort of renaissance these Rust Belt towns may hope to have.

Gray, who grew up going to Muckdogs games, was a lifelong restaurateur, having owned and managed several eateries in the Raleigh area before returning home to Batavia. He opened the Eli Fish brewery in 2018 and had a tough time keeping the business afloat during COVID, cutting staff and pivoting to take-out specials to survive lockdown measures. He was proud to have made it through the dark times, though, and was now surpassing pre-COVID levels of staffing and business. Fellow IPA connoisseur Bill Kauffman would capture my feelings about craft breweries pretty well in a speech extolling the virtues of "localism," saying, "The craft beer thing is mocked, but it inculcates homeward-looking habits and is a nourishing manifestation of do-it-yourself. The loyalty that both sippers and topers show to local beers is a true-blue example of patriotism of place."

Gray's enthusiasm for Batavia's potential was contagious. He was convinced that after decades of stagnation, the town had begun an upward trajectory. He felt that the "black cloud that had hung over Batavia since the downtown was bulldozed during urban renewal" was beginning to pass, with business occupancy on Main Street increasing and internal community resistance to change dissipating.

As I headed back to the third-base grandstand, I felt good about spending money buying a locally brewed beer, knowing the proceeds would support someone like Matt, his young family, and his local employees, as opposed to paying an exorbitant price for a generic beer at a major league game, knowing that my dollars were being funneled to large multinational corporations like InBev, whose revenues were over $57 billion in 2022.

A new pitcher was warming up, and kids began to converge alongside the left-field foul line fence in anticipation of the nightly opportunity to run the bases with the mascot, Dewey the Muckdog, following the top of the fifth inning. Seeing their excited smiles always reminded me of Bates and made me imagine how much he'd enjoy this. While my daughter, Shea, could not yet walk, much less run, I knew she would have loved seeing the mascot up close as well. Obviously there was no way for me to bring an infant along on my reporting trips, and while I would have loved to have brought Bates on some, at his age—he would be entering kindergarten in the fall—I wouldn't have felt comfortable just abandoning him in the bleachers while I bounced around visiting with people. There were too many miles separating us all. Right as I was settling into my seat for the fifth, Marcy would be feeding Shea as part of her bedtime routine, before helping Bates into his PJs and tucking him into bed. I missed being there to read him a *LEGO Star Wars* bedtime story, and of course to help Marcy handle the challenge of putting two young kids to bed at the same time, alone.

Some more walks, an error, a double steal, and a double off the bat of six-foot-four, 225-pound Gavin Schrader, who had played high school ball at Batavia's Notre Dame High School and was slated to begin his college career at Niagara University in the fall, led to three more runs for Batavia in the fifth, extending their lead to 5–0 over the visiting Pioneers. Dr. Ross Fanara and his wife, Shirley, the longtime season ticket holders who were raising their two great-grandsons, Kartier and Kamdyn, were in their usual seats two rows behind the Muckdogs dugout. The Fanaras each had $199 "VIP" season tickets, which featured assigned seats in Dwyer's "lower bowl" and included periodic visits from a waitress clad in a striped referee jersey to take food and drink orders. General admission season tickets, like Ginny's and Betsey's, included open seating that began a few rows up on the other side of a concourse that wrapped around the stadium. Both varieties offered the "No Waste Ticket Policy," meaning that unused tickets from games that were missed could be rolled over for use at future games.

Ross told me he still remembered playing under the lights here when it was MacArthur Park and he was a slightly built child recovering from polio. His fandom, meanwhile, dated back to 1951, when he began riding his bike to minor league Clippers games, setting him on the path to serve, decades later, with Shirley on the board of the Muckdogs (a position whose name belied the less glamorous reality that their work included tasks like minor painting jobs around the ballpark and pulling weeds from the stadium grounds). As I watched Ross watch the game, I could almost see him being transported to pleasant memories of summers gone by, content and unfrazzled as his great-grandsons sprinted through the stands. Watching the frantic energy of the young boys enjoying precious hours on the loose, well past their bedtimes, was a joy for me too.

*   *   *

Ross and Shirley Fanara shared a modest home a few miles from the ballpark. Ross told me it was only 1,200 square feet, as "we didn't anticipate raising any kids in it." It was a curious hybrid of the neatness common to grandparents everywhere—including plastic coverings on the lampshades—with a profusion of children's toys spilling over in all the corners. The boys' bedroom, with its *PAW Patrol* desk and bunk beds topped with stuffed dinosaurs, reminded me of my son Bates's room, where his longtime favorite stuffed animal, "Tail-ey" the dinosaur, resides. Ross and Shirley's most treasured possessions were housed in a five-foot glass cabinet near their front door that was filled with Muckdogs memorabilia like a Ryan Howard bobblehead and countless signed baseballs. Ross gestured around him at the tidy, comfortable home and said, "As you can see, I've chosen the path of simplicity at this point in my life."

Ross told me they tried to limit the boys' television consumption to thirty minutes a day, instead keeping them occupied with karate practice twice a week, tee-ball twice a week, and additional visits on the weekend to the Notre Dame High School baseball field, where Ross would tutor the boys in baseball before bringing them to the library to play on the computer and do some reading lessons. Thinking about how exhausted I am after watching my two kids for a long day, I had a hard time imagining how someone could do it in their eighties. When asked where he got the energy, Ross responded, "Love. All I can say is that I love them and love life and am thankful that God gave me another day to be with them."

Shirley obviously felt the same. "It's so neat to see how simple things are amazing to kids," she said, with Ross adding, "It keeps us going." Of course, underneath this happiness lies the sobering reality that they will not be around forever, and it is unclear what will happen to the boys when they are no longer around to care for them. At one point Ross told me that he sometimes cried at night and prayed that God would "give me three or four more years to raise them."

*   *   *

After Elmira scored twice in the top half of the sixth, Skip Martinez turned to last year's ace, imposing right-hander Julian Pichardo, whose grandparents Mike and Cindy Baluja were no doubt anxiously tuning in to the YouTube broadcast in their living room back in Tampa. Despite impressive velocity that appeared to be in the high 80s, Pichardo grew a little rattled at what looked like a botched call by the umps on a pickoff attempt, drawing his ire along with that of Skip Martinez. He allowed a two-run double over the course of two innings, to go along with three strikeouts.

As the crowd began to thin and the temperature dipped into the fifties, I noticed a middle-aged woman diligently keeping score in a notebook, recording the results of each at-bat using a form of shorthand code that's been around for over 150 years. She stood on the concourse above the lower-level seats on the third-base side, coughing a little and bouncing to keep warm despite being wrapped in a blanket and wearing a winter hat. Her name was Cathy Preston. Bill Kauffman had introduced us over the winter, noting that she was a longtime season ticket holder and one of the few remaining members of the vanishing tribe of those who regularly kept score at baseball games. She enjoyed how methodical the ritual was, like a puzzle that kept her engaged for every pitch. Such was her devotion to scorekeeping that she used to grow anxious leaving her seats to grab something at the concession stand for fear she would miss some of the action and fail to record it in her notebook. She now appreciated the fact Robbie had a local girl providing wait service to her section of VIP season tickets behind the third-base dugout. For Cathy, baseball was all about the Muckdogs; MLB teams barely registered on her radar. She dismissed MLB as "only caring about the almighty dollar, whereas the Muckdogs play for a pittance." In truth, the collegiate Muckdogs actually paid for the opportunity to play there. Cathy, like many other Muckdogs fans, "value[d] their blood, sweat, and tears."

Cathy's other passion was trivia, and she would take to greeting me with trivia questions as the summer progressed. Her weeks were structured around a regular circuit of local trivia nights she would attend—T.F. Brown's on Tuesday, Eli Fish on Wednesday, the Caryville Inn on Thursday. She even carried an almanac in her purse to occasionally study if she needed to kill some time—"that's the kind of nerd I am," she joked. Her efforts did earn her a spot on *Jeopardy* in 2003, though she was suffering with morning sickness from her pregnancy with her daughter, Aurelia, at the time, and said she was preoccupied just trying "not to throw up on Alex." She did note with pride, though, that she got the Daily Double.

After the Muckdogs extended their lead to 6–4 with a sacrifice fly in the bottom of the seventh, Alex Hale, son of groundskeeper and former Attica guard Larry Hale, recorded the first out of the ninth before Skip Martinez turned to flamethrower Carlos Rodriguez to close it out. Rodriguez was undoubtedly the hardest thrower on the team, topping out in the high 90s the previous summer before dipping to the low 90s this summer as he continued to rehab from an arm injury. Tall and well built, he had the unmistakable look of an elite athlete and hoped to make the jump from a Florida community college to Division I Eastern Kentucky the upcoming fall. Even Robbie stopped working long enough to lean against a garbage can near the first-base dugout to take some weight off his foot and watch Rodriguez.

Following the final out, a fly ball that was easily caught by the center fielder, Rodriguez joined the rest of his teammates in what would become a regular postgame gathering at home plate following victories, where the Muckdogs would congratulate each other and salute the crowd. Robbie posted up at the front gate to wish exiting fans a good night as they streamed out before retreating to his office, where he would fall asleep while settling the game's concession sales; the sellout crowd of 3,642 had led to a great night for them. Fighting to wake up long enough to finish his postgame tasks, Robbie shut off the light in his cinder-block office at around 1:00 a.m. and retreated to the small house a few blocks away that he crashed at during the season. He'd soon be back at Dwyer to prepare for an all-day youth tournament he would be hosting the next morning. The gates would open at 8:00 a.m.

*   *   *

I couldn't help but compare Batavia's Opening Night with the Pirates Opening Day at PNC Park in Pittsburgh, to which I had brought Bates a few months prior. I'd been conflicted on whether to go, as it felt wrong to me to spend money supporting the franchise of owner Bob Nutting, the billionaire whose payroll was always near the bottom of the league, resulting in mediocrity, year in, year out.

One of the primary sources of Nutting's personal fortune offers a cautionary tale of what happens when a single-minded pursuit of return on investment trumps any sense of corporate social responsibility. He is the CEO of Ogden Newspapers, and the fourth generation of the Ogden Nutting family to run the company, which has grown to include over forty daily newspapers from New York to Hawaii. The company's website pays homage to the importance of local journalism, stating, "We believe local newspapers should not only report the news of the day, but also tell the stories of their communities, and of the people who live there. We take writing the first draft of history seriously."

However, it appears as if they are following the business model favored by predatory private equity investors in the newspaper industry; namely, aggressively cutting expenses by reducing staff and news coverage while still collecting advertising and subscription revenue. Deborah Caulfield Rybak wrote on the website Politics on Maui:

> Here on Maui, however, it looks like Ogden's intent is to squeeze every last dime out of its investment and leave an emaciated skeleton in its wake . . . Staff has been decimated by layoffs, buyouts, and early retirements. Employee numbers have eroded significantly, from a one-time high of about 120 employees to the current staff of about 39 . . . In addition to its reduced news-gathering ability, the paper also has lost much of its local personality. During the tenure of publisher Joe Bradley, who retired last year, the *Maui News* ran community-focused editorials. It took stands on issues, political candidates, and other matters of importance to Maui County residents. Two publishers later, the paper's daily opinion page editorials are 95% reprinted from other newspapers.

Nutting was busy profiting from the gutting of local newspapers while simultaneously refusing to pay to field a competitive major league team, even though the Pirates' franchise value had appreciated over $1 billion under his family's ownership. Even more galling than owners making billions regardless of whether they succeeded on the field was Rob Manfred's defense of them—during the 2022 MLB lockout no less—in which he said, "We actually hired an investment banker, a really good one, to look at that very issue. If you look at the purchase price of franchises, the cash that's put in during the period of ownership and then what they've sold for, historically the return on those investments is below what you'd get in the stock market . . . with a lot more risk."

The statement was patently absurd, as even a cursory glance at the purchase price of MLB teams and their estimated franchise values today reveals remarkable appreciation. It was clever, though, in that the teams' financial books are generally closed, and therefore the assertion couldn't be proven false. Of course, if owners really believed they'd be better off investing in the stock market, they're welcome to sell at any time. In the case of the Pirates' Nutting, there are tens of thousands of Pittsburgh residents who would be thrilled if he did.

Despite my frustration with Pirates ownership, the possibility of a fun father-son outing led me to abandon principle in pursuit of potential happiness for Bates. Unfortunately, while PNC Park is a gem and a civic treasure, the game day experience was underwhelming. The $50 apiece we spent on two upper-deck tickets (which was actually cheap by MLB Opening Day standards) to go along with waiting in a thirty-minute line for $15 parking nearly half a mile away, dampened my enthusiasm before we even set foot in the ballpark. We were then left standing in another long line to pass through security, where disengaged employees had us empty our pockets and screened us, all the waiting and standing around leaving Bates exhausted and grumpy. Once inside, the two of us had to fight our way through thick crowds in the concourse to purchase a Dippin' Dots for Bates and a $12 lukewarm cheeseburger, served by bored employees, to go along with a $15 Iron City tallboy beer for myself. We hadn't even found our seats yet, and I was already down nearly $150. Still, the weather was wonderful, and the club had added some fun new family attractions along the riverwalk area like a pirate ship for kids to climb, which Bates scampered through happily.

As we eventually took our seats, it became clear that the field was too far away for a young kid like Bates to focus on, especially with the game moving along at the plodding pace that was ubiquitous in pre–pitch clock major league baseball. Furthermore, what amounted to a AAA roster for the Pirates didn't do much to capture my attention. Despite this, young twenty- and thirtysomethings seemed to be having fun gulping down beers with their friends in the sunshine, and I was reminded of some of my own wild trips to Shea Stadium fresh out of college with my buddies. But it quickly became apparent that Bates was ready to go home, and so we left after four or five innings, a bit poorer, and with little to share in the way of good memories.

It wouldn't be fair to extrapolate too much from one parent's less-than-ideal trip to the ballpark with a young child. Still, I couldn't help but wonder what it said about the future of major league baseball if it not only appeared incapable of capturing my son's attention but even I—a lifelong fan who played baseball through two years of college—wasn't all that interested in sitting through an entire game on a beautiful Opening Day at one of the sport's premier ballparks.

6

Auburn Doubledays at Batavia Muckdogs

June 6

I began my Monday morning in Batavia with a visit to the Pub Coffee Hub, a cool coffee shop located in the old Harvester Center on the east side of town. The hulking industrial building had been home to the Johnson Harvester Company beginning in the late 1880s, and, after being acquired by the Massey-Harris Company in 1910, its production of farm equipment became the largest industry in Batavia. When it closed in 1956 it drove unemployment to more than 20 percent, and residents were no longer able to mark their day by the steam whistle that would blow outside the factory. Since it would have been impossible to find a single tenant to occupy the nearly 900,000-square-foot facility, it was instead repurposed to become a "business incubator," providing emerging small businesses a place to grow, with over fifty now calling it home. The Pub Coffee Hub, occupying an inviting space on the ground floor, was one. It was owned and managed by Rob Credi, a 2001 graduate of Batavia High School. Bill Kauffman's wife, Lucine, had been his high school tennis coach. Rob wanted to provide an independent alternative to the town's two Tim Hortons, two Dunkin Donuts, and two Starbucks.

And indeed he had. His coffee shop was warm and pleasant, cozy on snowy days and bright and airy on sunny mornings like this one in early June. An impressive collection of new and used records for sale was displayed near the door. Panoramic views of the tree-lined cemetery across the street provided an aura of serenity, and it came as no surprise that Bill Kauffman, who often spoke and wrote of the mystical connection he felt with the ghosts of Batavia past, enjoyed working here with his morning cup of coffee.

Knowing that I was a Mets fan, Bill had tipped me off to a fellow devoted Mets fan (and avid reader) who was a regular at the Pub, which is how I came to meet Eric Zwieg. Eric, who looked to be in his midfifties, was immediately recognizable, sitting at the counter reading postmodern fiction (as I would discover he did nearly every day), often Don DeLillo. His literary tastes—which included some writers I never felt I could fully understand—humbled the English major in me.

Eric told me that he'd gotten his bachelor's degree five years ago, followed soon after by a master's, and was now at work on his MFA, for which he was writing a novel. He'd also authored several plays, in keeping with his interest in "community-based theater," many of which were funded by the Genesee-Orleans Regional Arts Council (GO ART!) and performed locally. He'd grown up in Jamestown, New York, where he'd played Little League baseball and been a fan of the local minor league club. Eric had gone on to travel the country with various theater and music groups, before settling down in Batavia to pursue his education and his writing. He was also a Muckdogs fan (though he went to games only when they didn't conflict with the Mets, which he tuned in to religiously, attending daily "church" when they played at 7:05 p.m., a service presided over by his "boys," the announcers Gary Cohen, Ron Darling, and Keith Hernandez). He said he began sitting near Bill Kauffman in the third-base bleachers at Dwyer Stadium in 2016 and credited new owners Robbie and Nellie with "changing the feel of the ballpark in one season" following the launch of the collegiate Muckdogs in the summer of 2021.

As we spoke that morning and subsequent ones like it, I detected a prickliness and contrarian impulse in Eric that, oddly enough, made him one of those people you couldn't quite help becoming interested in. Or maybe I just had a masochistic anthropological desire to try to better understand someone who seemed, almost intentionally, to be resisting my ability to do so. For example, he would say that he was an "old school baseball guy, and gimmicky promotions aren't my bag," before adding that as a "performing arts professional I'm always assessing the off-field experience" and crediting Robbie for doing a good job with it.

Fortified with a few cups of coffee, I made the short mile-and-a-half drive over to Dwyer from the coffee shop. I'd grown to appreciate how nothing in Batavia was ever more than a mile or two away. Arriving in the early afternoon, I watched the ballpark come slowly to life, the field looking sharp after Larry had prepped it that morning, and the players wandering in slowly, some having already adopted a nocturnal schedule and enjoying their first meal of the day in the leather recliners in the locker room. A few then stretched and jogged before taking some extra infield practice in their shorts and red short-sleeve uniform hoodie pullovers. Baseball, more than perhaps any other sport due to the sheer number of games, develops a daily rhythm that is reassuring and comforting in its constancy.

Tonight's opponent was the Auburn Doubledays, who had made the short trip about ninety miles west on the New York State Thruway to visit Batavia. Auburn was another blue-collar community—famous for the hulking maximum-security prison located right in the heart of town—that had been stripped of its major league affiliate and replaced it with an amateur team in the PGCBL.

Some clouds had rolled in, and I asked Robbie if he expected rain to interfere with the evening's game. He gave me an icy look and confidently declared they'd be okay, adding, "We don't use the R-word here." On cue, it began to pour at 5:15 p.m. as the Doubledays were taking batting practice, a little more than an hour before the first pitch. Larry Hale, Muckdogs groundskeeper, ran onto the field, where he was joined by some visiting Doubledays players in a scramble to cover the infield with the tarp. "Who'll Stop the Rain" played on the PA system. Predictably the rain stopped as soon as the tarp was down, and the game was cleared to begin with a delayed 7:40 p.m. start.

Tonight was Elba Night at the ballpark, meaning that general manager Marc Witt had chosen groups from the nearby village to participate in the off-field events that surrounded every game. Elba, situated a few miles north of Batavia on the fertile muckland soil that inspired the team's name, produced rich harvests, especially of onions, leading to its being dubbed the "Onion Capital of the World."

The game would begin with an assembly of tractors driving across the gravel warning track as part of a ceremony featuring the Elba chapter of the Future Farmers of America, an agricultural student group, followed by the Elba Elementary School Student Council leading the crowd in the Pledge of Allegiance. As adults we sometimes forget how exciting it is to hear your name broadcast over a PA system as a child, but you could see the pride in the kids' faces when they heard their names announced by public address announcer Paul Spiotta. Following the national anthem, which was sung by the Elba Upper Elementary and High School chorus, Paul announced:

> Throwing out the first pitch today will be the Onion Queen herself, Georgia Luft. Georgia is a three-sport athlete participating in soccer, basketball, and softball. She has participated in National Honor Society, Student Athletic Association, and FFA as a member and past officer. She has been a member of the Genesee County Dairy Princess program for several years and will be attending Finger Lakes Community College for physical education.

Paul failed to note that she would be throwing an onion in place of a ball, which she did, delivering a nice pitch and receiving a warm round of applause.

Elba was a pretty place, a place Bill Kauffman called home, having lived in the same charming but modest century-old Greek Revival house tucked alongside farm fields for three decades since returning home from Washington, DC. As a young man, he'd worked in DC for the legendary senator Daniel Patrick Moynihan, and later as an editor for the libertarian magazine *Reason*. The more he saw how things worked in the capital, though, the more he developed a renewed appreciation for home. While DC was a fun place for a guy in his twenties, he'd grown disenchanted as he'd gotten closer to the political machinations that define life inside the Beltway. This disillusionment was compounded by the sense that as someone who had begun to feel like "an anarchist philosophically"—or at least what those in polite company would classify as a libertarian—"why would I be in DC?"

Even more importantly, though, he had experienced a "powerful homesickness" for Batavia, where "every corner and building had the weight of myth and memory and stories." And so he had moved back.

The Onion Queen was a sought-after local honor and just the sort of tradition that, along with countless others like it, had helped pull Bill back home. Bill Kauffman's daughter, Gretel, had even written a college application essay about the competition that began, "While earning the title of Onion Queen is not necessarily the dream of every little Elba-bred girl, competing in the contest is certainly a rite of passage for those who have grown up watching the prom gown–clad 'big girls' parade through the village park on the arm of a mortified Boy Scout." Bill Kauffman said his mom still joked about how she would have won had the eventual winner not "been making eyes at the judges."

After the Elba students exited the field, and the catcher substituted the opening-pitch onion for a ball, the game began. The Doubledays jumped out to an early lead in the top of the first with a sacrifice fly to right field, taking advantage of two hit batsmen and a single allowed by Batavia starter Josh Milleville, a right-hander from nearby Lockport, New York, who pitched for Division I Fairleigh Dickinson.

Bill Kauffman had badly wanted to come to the game, but, despite his feeling well, his wife, Lucine, had prevailed upon him not to, since he was still technically within the ten-day COVID quarantine period following his positive test. Longing to experience the soothing rhythms of baseball at Dwyer after almost ten months since the final out had been recorded the previous summer, he hatched a plan to take it in without putting anyone at risk. He told me he would sit alone beyond the right-field fence in a lawn chair. I wanted to see how he was doing and called to confirm he was out there. And called again. And again. No answer. I was puzzled. So I reluctantly exited Dwyer and made my way out toward the expanse of grass beyond the right-field fence, where I quickly spotted Bill, sitting in his chair with a sheaf of papers on his lap, wielding a pen, and, from the looks of it, busy editing. I told him I'd been calling, and, with a bit of pride, he informed me that he didn't carry a phone. I knew a handful of proud flip-phone owners—including my mom and father-in-law—but hadn't run into anyone who didn't carry any sort of phone (even including my ninety-eight-year-old grandmother). Bill told me he didn't like how people had grown "enslaved to their phones," and that the only time he made an exception was when he traveled for work, when he'd borrow his eighty-seven-year-old father's phone in the event someone needed to reach him in an emergency.

"The more people insist I get one, the more determined I am to resist," he said.

As Bill, looking every bit the writer in his rumpled button-down oxford shirt, gray slacks, and blue ball cap, sipped on a can of seltzer, I mentioned how we could barely see the field beyond the tall right-field fence featuring miscolored pieces of plywood. He didn't seem to mind, telling me how he often brought his work to a nearby copse of trees to edit, and how just being there led to a feeling of inner peace, being "near the stadium where I've spent a thousand nights, the nearby playground where I scampered as a child from dawn to dusk. It's not so much specific memories as a feeling that washes over me and makes it easier to work." Noticing how he had retreated into a place of rumination, almost talking to himself as much as to me, I kept quiet. "Sometimes I get a sense of overwhelming gratitude and sense that I can't believe I get to live here, which is amazing, as some people think it's just a scummy town, but it brings balance and heft to my life," he said. The remaining white clouds in the sky had given way to the dark blue of impending nightfall, the lights of Dwyer now doing the work of illuminating the field. Bill, unmoved from his reverie, told me that even though he couldn't really see anything, "I like the sound of the bat and ball and Paul's voice over the speakers."

"I'm reminded of Billy Pilgrim in *Slaughterhouse-Five*," he concluded. "I become unstuck in time here."

* * *

Meanwhile the game continued its deliberate march into the night. Shortly after I returned to the grandstands, the teams traded runs in the third, at which point Paul made an announcement:

> The night's Turnbull Heating and Cooling Veteran of the Game is our own volunteer and security guard Dave Fisher. Dave joined the U.S. Army right out of high school, serving four years of active duty. He served overseas during both the Noriega Conflict in Panama and Desert Storm in Iraq as a member of the Third Armored Division. Dave received a

number of medals while in service, including the Good Conduct Medal, Civil Defense Medal, Southeast Asia Medal, an
Iraq War Vet Medal, and Overseas Medal. Please give a round
of applause to our very own Dave Fisher.

Moments later Dave shouted, "Incoming"—not entirely
ironically—as a foul ball sailed into the bleachers, as he was wont
to do.

The Muckdogs had a huge bottom of the sixth, capitalizing on
a flurry of hit batsmen, walks, singles, and a double to push four
runs across the plate and pull out to a 5–2 lead. The team's hot start
to the season appeared poised to continue, delivering smiles to the
1,722 in attendance. It was a steady and reassuringly positive vibe, as
much connected to human interactions off the field as to what was
happening on it. Dallas Young, an outfielder from Detroit who had
joined the Muckdogs from Henry Ford Community College, captured this aura when Jerry Reinhart asked him how he was doing one
afternoon, and he replied, "Just vibing." The phrase took off in the
locker room and then spread to social media. Soon after, the players
noticed a young fan holding a posterboard sign with a related phrase
on it during a game: "Just Vibes." The boy gave it to Dallas, who
would hold it aloft during the team's home plate celebration following games for the rest of the summer.

*   *   *

I would later ask Dallas, a Black player from a big city, how he found
life in small and overwhelmingly white Batavia (which had only
about 6 percent Black residents, according to the most recent cen-
sus). Dallas told me that it had been an overwhelmingly positive
experience, beginning not long after his arrival, when a gaggle of
little girls nervously approached him at Target and asked if he played
for the Muckdogs. They mumbled a nervous "Hi" before darting
away. "I've never been around so many nice people," he said. "They
care about the team, and they care about each other. They have to . . .
It's a small town, everyone knows everyone, and they want to see
each other succeed."

Pitcher Julian Pichardo had his own, slightly odder, introduction to the support of the Batavia community when he trespassed onto a "heaven-like" piece of property just outside town to access a small lake he'd spotted as a potential fishing hole. He loved to fish on the few days the team had off—rewarding himself for a good performance or helping to clear his mind of a bad one—and was always on the lookout for a good spot. Suddenly he heard some shooting, followed by a man shouting at him from a distance. It turns out the owner of the land had been out shooting before spotting Julian's bright orange waterproof bag. When the man approached and angrily warned him that he could have been inadvertently hit with a stray bullet, Pichardo apologized. The landowner then recognized the tall pitcher with the goatee and long hair, and even mentioned that he'd once bought him and teammate Trey Bacon breakfast at the local diner. He gave Pichardo his card and invited him to come back anytime to fish, as long as he let him know in advance to make sure there weren't any more dangerous surprises.

These stories of the "good vibes" shared by the Muckdogs and the local community were a balm to my psyche, which I feared had been heading to a bad place, as the news assaulting it from both traditional and social media was almost uniformly negative, and often framed in virtually apocalyptic language. A professor friend of mine in Pittsburgh had taken to calling this constant drumbeat of crisis "the panic industrial complex," and it was taking its toll on mental health and social cohesion. It wasn't so much that I fell prey to the panic of the day—if anything, I was aware that most of the stories were hyperbolic. But I was bothered by the corrosive impact this was having on our society, with political leaders and media personalities incentivized to keep us on edge and at each other's throats.

*   *   *

After the visiting Doubledays bounced back with three runs in the top of the seventh to tie the game, I went on a walk to stretch my legs and see how Robbie was doing at the concession stand. As I did, I ran into a bespectacled gray-haired gentleman wearing a Hawaiian shirt and standing next to a folding table with a display seeking new members for the Landmark Society of Genesee County. He looked a bit lonely and eager to chat, and as the son and grandson of community-minded history buffs, I had a soft spot for just this sort of person. I walked over and explained how I was writing a book about the community and the team and was curious about his display. He introduced himself as Richard Beatty and said that he'd retired in 2016 from his job as a state industrial property appraiser, in the hope of getting more involved in the community. He told me he was now president of the Landmark Society, which had been formed in 1965 to fight the urban renewal movement, joking that he began as a volunteer with the society but, after finding himself the "last man standing," became the president.

Beatty had grown up in Florida and also spent time in New Hampshire and the Southern Tier town of Deposit, New York, before landing in Batavia in 1999. He launched into an enthusiastic description of a new play, based on the work of a city historian and funded by GO ART! that told the story of a prominent downtown mansion that once housed city hall and, more recently, the police station, and whose future was now being decided by civic leaders. Beatty echoed Bill Kauffman's disgust with the impact of urban renewal on Batavia, voicing his frustration with the community's track record of preserving historic infrastructure, and sadness to see some of its most impressive downtown buildings and mansions bulldozed in the name of "progress." He shook his head when describing Batavia neighbors of his who now rarely frequented any of the remaining downtown restaurants, preferring Applebee's.

To read about the Batavia of old, before outsiders descended on the town preaching the gospel of urban renewal, is to discover a place that had texture and charm. Ruth McEvoy captures a bit of this in her book *The History of the City of Batavia,* writing of John Brown's grocery store at 18 Main Street, where, until he died in 1928, Brown would make a point of warmly greeting each customer. McEvoy describes a downtown featuring an array of local restaurants ranging from the Dagwood, known for serving tasty sandwiches to office workers on Main Street, to Ange's, where Ange's personality was reportedly as much a draw as the food. For decades beginning in the late 1800s the Hotel Richmond was one of the best places for travelers between Albany and Buffalo to stay. Large leather chairs greeted tired guests in the lobby, and they could retire to a pleasant coffee shop to enjoy treats prepared by the hotel's resident baker. Organizations hosted balls in its private dining hall, where Batavia residents would don their finest outfits to enjoy a night on the town. The Hamilton Hotel, the American House, and the Ellicott House were other downtown options for travelers in the days before Interstate 90 was developed and led to their being replaced by chain hotels alongside the highway. Richard Beatty and the Landmark Society knew that "old Batavia" could never be resurrected, but they were devoted nonetheless to at least stopping the bleeding and preserving the few remaining historic buildings that had escaped the wrecking ball.

Beatty had no use for pro sports, finding the "absolute greed that characterizes the business disgusting," but did enjoy his visits to Dwyer and wanted to support the new owners, Robbie and Nellie, and so bought season tickets. He told me that he generally spent more time "socializing than watching the game," which didn't come as a surprise, as he had by now been animatedly telling me about Batavia's architectural evolution for over an inning. As fascinating as his history was, I didn't want to miss what was now a 5–5 tie as the game entered the late innings. I politely thanked Richard for his time and pledged to get together with him soon at the Pub Coffee Hub to continue our conversation.

I'd found the discussion with Richard to be surprisingly uplifting. He knew I was working on a book about Batavia, so perhaps he was just doing a marketing pitch for the town he had grown to love. But beyond that, maybe there was something to the gospel of localism Bill Kauffman had been proselytizing. Rather than spending our time raging at our TVs or iPhones over national issues we have limited ability to influence, perhaps it's healthier and more satisfying to focus our attention closer to home, as Richard was, where we could make a difference.

Somehow Batavia survived the top of the eighth despite two errors by usually sure-handed shortstop Caleb Rodriguez. Brian Fry, a rising sophomore at the University of Toledo from nearby Medina, New York, led off the bottom of the eighth with a double, one of his four hits on the night. After six-foot-five, 250-pound cleanup hitter Tyler Cannoe popped out to first, six-foot-four, 220-pound Daniel Burroway, who rounded out the hulking middle of the Muckdogs batting order, singled and stole second, putting runners on second and third. The next batter flicked a fly ball to shallow left field. As the ball dropped just in front of the oncoming left fielder, one could feel a moment of tension as the crowd collectively wondered if Skip would send Fry home. It would be a dangerous call, as the ball seemed shallow enough to make for a relatively easy putout at the plate, but Skip waved Fry home nonetheless. And he made it, bringing the crowd to its feet and prompting Muckdogs play-by-play YouTube announcer John Carubba—whose enthusiasm sometimes seemed to eclipse that of the players—to proclaim, "This is great baseball, folks, this is why you should come to the ballpark, all kinds of strange twists and turns!" It wouldn't be the last time that Skip went with his gut making decisions with baserunners. It was fun to watch, as the team embraced this gunslinger mentality, always pushing for the extra base or steal, challenging the opponent to make a play.

Skip's seat-of-the-pants style called to mind colorful managers of old like Billy Martin and Earl Weaver, whose teams had unique identities molded by their managerial vision and style (and no short-age of flair). This, of course, was before the ascendence of quants from places like MIT and Harvard Business School into baseball's upper management, producing, in the words of three-time Manager of the Year Joe Maddon in his memoir *The Book of Joe*, a "brutally efficient" game that had been excised of so much of what had made it compelling.

Reliever Trey Bacon, whose live arm and low-90s fastball belied his slight build, made short work of the visiting Pioneers in the top of the ninth, striking out the final batter of his three strong innings, in which he gave up only one hit while striking out four. The win would mark the third for the Muckdogs in their first four games. As "Hit the Road Jack" played, and the team congregated around home plate for their postgame salute to the crowd, I began to sense that this team could be going places. They had a productive offense coupled with strong pitching, even if their defense had been spotty at times. More importantly, though, I'd begun to detect something in their chemistry that was intangible yet palpable, that combination of a commitment to winning while having a good time that character-izes so many successful teams. This developing identity came across on the field as they did things like hustling to take an extra base, and off the field when their chemistry was apparent as they played the imaginative role-playing game Mafia on the team bus. The collaborative storytelling game recalled summer camps of decades gone by and seemed delightfully anachronistic in today's age of iPhone amusements.

Public address announcer Paul Spiotta, buoyed by the night's Muckdogs victory, sent the happy crowd home with the reminder "See you here tomorrow night at 7:05 as Jamestown comes to town with the Arc GLOW [a local nonprofit designed to help people with developmental and intellectual disabilities] giveaway, and remember, Go Dawgs!"

I caught up with Robbie as he stood at the gate saying good night to the fans, grimacing a bit as he shuffled around. He told me it had been a bad day for his foot, which was a noteworthy departure from his usual upbeat determination. He shared with me the dizzying array of things he did just to remain ambulatory, such as hot and cold therapy in the team's training room and an entire home filled "with crap for my feet like marbles to pick up with my toes, creams, massagers, and everything else that Amazon recommends." Few of the passing fans understood the extent of his pain, and it was a testament to his stoicism that few would discover just how bad it had gotten.

I picked up some Labatt's at the gas station and a midnight snack of McDonald's on my way back to the La Quinta, which had become my preferred resting spot in Batavia. I tried to get some work done for as long as I could keep my eyes open before passing out into a deep sleep. Though initially worried that it would keep me awake, I discovered that the steady stream of passing traffic on the nearby thruway was actually quite soothing. There was something comforting about surrendering to sleep under warm covers while listening to the hum of big rigs plowing onward, ferrying their wares deep into the night.

The next morning I headed to the sixty-seven-year-old local institution the Pok-A-Dot restaurant for breakfast. The regulars eyed me warily as I made my way to a table. My casual dress—shorts, T-shirt, and ball cap—shouldn't have invited any scrutiny, but in a town the size of Batavia the locals still had a sixth sense for outsiders. Usually I found that this translated into a friendly welcome, but for some reason I would always get a cold reception at the Pok-A-Dot (which was one reason I eventually stopped trying and chose the friendlier Miss Batavia Diner as my go-to breakfast spot).

The same talkative young waitress Bill Kauffman had introduced me to on a preseason visit to the Pok-A-Dot months before greeted me and asked if I was "waiting for Bill," but that still didn't result in quicker or friendlier service. If anything, it made me feel more uncomfortable that she immediately remembered me as an outsider. I sat alone for a long time before sheepishly making my way to the counter to flag her down and place an order. Meanwhile I listened in as the same regulars I remembered from my first visit sat at the same cluster of nearby tables, almost as if they'd never left, complaining about a list of topics that could have been lifted from the previous night's broadcast of *Hannity*. This morning they were especially worked up about new gun control measures that had supposedly been introduced by Governor Kathy Hochul. One offered the evergreen "If you take away guns from good people, only bad guys will have them," while another griped, "She stood up there yesterday announcing new restrictions like she was accepting the Nobel Peace Prize—just like Cuomo used to—they just want more power."

While I hadn't been too impressed with the governor, and was a gun owner myself, I still found their talk to be unsettling. The angry discussion over breakfast orders the waitress now knew by heart resembled the clichéd "diner full of MAGA Republicans" that one reads so much about in the national media, but the coverage of which is so often insultingly simplistic and inaccurate. But where were the Bill Kauffmans and Cathy Prestons and Russ Salways in these parachute visits into Red America? I had often wondered. Where were the intellectuals and eccentrics and just fundamentally nice people that I'd spent time with over the course of years of reporting in small towns, people who would happily show a stranger around town to make them feel welcome? This morning offered a taste of a less welcoming, and more angry, place. Some of their grievances were legitimate, but that made them no less demoralizing to listen to, as it was a sobering reminder of the toxic politics that had seeped into every nook of our country. All I could do was hope that they would spend some time enjoying a ballgame with their neighbors at Dwyer (where I had not seen them) and less time consuming the national media whose business model was brilliantly captured by Matt Taibbi in the title of his book *Hate Inc.: Why Today's Media Makes Us Despise One Another.*

7

Jamestown Tarp Skunks at Batavia Muckdogs

June 10

After a short visit home, I threw some clothes into my old army rucksack and hit the road for the four-hour drive northeast to Batavia for a game against the Jamestown Tarp Skunks. As I traversed the rolling Pennsylvania farmland heading toward Erie, I was struck by how, despite its myriad problems, this country was still remarkably beautiful.

I arrived in Batavia in the early afternoon, in time to grab a sub at the Northside Deli a few blocks from the ballpark. I'd quickly discovered why Northside had long been a local favorite, and on my drives up to Batavia—somewhere around Buffalo—I began to eagerly anticipate the chicken Parmesan that awaited at Northside. The deli, which had Muckdogs paraphernalia displayed alongside the ubiquitous Bills and Sabres pennants (as well as a small sticker on the cash register with a picture of President Biden pointing to the price display and saying, "I did this," a barbed reference to inflation), was also a favorite of the players, and I would often see them there wearing their red pregame hoodies, carb-loading before batting practice.

While I waited for my sandwich, and despite my growing disenchantment with MLB leadership, I nonetheless picked up a copy of the *New York Post* to check on how the Mets were doing. My New York Mets fandom had blossomed living in Manhattan in the late 1990s, when I had grown to love the colorful and overachieving squads led by Bobby Valentine. As a twentysomething college grad new to the big city, I loved catching the 7 train to Shea, or even just watching Mets games at a nearby Irish pub with my buddies. There was an energy to the team that was infectious, one that complemented the general buzz of those days in Manhattan that I found intoxicating. The Derek Jeter–led Yankees dynasty coupled with the advent of the regular-season Subway Series (and an eventual Subway World Series in 2000) injected yet more juice into baseball in the city. I became a WFAN sports radio junkie, each summer a roller coaster of highs and lows depending on the previous night's Mets performance, listening to afternoon host Mike Francesa insult callers of all stripes in his trademark fashion. Mike Piazza's home run against the Braves in the first game at Shea Stadium after the attacks of 9/11 remains one of my most cherished memories as a lifelong fan, helping me—and much of the city, it seemed—get back on our feet and rediscover what it was like to smile.

Oddly enough, another of my most treasured memories of major league baseball took place while deployed to Iraq in 2006 as an army infantry officer. Though the team had begun to evolve from the scrappy underdogs I'd grown to love in the late 1990s to underachieving favorites, I'd remained a devoted fan. I'd been proud to sport my Mets cap while stationed deep in Braves country at Fort Benning, Georgia, and later while drinking hefeweizen in the bars of Bad Nauheim, Germany, my next duty station. My interest in the Mets had not even dissipated nine months into a rough deployment to Iraq. That October, with my infantry battalion suffering considerable casualties in what was at the time the epicenter of Iraq's Sunni insurgency, Anbar Province, the Mets faced the St. Louis Cardinals in the National League Championship Series. This was after they had run away with the National League East with a dominant 97-win season.

My nightly ritual during those games was always the same. I would awake at about 3:30 a.m. (as Iraq was eight hours ahead of New York City), slide into my flip-flops, shake the cobwebs from my head, maybe grab a nonalcoholic beer and a frozen microwavable pizza from the fridge, and join my buddy (an equally obsessive Cardinals fan) in our little chow hall to watch America's pastime in the fertile crescent, courtesy of the Armed Forces Network. Our lonely vigil was interrupted only by the occasional soldier stopping in to grab some coffee before starting a guard shift in the desert night. These nights are frozen in my mind, marking the only prolonged distraction from what was otherwise a long year in a violent place.

Watching the games, listening to Shea Stadium rock to the chants of "Let's go Mets," I was temporarily transported to a different—better—place. I would've thought my interest in the Mets at night would have lessened after confronting a Sunni insurgency by day, but I found myself as emotionally invested in the outcome of the games as if I had been back home.

And then, as Mets fans will never forget, Yadier Molina shattered our dream on a chilly October night in Flushing, a crushing ninth-inning home run in Game 7 sending Shea's faithful back to the 7 train in dismay, and me—demoralized and exhausted—to face the dawn of another day in Anbar.

I volunteer all of this to show that whatever frustration I now have with MLB leadership marks a departure from the attitude I'd always had toward baseball, and that saddens me. The more I studied the economics of baseball, and as I absorbed the infuriating news of MLB's decision to strip forty-two communities of their minor league teams, the harder it was for me to recapture the naive innocence of a fandom undisturbed by an understanding of the organization's cold-blooded business decisions that are at odds with the sport's carefully cultivated image of Americana. I can't unhear comments such as those volunteered by one MLB executive who said, "MLB is about money. It's pure economics. If one minor league town won't pony up to fix a field, another one will. We can always find a better partner. These are sophisticated businesspeople." This was the embodiment of so much that was wrong with the sport. It was the ultimate betrayal of small towns across the country that had in many cases hosted minor league teams for a century. Part of me regrets having pulled back the curtain to better understand those who governed this "land of Oz," their values, and the motivations behind their decisions. Wearing my Mets cap now makes me feel like an accomplice to an enterprise I feel guilty supporting. And that really sucks.

*   *   *

When I arrived at Dwyer, Northside chicken Parm sub in hand, Robbie told me that they had a "motivational speaker" scheduled to address the team before batting practice, and so I went to the locker room to check it out. I figured it might also be a good chance for me to briefly introduce myself to the entire team, as so far I had just met a handful of the players individually. I asked Robbie, and he agreed. He had, in fact, agreed to all my requests, essentially providing me unlimited access anywhere I wanted to go all summer, from the locker room to the manager's office to the press box to the front office. I suspect this was partly because Robbie was a good sport and partly because he didn't seem particularly interested in what—if anything—I ended up writing. I suppose this shouldn't have been entirely surprising coming from a former minor league hockey brawler who wasn't a regular consumer of narrative nonfiction.

Neither did the team seem especially curious about my project. I know this, in part, because I left a few copies of my first book in the front of the locker room, inviting them to grab a copy and check it out if they needed something to read on their next long bus trip. I also figured it was important to provide some concrete evidence that I was in fact a published author, and not just some weirdo lurking around, notebook in hand. Alas, as the summer wore on, I'd steal a glance at the books in the hope that at least one player may have grabbed a copy—perhaps wanting to learn more about this author in their midst—but, alas, no, they sat untouched, collecting dust.

The motivational speaker that afternoon turned out to be Guy Allegretto. Apparently Allegretto was a decorated Vietnam veteran of the Marine Corps, and a friend of Dr. Ross Fanara. Allegretto, clad in a camouflage Marine ballcap and an extra-large red football jersey with the USMC globe and anchor crest on the front, wasted no time accelerating from 0 to about 150 on the intensity scale, adopting the persona of a drill instructor as he bellowed at the assembled college players, who were seated before him in their pregame uniforms on recliners and folding chairs.

He demanded they respond with shouts of "Yes sir" and "No sir," regaling them with tales of his six thousand Marine "brothers" holding out at Khe Sanh despite being surrounded by "forty thousand North Vietnamese Commies." He then drew the parallel between the marines overcoming the adversity of rockets, mortars, and hand-to-hand combat and the upcoming summer of baseball, shouting that just as "no one on Earth is gonna intimidate a US Marine, no one is gonna intimidate a Muckdog."

Though I liked Allegretto and wanted to buy in to his talk, I couldn't make the leap from combat—whose brutal reality I had experienced—to summer league baseball. Remarkably, though, it somehow seemed to resonate with the players, who, whether out of fear, shock, inspiration, or some peculiar mix of all three, were now on their feet shouting back in response to his commands. Somewhat taken aback by their enthusiasm, I realized that this summer would in fact be the highlight of many of their baseball lives, the end of roads that in many cases had begun ten or fifteen years earlier in backyards with parents and grandparents just as mine had. Perhaps this awareness helped fuel their will to win and to see the season as more than just an opportunity for additional practice.

As game time approached, a handful of Muckdogs sat at a folding table near the stadium entrance to sign autographs as fans began to stream in. Little kids tentatively approached, steered toward the table by their parents. When one got an autograph and shuffled away without saying thank you, his mom corrected him, saying, "Manners!" One boy, probably eight or nine, asked the players to sign his shirt. Both sides seemed to be benefiting from the ritual, as the assembled Muckdogs—many of whom were average players from middling college programs—enjoyed being treated like celebrities, while the younger kids, who wouldn't know the difference between Jerry Reinhart and Aaron Judge, were just thrilled to be interacting with these "famous" athletes.

I got a text from Betsey Higgins, who, along with her friend Ginny Wagner, had just arrived from Buffalo. She invited me to join them for a few innings and let me know that they'd brought some carrots and raw broccoli for me, as "you can't eat hot dogs five nights a week." It occurred to me that this would in fact be my first vegetable in quite some time, and, eager to catch up with them, I made my way over to their seats alongside the third-base line.

They were sitting alongside another Muckdogs regular, Hal Mitchell, and his girlfriend, Theresa Rumble. Hal was wearing a disabled veteran cap and the black and white Batavia jersey from the previous summer, and enjoyed sharing stories of Muckdogs alums they had gotten to know who had gone on to make the big leagues. While he and Theresa had embraced the college kids who had taken the place of the professionals who preceded them, something special had been lost. The direct connection between small ballparks—and the unique ecosystems of players, employees, and fans that they housed in forty-two towns across America—and places like Yankee Stadium and Fenway Park had been severed.

Average college players now threw fastballs in the high 80s from mounds in places like Bluefield, West Virginia, where the likes of Jacob deGrom and Noah Syndergaard had once squared off against each other in the Appalachian Rookie League, each bringing 100-mile-per-hour heat. Being able to track alums from your team as they fought to make their way up the ladder to the big leagues was part of the allure of minor league baseball that couldn't be replicated with college kids, the vast majority of whom wouldn't get drafted, much less play in the majors. Just as importantly, the relationship with a major league "parent" had provided these communities a certain local pride, an enduring connection to big cities that in many other ways had left them behind. As one longtime minor league fan wrote to me, "When you live in a small town, there's something about minor league baseball that gives you illusions of grandeur. The connection to professional baseball as you watch guys that you saw in your small town make it to the majors helps you to imagine that your little town isn't as small as you know it is."

*　　*　　*

One of the rumored architects of MLB's decision to cut 25 percent of minor league franchises, including Batavia, was the disgraced former general manager of the Houston Astros Jeff Luhnow. Luhnow would later be suspended from Major League Baseball—and fired as general manager of the Astros—for his role in the sign-stealing scandal that corresponded with their 2017 World Series title. Luhnow was familiar with Batavia, as he'd been the Cardinals' farm director when the Batavia team was a Cardinals affiliate.

Before his fall from grace, Luhnow was a celebrated alum of the University of Pennsylvania's Wharton School. He spent several years at McKinsey consulting, famous for its ruthless approach to corporate governance and, according to critics, sometimes loose sense of business ethics. Luhnow was part of a new generation of baseball leaders adhering to the gospel of efficiency to guide business decisions, and analytics to guide baseball decisions, from off-the-field personnel direction to in-game strategy.

In his book *Winning Fixes Everything*, former Astros beat writer Evan Drellich writes about how the Astros, under the ownership of Drayton McLane, still maintained the feel of a family-first organization, but how beginning in 2011, following Jim Crane's purchase and Luhnow's management, "cost cutting and the drive for efficiency" became paramount, the Astros becoming trailblazers in an overall "shift to a more corporate outlook" in the business of baseball.

Luhnow would embrace a clinical, quantitative approach to baseball decisions, telling the *McKinsey Quarterly* (he had, not surprisingly, also hired the firm to advise the Astros on their new direction):

> Big data combined with artificial intelligence is the next big wave in baseball . . . It's an area that I consider to be highly proprietary, so I don't discuss in front of my competition. But we're making a big investment in this area. There's radar and video at every facility in baseball now, not just the major leagues, but the minor leagues, colleges, starting to go into high schools. We know what every person is doing on the field at all times . . . If we're not making some mistakes along the way, we're not being aggressive enough . . . We now have so much technology around the ballpark and information about the trajectory of the ball, the physics of the bat swing, the physics and the biomechanics of the pitcher's delivery . . . It's quite frankly overwhelming in terms of the amount of information that we have access to and intimidating to figure out how to analyze all that information.

His comments echoed Mark Zuckerberg's guiding principle during the early days of Facebook to "move fast and break things." Left unsaid in Luhnow's interview was that the Astros ability to "know what every person is doing on the field at all times" would include using live video to steal signs from the opposing team's catcher and then communicate what pitch to expect to their batters, in violation of league rules.

While the cheating scandal has damaged the sport's integrity in the near term, the ongoing transformation of the system by which teams scout and develop talent will have an even more enduring (and, arguably, pernicious) impact on the sport's future. Towns like Batavia who were stripped of their teams were victims of the first broadside in the evolution of player development away from assuming a vast infrastructure of minor league clubs was necessary so that scouts could observe thousands of games played in 160 cities each summer. Receding into the past were the days of relying primarily on the accumulated wisdom of rumpled scouts fueled by fast food who dragged radar guns, stopwatches, and notebooks to dusty ballparks, logging thousands of miles every summer scouring the countryside for the next big prospect. In its place would be a reliance on data. Many major league executives now believe it is more efficient to capture the data digitally and have a small cadre of highly educated quants analyze it than to have scouts traveling the back roads of America to watch players in person.

Luhnow was certainly not the first to embrace these ideas, which had been circulating and increasing in popularity since Michael Lewis's 2003 book *Moneyball*. A famous passage highlighting Oakland general manager Billy Beane's embrace of "sabermetrics," or a focus on an empirical study of statistics when making baseball personnel decisions, referencing the pioneering work of his assistant at the time, Harvard graduate Paul DePodesta, describes how:

> Billy had his own idea about where to find future major league baseball players: inside Paul's computer. He'd flirted with the idea of firing all the scouts and just drafting the kids straight from Paul's laptop. The Internet now served up just about every statistic you could want about every college player in the country, and Paul knew them all.

Over the course of the next decade or so, Ivy League–educated technocrats, once outnumbered iconoclasts, would begin to dominate the baseball operations departments of many teams. Luhnow had been on the vanguard of this tribe, and his success with the Astros only served to reinforce baseball's embrace of this brave new world. In particular, the notion of cutting back on the minor leagues found a receptive audience among a number of MLB owners who felt that having so many clubs scattered in smaller towns across America was an antiquated method of assessing talent, a wasteful anachronism they'd be better off dispensing with. In the words of the University of San Francisco's Nola Agha, who has studied and written extensively on sports economics, with special attention to the minor leagues, "All they [MLB owners] care about is short-term profit maximization. They are worse than any other pro sports owners in this regard. When it comes to the minors, they're penny pinching and trying to save every last dollar. It's extraordinarily short sighted. It's like, 'We're already losing fans, so let's cut off our grassroots fans.'"

Luhnow has moved on, untroubled by the impact his sports management philosophy had on small town America. He is now focused on soccer teams he owns in Spain and Mexico. A *Sports Illustrated* profile says, "If Luhnow misses baseball, he doesn't show it. He was never really romantic about the national pastime. He saw the right set of circumstances for him to create change. Now he sees that in soccer." Luhnow explained that for him the excitement resided not so much in the particular sport but rather from "being in an industry where there's a lot of skepticism around the use of technologies, analytics, and data, trying to do what we did in baseball, which is demonstrate through wins that this stuff works." And it seems to have worked on the field. But in the eyes of many fans, like Batavia's Bill Kauffman, the embrace of analytics caused massive collateral damage to the appeal of the game. Kauffman would lament:

> The bloodless analysts have done their best to squeeze the last drops of life from professional baseball—especially the majors—by purging the game of its human factor. They don't understand that baseball's hold on the imaginations and emotions of fans is due to two things: stories and community. By eliminating or severely restricting managerial decisions, umpires' calls (and, with instant replay and the coming robot umps, the resulting arguments and rhubarbs), and hunches and gambles and bunts they are removing the raw material of

the stories that keep baseball alive across the seasons and the generations.

*   *   *

Barry Powell, the assistant coach for the visiting Jamestown Tarp Skunks, was in his forty-seventh year of playing, coaching, and scouting baseball. After years bouncing around independent and semipro ball as a young man, an arm injury ended his playing career, leading Powell to embrace coaching and scouting as a way to remain involved with the game he loved. Thus began a decades-long journey across high school, junior college, collegiate summer league, and minor league ballparks, where he coached and, at various times, scouted for the Royals, Marlins, and now Phillies. Deeply tanned, with a square jaw, athletic gait, and ability to toss batting practice at age sixty-seven just as smoothly as a man decades younger, he looked as if he'd been born hitting fungoes at a Florida spring training facility. He says, "I don't know how to do anything else. I don't hunt, fish, or golf. Baseball's my life." Supremely disciplined, he avoided the midlife paunch that characterizes so many of his peers, explaining that he ate healthy, packing as much "nonperishable healthy food into a cooler" to eat on the road as possible, sometimes splurging for "grilled chicken or salad somewhere like Ruby Tuesday, Golden Corral, or Applebee's." He does confess that, on occasion, the smell of a burger at the ballpark "makes me lick my lips and hunger overrides healthy, but I try not to make it a habit." And, of course, there is the occasional high school prospect who can be found only "off gravel roads in towns with one stop light, and then I'll sometimes find myself walking around in a country store picking up items to check their expiration date . . . When this happens I try to remind myself that tomorrow will feature a better menu."

Powell was also the sort of man being rendered obsolete by the powers-that-be in professional baseball, and he knew it. He knew Batavia assistant coach Thomas Eaton from when they were both players crisscrossing the Carolinas in the low minors decades ago, and he nodded in agreement with Eaton's assessment that "scouting's over now, analytics took over. *Moneyball* killed us. Velocity and spin rate are everything for pitchers now. If you throw eighty-eight with control and succeed at every level, it doesn't matter, no one's interested." Today a cerebral, control-oriented pitcher like Greg Maddux, whose fastball never rose above the low 90s and dropped to the mid 80s by the latter stages of his Hall of Fame career, would be quickly passed over in favor of the latest flamethrower. Powell lamented how today MLB clubs send twenty-six-year-old scouts to games just to sit, not talking to anyone, and tape prospects on their phone. He contrasted this with his approach, and that of scouts of old, who would get to games early, watch the players get off the bus, take note of how they dressed and carried themselves, how they interacted with their teammates and fans during batting practice, and if they "drank all the liquor in town, chased all the girls." These evaluations of the complete player (and person) went far beyond a narrow set of quantitative metrics that could be derived from a splice of film. They required a human eye coupled with years of experience and therefore violated the preeminent tenet of the game's new quants: efficiency. An iPhone recording is a heckuva lot cheaper.

Few in the Dwyer grandstands were aware of the extent to which the new collegiate product on the field was the result of these larger forces, conceived of in elite business schools and sports science labs, and adopted by well-credentialed and highly compensated businessmen in executive suites. They were simply excited to be back with their summer friends enjoying some good food and beer and rooting for this year's squad.

*   *   *

Dwyer was about half full as local product Tyler Prospero took the mound. As a young child Prospero had watched minor league games at Dwyer through a crack in the fence. This summer he was hoping to take advantage of one last chance to catch the eye of a scout or land a contract with an independent-league club. Tonight he made short work of Jamestown in the top half of the first, retiring the first three batters he faced.

The Jamestown starter didn't match Prospero's command, walking two batters in the bottom of the first before hitting the third with a pitch to load the bases. It was a good example of how pitching in the league could run the spectrum from impressive to sloppy, with most teams carrying a few "aces" who threw in the low 90s with control, augmented by a number of pitchers whose stuff was far less impressive. Batavia soon plated their first run when Tyler Cannoe, the bulky and bespectacled first baseman from Division III Salve Regina University, lumbered into a fielder's choice, scoring the runner from third.

Prospero, meanwhile, continued to cruise on the mound. He gave up one run in the fourth, the only one he would surrender before the Muckdogs broke the game open with four runs in the bottom of the sixth, highlighted by Cannoe's bases-loaded single to right for two more of what would be five RBIs in the game.

*   *   *

By this point I'd been to enough games without seeing a home run to conclude that the absence of power wasn't just a temporary result of transitioning to wooden bats from the metal ones the players had been using in college. Most of them simply weren't as good as the professional drafted players who had populated Muckdogs rosters in previous years and for whom Dwyer's home run fence did not constitute a seemingly insurmountable obstacle. However, I was also surprised to notice that the resulting brand of baseball—a throwback of sorts featuring lots of hits, bunts, and stolen bases—had its appeal when compared to the major league game. MLB games now, as a result of analytics highlighting the value of power pitching and power hitting, featured fewer balls batted into play, which resulted in less defensive and baserunning action. MLB games had become long slogs often clocking in at over three hours, with sustained periods of inaction punctuated by the occasional home run. While the pitch clock would help with this, it wouldn't change the fact that over one-third of plate appearances were now "inert," with no need for anyone on the field but a pitcher, catcher, and batter. Aware of my young son Bates's attention span, it was impossible for me to imagine him—or young kids like him—sustaining any interest in a game where nearly five minutes could go by without a ball being put in play.

The MLB game has begun to resemble a computer simulation. Suffocating talk of "spin rates" and "launch angles" has taken away from baseball's abstract beauty, with references to computer modeling dominating broadcasts and replacing the poetic cadences of the great sportswriters and broadcasters of old. Roger Kahn, in the 1972 classic *The Boys of Summer*, seems to have as many references to classical literature as he does to statistics, and elegantly captures the beauty of the game with simple descriptions like a speedy outfielder "making the outfield seem too small," so much more evocative than a sterile number telling us how many feet he covered when tracking down a fly ball. Nearly gone are the creative calls of iconic announcers like Red Barber, ones my late uncle used to listen to as a child tuning in to Brooklyn Dodgers games on the radio, fifty years later still recalling with a smile specific expressions Barber used. Now, instead of hearing a "Barberism" about a speedy player "running like a bunny with his tail on fire," we are more likely to have an analytic dissection of how long it took him to get to first—down to the millisecond— and then how that stacks up to average speeds when broken down by position across the league.

MLB's seemingly insatiable appetite for "innovation" has led to the incursion of technology into just about every corner of the game, to include officiating and broadcasting, with Triple-A ballparks using robot umpires in 2023 to call balls and strikes. Meanwhile, MLB also proudly celebrated a partnership with AI-driven sports streaming service Pixellot to provide the new collegiate Appalachian and MLB Draft Leagues with a "multi-camera system that fully automates the entire game production without the need for a single camera operator, director, or producer. Utilizing artificial intelligence, Pixellot's technology is able to automatically detect the game state, switch camera angles, zoom in on the ball, track the players, and provide a professional production."

In other words, MLB seems intent on racing headlong into a future that threatens to leave behind a portion of its fans who don't see the inherent appeal of more technology, which they feel too often strips away elements of the game's human texture they have grown to love and appreciate. Bill Kauffman captured the sentiment of those attempting to resist the onslaught of the machine in a speech at the University of Wisconsin, saying, "As the rationalization, the computerization, of baseball at the 'highest level' proceeds, ominously, apace, we traditionalists—that is, people who prefer humans to machines— must take refuge in the lowest minors, the independent leagues, the high schools, Little League, and, best of all, gloriously unorganized sandlot baseball . . . If the majors disappeared tomorrow, baseball would still be played where it matters."

*   *   *

After a strong six innings in which he allowed only one run on five hits to go along with six strikeouts, starter Tyler Prospero was pulled by Skip Martinez and replaced with the groundskeeper Larry Hale's son, Alex. Alex looked impressively composed for someone with only a few innings at Niagara County Community College under his belt. He would acquit himself reasonably well, allowing only one run while his father looked on, a soft smile on his face. It had been a long journey for the two of them that had begun over a decade ago with Larry juggling shifts at the Attica Correctional Facility so he could coach his young sons on the Little League fields just beyond Dwyer's left-field fence.

As the Muckdogs extended their lead over Jamestown to 7–2 with two more runs in the bottom of the seventh, a little girl wearing a pink batting helmet dutifully arranged helmets on their rack in the dugout. Her name was Jaelyn Christie, and her mom had been periodically peeking into the dugout from her seats along the third-base line to check on her. Jaelyn's dad had seen an ad on the Muckdogs Facebook page asking for guest batboys/batgirls, and his young daughter had eagerly volunteered. Clubhouse manager Erik Moscicki had taken her under his wing, earnestly explaining the responsibilities of the job. As the game now moved into the latter innings, Jaelyn quietly approached each Muckdog and asked him to sign her pink helmet. Even the most stoic players couldn't help but smile at her request.

By 9:00 p.m. the sun hadn't even disappeared beyond the horizon. The evening marked a far cry from the late afternoon in the dead of winter when Betsey Higgins and Ginny Wagner had briefly taken their seats in the bleachers for a quick reminder that Dwyer Stadium still stood and would again welcome them for nights like this, if they could just survive a few more months of dark and cold. It was the sort of night Ginny had imagined on those days when a gray pall shrouded Buffalo and she would glance at the Muckdogs ticket stub she kept on the fridge to reassure herself that sunshine and baseball would eventually return. The late innings were Ginny's favorite part of the game, when "the hubbub calms down and the only people left are the real fans." She described how, during these quieter moments, she experienced an almost "mystical feeling because the remaining fans truly love it and aren't distracted."

"We can even hear Bill laugh now," Ginny observed, noting how he sat nearby but that his trademark belly laugh had been drowned out by neighboring fans when the bleachers were packed.

As Ginny spoke, Betsey stared at the field with the serene expression I would become familiar with, lost in a kind of reverie. I was hesitant to even address her, lest I break the spell.

She finally turned to us, though, and agreed that these innings were also her favorite, though for a different reason. Betsey has a special affinity for twilight at Dwyer, when the sun casts its final rays from beyond the left-field pines. In language befitting the librarian she is, she said, "When the lights go on during the crepuscular hour you forget everything, see the pink clouds, and it's almost like a religious experience." Ginny couldn't let the word "crepuscular" escape without some gentle teasing, chuckling that Betsey used it so much she would sometimes leave voicemails for her saying, "It's the crepuscular hour, I hope you're outside."

"Sweet Caroline," a song they'd hated before associating it with Muckdogs games, then played, its familiar refrain a reminder that they'd emerged from another Buffalo winter and been delivered into the warm embrace of Dwyer's summer grandstands.

The game itself passed without further drama, with Batavia cruising to an easy 7–2 victory. Hometown starting pitcher Tyler Prospero and slugger Tyler Cannoe, with his 5 RBIs, were chosen as dual players of the game and rewarded with buckets of Gatorade poured over their heads. As they shook the ice from their jerseys, the team circled home plate and doffed their caps to salute the remaining fans, who then spilled onto Bank Street, buoyed by another victory.

While the exiting fans would soon be in bed, the most demanding part of Erik Moscicki's night had just begun. As clubhouse manager, he was responsible for ensuring the locker room was tidied up and that everyone's uniforms were clean and ready to go when they reported to the ballpark the next afternoon. It was a job the twenty-

six-year-old Batavia native took on with remarkable enthusiasm.
While the cerebral palsy in his right leg prevented him from participating as a player at higher levels, he remained determined to find a
way to actively contribute to Batavia's teams, which he now did by
serving as the clubhouse manager of the Muckdogs, as well as an
assistant high school hockey coach.

"My entire life is sports," said Erik, adding that "every relationship I have I can connect to sports somehow."

As the players kicked back in the leather recliners lining the locker
room and dug into plastic plates overflowing with postgame pasta,
Olivia Rodrigo's "good 4 u" playing on the speakers (the "breakup
anthem" would become an unlikely victory song in the clubhouse),
Erik darted around and began to straighten up. The sooner they finished eating and shed their uniforms, the sooner he could begin the
process of cleaning them to his own exacting standards. This usually
took around three hours. Erik would start by throwing the "loops,"
hooks containing the player's undergarments, in the laundry before
stripping down to his boxers and heading into the showers, where he
would proceed to scrub each of the nearly thirty sets of jerseys and
pants by hand with a brush and Dawn cleaning spray on a folding
table under the running shower water. It was a lonely and thankless undertaking. Pools of dirty brown water massed above clogged
drainpipes as the clock passed midnight, Erik still scrubbing, the
players long since having returned to the nearby dorm rooms where
they spent the summer.

Aside from some of the older players heading to the Copperhead
Creek bar to play some pool and relax with a few beers after a big
win, there wasn't much partying during the summer. This was in
part because many of the players weren't yet twenty-one and Batavia
didn't have the world's most exciting nightlife for college kids (it was
a far cry from the bars packed with fetching townies and wealthy
tourists depicted in the rom-com *Summer Catch* about the Cape
Cod League), and in part because the grind of games almost every
day meant that most were too exhausted to go out after midnight.
That, and they wanted to win. Dallas Young, the talented outfielder
from Detroit, said, "There wasn't a lot of partying. We took it serious
because we knew we had a shot at the championship and our team
chemistry was through the roof."

So on nights like this, most players simply returned to unwind in common rooms with their video games—*MLB The Show* and *Call of Duty* were favorites—and movies until the early morning hours, when they'd finally fall asleep.

Still, Erik toiled away, taking on his postgame tasks in the empty locker room with an almost manic fervor. Admitting it was hard work, Erik nonetheless insisted, "It's work I take pride in." He said, "This is their [the players'] sanctuary, and I want to make sure they can focus on playing tomorrow without needing to worry about where their stuff is or if it's clean." And indeed, he must have derived satisfaction from the work, since he could have gotten away with doing a lot less. As he scrubbed, he grew more philosophical about his role on the team, earnestly saying, "I want to use my energy to make a difference in people's lives . . . At the end of the day, we are all people and should support one another and be kind to each other." Coming from someone else, this might sound corny enough to cast doubt on the speaker's sincerity, but Erik was the antithesis of snark. He exuded an honesty that left no doubt that this really was a guiding principle in his life.

"Erik is the heart and soul of the team," said Florida native Brice Mortillaro, who had played catcher for Batavia the previous summer and grown close to Erik, adding, "He's also one of the nicest people I've ever met." I was beginning to understand why the team brought a cardboard cutout of Erik's likeness on the road trips he couldn't go on. Erik suspected this idea had originated with Jerry Reinhart, the fellow Batavia native he'd known for years. The pride with which Erik shared this story suggested that this act of kindness went further in solidifying his devotion to the Muckdogs than any amount of compensation would. And that's good, since, knowing Robbie's parsimonious ways, I doubt Erik was paid much in relation to the grueling hours he put in.

I walked to my car, accompanied by the soothing sound of chirping crickets where crowds had cheered and "Sweet Caroline" had played just hours before. The ballpark and surrounding neighborhood were dark, save for a sole light emerging from the front office, still illuminated as Robbie "settled" his receipts. He would be back at Dwyer later that morning—it was now past midnight—to embark on his "Be the customer" routine of walking the stadium to ensure it was clean in advance of another youth baseball tournament he'd be hosting.

Finally Robbie would leave, and one person would remain in the windowless cinder-block clubhouse beyond the third-base bleachers, still scrubbing in the shower. Erik Moscicki would carefully place the last uniform in its locker just before 2:00 a.m. Then he would finally go home, tired, but proud to have done his part for the Muckdogs.

8

Syracuse Salt Cats at Batavia Muckdogs

June 13

Following the win, I'd made my way to Batavia's FairBridge Inn & Suites, since I'd discovered that my preferred La Quinta was prohibitively expensive on summer weekends as northeasterners heading to and from westward vacations swallowed up its rooms and drove up the price. It was a humbling night in a depressing room complete with a brown-stained chair, a reading lamp that didn't work, and a bathroom floor that my shoes stuck to. In other words, it was the worst time to scroll through Facebook and Instagram and be greeted with photographs of friends and acquaintances on summer trips enjoying deluxe accommodations accompanied by clever humblebrag captions. Reflecting on various career decisions I'd made over the years that had seemingly led to that decrepit place, I couldn't help but chuckle recalling Jerry Seinfeld's joke "Sometimes the road less traveled is less traveled for a reason."

Waking up the following morning, I was eager to escape the Fair-Bridge as quickly as possible and made my way to the Pub Coffee Hub to grab some breakfast before heading home to help with the kids and hopefully find a way to mark my and Marcy's anniversary. As I sat down at the Pub on a quiet Saturday morning with sunlight streaming through the windows, sturdy century-old trees providing a canopy of shade over the sagging gravestones across the street in the cemetery, I experienced a taste of the tranquility Bill Kauffman often commented on when admiring that same view. I felt cleansed.

After a quick thirty-six-hour visit home, during which we were unable to do anything special for our anniversary but did manage to bring the kids to Pittsburgh's legendary Kennywood Amusement Park (which has been around since 1898), it was back up Interstate 79 toward Batavia. I felt a little uneasy leaving, as Bates's behavior at the amusement park had been spotty, and even one full day of helping out with two-month-old Shea had reinforced to me how tough a job I was handing off to Marcy every time I left on these reporting trips. But, to her credit, she reassured me that she had things under control, and so I headed up to the evening's Muckdogs game against the Syracuse Salt Cats, an exhibition game against a collegiate team from another league.

The Le Roy Marching Knights from the nearby school district performed at the entrance to the stadium as their cheerleaders lined up nearby to greet what appeared to be a large crowd streaming into Dwyer. The simplicity of entering Dwyer was so refreshing, especially in contrast to the technological advances that seemed to be accelerating in dizzying fashion at MLB games, despite little evidence that there was a hunger for it from paying customers. According to Ballpark Digest, the Yankees had boasted of adding "GameOn technology that will enhance ticketing and guest experience via Yankees.com . . . implementing Generative AI and GPT technology. The goal is to use queries to build out a fully managed chat experience to provide fans with faster support for ticketing, premium experiences, Yankee Stadium tours, concessions, transportation and more." The CEO of GameOn Technology added, "We're excited to implement our industry-leading platform to benefit Yankees fans as they navigate their most important questions related to attending games at Yankee Stadium."

Bill Kauffman's response to such a shift was perhaps not surprising. "God help us! I dunno, you buy a ticket, you get and follow directions to the stadium, you find your seat. Human intelligence has accomplished these modest tasks for well over a hundred years. Why do we need artificial intelligence?"

Meanwhile, Diamond Baseball Holdings, which had been busy buying up minor league franchises that had escaped MLB's scythe, had clearly embraced this high-tech future for the game, issuing press releases such as this doozy:

Diamond Baseball Holdings (DBH), which owns and operates select Minor League Baseball clubs, today announced a
three-year enterprise partnership with global fan data company FanCompass as part of the ongoing development of a
technology stack ... FanCompass technology will help DBH
clubs create more touchpoints with fans, provide meaningful
engagements for brand partners, and enhance organizational
data proficiency across the club portfolio ... FanCompass will
deliver the zero and first-party fan data collected through the
platform directly into the clubs' data ecosystem for immediate
access by marketing, sponsorship, and ticketing teams.

Even attempting to dissect the meaning of the release made
me long for the days where the consumer element of a visit to the
ballpark—a "touchpoint," if you will—didn't extend far beyond buying some peanuts and Cracker Jacks, and so I sent it to several people
knowledgeable on the business of baseball to see if they could make
sense of it. Even they had a hard time deconstructing the corporate jargon, though one ventured to say that his best guess was that
it essentially meant, "Diamond is trying to use creepy Google-style
tools to mine fan data and milk a few more bucks out of the fans for
themselves, and then sell the data to other corporate douchebags."
  Thankfully elements of this technological dystopia had not yet
infiltrated Dwyer Stadium. I happily surrendered myself to the now
familiar sense of calm reassurance—without the need for any apps
or AI assistance—that enveloped me after I handed off my paper
ticket to Dave Fisher (careful, as always, to keep the stub he returned
to me as a souvenir) and made my way inside. As I walked across
the concourse before the game, an older woman seated at a nearby
folding table tossed me a box of Jell-O from what appeared to be a
large collection, which confused me until I soon learned that Le Roy,
New York, whose school and civic groups were leading the evening's
off-field pageantry, was the "birthplace of Jell-O."
  As the Syracuse pitcher—a lanky beanpole who looked as if he
might blow away if there was a strong gust of wind—took the mound
and began delivering fastballs that couldn't have topped 80 miles per
hour, I felt a bit bad for the large crowd, most of whom didn't appear
to even know this was an exhibition game (a fact Robbie wasn't eager

to publicize). One of my barometers for the quality of pitching was that if it looked like I would've had a good chance of hitting it back in my college days, it probably wasn't very good. And I felt like I would've had a decent shot of hitting this guy tonight, at age forty-five, much less twenty years ago.

Sitting with Buffalo friends Betsey and Ginny, I was offered a snack of hummus, crackers, and celery by Betsey. Ginny gently teased her, saying she had never seen her "so domesticated," observing how it was quite the contrast from her days watching Ginny's boys (who were Betsey's godchildren), when she would invariably rely on take-out. The twosome were blissfully unconcerned with the quality of the awful Syracuse pitcher, who appeared to now be throwing off-speed curveballs that weren't curving, walking batter after batter to eventually load the bases. Betsey commented on the "tension and adrenaline" of the bases-loaded situation, and I decided to let her enjoy the moment without critiquing the quality of the opponent.

When I lamented the fact that Bates had thus far not caught the sports bug from me—instead developing an obsession with LEGOs and *Star Wars* (or, better yet, the animated *LEGO Star Wars* on Disney+)—Ginny told me that her boys, now twenty and eighteen, were "kind of nerds and not into sports . . . They're more the Dungeons and Dragons types." This revelation didn't reassure me, as I found the idea of debating the finer points of Kylo Ren's complicated allegiances with Bates for the next ten years, as opposed to enjoying sports, to be a bit frightening, no matter how much I told myself I wanted him to be his own person and discover his own sources of happiness.

As Ginny and I discussed the mysteries of child-rearing, Batavia continued capitalizing on Syracuse's poor pitching and spotty defense to pull out to a 4–0 lead in the early innings.

Meanwhile, in the press box, public address announcer Paul Spiotta was growing less and less patient with the sloppy baseball on display from the visiting Salt Cats of Syracuse. This response to the new collegiate product was not uncommon in the small towns robbed of their affiliated teams. Whereas many fans seemed happy to still have a place to go and have fun with their friends, and were generally unfazed by the lesser quality of play, some of the more "hard-core" former diehards struggled to overlook a subpar game. Paul told me that the starter had walked five and now the new reliever had already walked two and hit two other batters with pitches.

As he spoke, Syracuse walked another run home to push Batavia's lead to 7–0.

"This game could go on till eleven," Paul muttered. "I hope they hit the mercy rule." While Paul was too loyal to Robbie and the "new" Muckdogs to openly gripe about the degraded quality of play, I knew it was impossible for him not to notice what Batavia had lost.

I could see both sides of the equation. I understood the fans for whom it was more about the overall ballpark experience than whether pitchers were throwing in the 80s or 90s, or whether long fly balls cleared the fence or landed on the warning track. I also understood the frustration of those who felt they had been stripped of a superior product for no good reason and forced to accept an inferior one. What bothered me most, though, was the disingenuousness of MLB officials in arguing that contraction would not result in a degradation of the quality of play in impacted communities.

"Same schedule, same tickets, same age and quality of play," an MLB official had told ESPN. "Literally nothing changes. Instead of low-level minor league players, it's guys that go to Vanderbilt, etc." Needless to say, there were no guys from programs like Vanderbilt on the Muckdogs roster, nor many in the entire PGCBL. Statements like that from MLB—and there were many—were simply not true, and almost everyone involved had to have known it.

Though the semiretired IT professional Spiotta was paid a modest amount to serve as the public address announcer, his enthusiasm for the job—even on nights featuring ugly play like this—suggested that he would have done it for free. When he learned that my son Bates was the same age as his grandson, Gabe Dentino (a rabid Muckdogs fan who had been thrilled when his favorite player, Batavia's Jerry Reinhart, had sent him a video message from college and a signed bat for his birthday), Paul told me that he sometimes invited young kids into the press box to announce the next batter as they approached the plate, and that my son would be welcome to do so. Already missing Bates after only a few days on the road, I appreciated the kind offer. I knew Bates would take him up on it.

Returning to my seat in the grandstands along the third-base line, I discovered Guy Allegretto, the Vietnam veteran who had delivered the motivational talk the week prior, sitting with his friend Dr. Ross Fanara. Allegretto was easily identifiable in his oversized red USMC football jersey. I'd learned that he'd been a part of the 1st Battalion, 9th Marines, the famed "Walking Dead," so named due to their having the highest casualty rate in Marine Corps history. Allegretto had fought at Khe Sanh, where six thousand marines spent months surrounded and under siege from forty thousand North Vietnamese troops. Only later would I discover the truly horrifying details of his experience. For now, our talk revolved around baseball. He explained that he would soon be sidelined by a surgery and asked me to send him the link to the team's YouTube channel so he could watch the games from home, which I promised to do.

Allegretto then did something that I was totally unprepared for. He opened his wallet and pulled out three $50 bills and handed them to me. I tried to politely refuse the money, not only because it seemed inappropriate to accept money from someone I was writing about, but also because I knew he wasn't a rich man, and I felt really uncomfortable taking a considerable sum of money from someone of modest means. But this proud veteran wouldn't take no for an answer, and insisted I keep it and use it to take Marcy out for a belated anniversary dinner—I had mentioned to him that it was tough to find time to do stuff together, like mark anniversaries, when I was home only for short visits—and buy Bates a special toy to make up for the time I was missing at home. Even as I tried to push the money back into his hands, I sensed how important this was to him.

Despite the bravado he brought to those motivational speeches, I also saw a scarred and lonely older man in Allegretto. His entreaty to use his money to celebrate my anniversary didn't come from nowhere; he'd spent some time telling me about the heartbreak he'd experienced when he and his wife of thirty years went through a devastating breakup (though he now had a girlfriend with whom he seemed quite smitten). He'd had no shortage of challenges in his life and seemed to derive real happiness from his association with me, a fellow veteran of the next generation in whom he could confide. And so I reluctantly took the bills and sincerely thanked him.

Eventually the game approached its merciful conclusion. Only about 10 percent of the fans remained, as it had grown quite cold and the game had been noteworthy only for its sloppiness. The last pitch was delivered at 10:28 p.m., marking a 10–7 Batavia victory over a Syracuse team whose offense had managed to score a few late runs and make the final score closer than it should have been based on the woeful performance of its pitchers. Kyle Corso, a soft-spoken and smoothly athletic six-foot-three Batavia infielder from Columbia University, was named Player of the Game after going 2-for-2 with a double and two RBIs. Recalling my admittedly undistinguished two-year baseball career at Princeton, I was glad to see this fellow Ivy League ballplayer beginning to distinguish himself as one of the team's more consistent offensive contributors.

As I walked to my car, parked nearby on a darkened street, it occurred to me that it was nice to feel safe no matter the time of day or part of town I was in. Retired Batavia policeman Rich Schauf told me that this was a potential benefit to the otherwise unenviable fact that the city hadn't grown much over the years, resulting in a closeness, a place where "people know each other and will notice when something looks different and is potentially dangerous." He also noted that the violence associated with the drug trade in parts of western New York may have been less pronounced in Batavia since dealers could always find demand in nearby larger cities like Rochester and Buffalo, whereas they would fight more vigorously to defend their turf in more remote cities like Elmira and Jamestown, where there was nowhere else nearby to sell. As a result, Schauf said, Batavia had only one homicide for every seven or so years he had been on the force.

As I headed to Burger King to grab a late-night dinner, one of my favorite songs, the Grateful Dead's "Fire on the Mountain," started to play on the car radio. For the moment, all seemed well in the world. I'd just enjoyed three hours with people who a few months ago had been strangers and were now friends, my family was safely slumbering at home, and I had a nice clean room to look forward to at the La Quinta.

The next morning I went to the Pub Coffee Hub, hoping to find the resident contrarian Eric Zwieg perched at his usual spot at the bar with a postmodern novel, but alas he was nowhere to be seen. The young man working there laughed when I asked about Eric, saying, "Yeah I know Eric, he's the most unpredictable predictable customer we have. He's a nice guy, but man he likes to argue." The Pub's owner,

Rob, mentioned Eric with the sort of chuckling bemusement Seinfeld used to refer to Newman with, also noting Eric's sometimes maddeningly contrarian nature. He said one time Eric "spent half an hour explaining why the third-base side was better than the first-base side at Dwyer," but that if you'd begun the discussion contending that the third-base side was better, Eric would've surely spent an hour arguing the opposite. When I told Rob that Eric said he was reading my first book, an account of the soldiers tasked with guarding Saddam Hussein in the months preceding his execution, exploring the unlikely relationships that developed, he warned me to "be prepared for a long no-holds-barred critique of it."

Bill Kauffman soon arrived to work on some ghostwriting, joined shortly after by Paul Spiotta, who dropped in from his part-time office upstairs in the Harvester Center. We found ourselves resuming a spirited debate concerning whether a particular play during the previous night's game should have been ruled a hit or an error. Paul said he'd left a voicemail for Bill, jokingly admonishing him to "stick to being a world-famous author and leave the official scoring to me." Bill soon left to wander the cemetery across the street, a habit when he was struggling with writer's block. It was a hot, sunny day and I hoped the weather would continue to hold for the following weekend, when I planned to bring my family to Batavia.

While I sipped my coffee, I received a text from Allegretto, whose cash was still residing uncomfortably in my wallet, congratulating me again on my wedding anniversary and explaining, in his typical stream-of-consciousness style, "In life I have always been a giver, which makes me feel good. I love to give. I am sure you will find something nice for your kids. One team, one fight, Let's Go Mets, baseball ... the greatest game ever!" He then referenced an article I'd written on Army Ranger School, in which I had returned to the school to chronicle current Ranger candidates as they experienced the course fifteen years after I'd attended. He wrote:

Absolutely brilliant article on the challenges it takes to be an Army Ranger. Trust me, when you approach being 50 years old your horrific war experiences will come to the forefront. Anything I can do to possibly help you in this area I will always be there.

As I sat in the Pub, bathed in sunlight, it occurred to me that I was starting to feel at home here, having grown accustomed to a pleasant daily rhythm amid people and places that had begun to feel familiar and welcoming. This realization coexisted, though, with the fact that I missed Marcy, Bates, and Shea a ton, a feeling that was magnified every time I received a text message and photo of them going about their lives back home, a reminder of the moments of childhood happiness they were experiencing and that I was missing due to these trips back and forth to Batavia all summer. Of course, along with the good times I was missing, I also wasn't there to help with the seemingly endless runny noses, earaches, rough nights, and bouts of poor behavior that also define parenthood.

I'd also established what in retrospect was probably a bad custom of bringing Bates home a small toy from each of my reporting trips to reward him for good behavior (poor Shea, at only two months, was too young to really appreciate gifts . . . That, and perhaps I was simply guilty of spoiling the firstborn Bates and overlooking his new sidekick). Of course, this was a dangerous habit to begin, since, in a development parents everywhere could have seen coming, he soon assumed I'd arrive home with a present in tow every time, regardless of whether his behavior had actually earned it. One problem I had in fulfilling this promise was reconciling Bates's obsession with LEGOs, *Star Wars,* and Pokémon with my desire to support local businesses in Batavia. Unfortunately, the local Adam Miller Toy Store didn't carry the things Bates most liked, and I didn't want to resort to Walmart.

And then I made an amazing discovery. I was driving down Ellicott Street, one of Batavia's main drags, when I spotted a quirky-looking storefront advertising "Toys and Comics" on it. Always on the lookout for places to get a "special treat" for Bates, I impulsively did a U-turn to check it out. When I entered Foxprowl Collectables, I was first struck by a funny smell, like a skunk or natural gas or perhaps weed from the tattoo shop next door. While I tried to identify the source of the peculiar odor, I noticed a man in a Hawaiian shirt with a small dog perched on his shoulder carefully studying some action figures nearby. Even more remarkable than the odd smell and the eccentric customer, though, was the sea of *Star Wars* figurines and spaceships, as well as Pokémon trading cards, that lined the shelves of the store. I felt as if I was seeing it through the eyes of five-year-old Bates, and I was overwhelmed at the smorgasbord of treasures. As I browsed the shop and its seemingly infinite supply of every piece of *Star Wars* merchandise imaginable—both new and used items, all for reasonable prices no less—I was thrilled to rediscover the pleasure that could come from old-fashioned in-person browsing, as opposed to clicking on whatever product Amazon algorithms steered me to.

And that was before I'd even met the owner of Foxprowl, Bill Hume. With unkempt shoulder-length hair, salt and pepper beard, gold chain, and a ball cap featuring Stewie from *Family Guy*, he was right out of central casting for the owner of a collectibles store who traveled to Comic-Cons in his spare time. And he had a personality to match. Born in 1970, Hume told me he got the *Star Wars* bug early, while also falling in love with comics "before discovering girls and beer and hiding my collectibles under my bed." Dissatisfied with an auto parts delivery business he worked for after community college, he dusted off his collectibles and began selling at flea markets and on eBay, before ultimately taking the plunge and turning his side hustle into a full-time business. He'd now been running Foxprowl Collectables for twelve years.

Bill took obvious pride in his business, and what it delivered to Batavia, a town he said was primarily known for Oliver's Candies, Batavia Downs (the harness racing track and casino), and, curiously, Long John Silver's (since it was the only one in western New York, Bill explained). As I imagined how delighted Bates would be to open the eight-dollar stormtrooper figurine I was planning to buy him, Bill practically read my mind: "Money's tight, gas costs a fortune, and a lot of things in the world suck, but this place makes people feel good. A five-dollar figure can make a kid smile."

9

Strat-O-Matic

March 15

S pending time with Paul Spiotta in the press box during the game against Syracuse had sparked memories of a much different experience a few months earlier, when I'd visited him in the den of his neatly kept home in a subdivision to the east of downtown Batavia. A flag was displayed on the wall in honor of Staff Sergeant Dominic Spiotta, Paul's father, who earned a Bronze Star and Purple Heart serving in World War II. It was the middle of March and yet another of the cold and rainy days that hovered over Batavia as winter began its agonizingly slow transition to spring. Paul was logged on to a Zoom call with a best friend, John Kemnitzer, now sixty-four years old but a good friend since they had gone to college together at Niagara. A little over twenty years ago, John had made the decision to move to Glendale, Arizona, a decision that seemed especially smart on this gloomy western New York afternoon, as it was now eighty-one degrees with sunshine pouring in the windows of John's Arizona living room.

They were about to begin the 561st of the nearly daily Strat-O-Matic games they'd played against each other beginning shortly after COVID emerged in March 2020. Strat-O-Matic is a sports simulation game dating back to the 1960s that has engendered cultlike status. Its devotees serve as the "managers" of teams composed of real major league players, past and present, using a combination of dice rolls that lead to outcomes for each at bat depending on statistical probabilities determined by real-life stats. Think of it as a fantasy game akin to Dungeons & Dragons, but for sports nerds. Paul and John began playing in high school and continued into college, but, as with so many youthful hobbies, family and job responsibilities soon intervened, and their days of squaring off at the helm of their imaginary teams appeared to be over . . . until COVID hit. It was then that Paul called his buddy and suggested they dust off their old player cards and commence with daily games. They agreed that it would be a good way to break up the depressing tedium of various COVID lockdowns and restrictions and decided to play out an entire season for a league consisting of eight teams. On the afternoon I joined them as perhaps the world's first Strat-O-Matic spectator, John's teams enjoyed a narrow 282–279 lead with only a few weeks remaining.

The game I observed featured the Negro League All Stars managed by Paul against a collection of National League All Stars from 1910 to 1947 coached by John. As the game began, they quickly settled into familiar banter, with Paul grumbling, "He's catching all the breaks as usual" at one point early in the game. A famous Negro Leaguer, Martín Dihigo, was pitching, one of the seven positions he played over the course of his career, and I shared with them how my grandfather had often told me stories of watching Dihigo play for the Negro League's New York Cubans as a boy growing up in New York City's Washington Heights neighborhood. It was almost as if my late grandfather had briefly joined this cross-country showdown, a shared love of baseball allowing this fraternity of enthusiasts to connect effortlessly across time and space, sunny desert to dreary snow belt, heavens above to computer terminals below.

The play-by-play man in Paul couldn't be repressed, and the game was punctuated by pithy observations, such as his lamenting the fact that his team "appears to be suffering a little jet lag in Glendale." Down 5–1 in the fifth, Paul began to mount a rally, as John observed, "That's how he always does it . . . claws back in the late innings." I was struck by their carefree smiles, reminiscent of young boys playing ball at the playground.

Though a lifelong baseball fanatic, Paul found his enthusiasm for the major league product was seriously damaged, like that of many in this area, when MLB eliminated Batavia's minor league club. Not only did he feel the loss as a fan, but it also could have cost him his job as a public address announcer—a job he loved—had Robbie not stepped in and stood up the collegiate Muckdogs, smartly deciding to retain Paul.

Like so many of the fans I spoke to in the communities whose teams were eliminated by MLB's contraction of the minors, Paul expressed a mix of anger and bewilderment that such a decision could have been motivated by what amounted to an inconsequential amount of money to the entities involved—with MLB clubs owned almost entirely by billionaires saving something akin to a single major league minimum salary for each entire minor league team that was cut.

Or, as a former minor league owner told me regarding contraction, "From the business sense you can make a good case, but from the perspective of Americana, why would you do this to the fabric of the game for a decimal point of dollars?" When the Blue Jays played in Buffalo for a portion of two summers due to Canadian COVID restrictions, Paul noted how ordinarily he would've jumped at the chance to watch major league games nearby, but after MLB took the Muckdogs away he simply didn't care and hence didn't go. He told me he used to wear two necklaces, one with the logo of the NHL's Buffalo Sabres and the other with the logo of his beloved Yankees. He no longer wore the Yankees necklace.

While Paul's friend John had also grown disenchanted with the decisions made by Major League Baseball, he tried to "compartmentalize" his dissatisfaction with its leadership with his ability to still derive enjoyment from something that had been a part of his life for so long. Like so many fans I met, he immediately shared with me the memory of his first major league game, when his father drove him to Pittsburgh to see the Cubs play the Pirates, a game highlighted by a Willie Stargell home run he still remembered. He said watching games today "takes me back to the innocence of being a kid," before continuing, "but I'm ticked off by the business side of baseball . . . MLB is playing all of us real fans, because they know that if we stop watching as a result of our frustration, we'll be punishing ourselves more than them, and so they cynically exploit this weakness."

He captured precisely the sentiment I'd felt in recent years raising a young son in Pittsburgh. On the one hand, I feel like a stooge paying major league prices to watch a perennial loser, yet on the other hand boycotting the games would deprive my son and me the chance to spend a beautiful afternoon together in a fantastic ballpark, while doing nothing to dent the miserly owner's personal fortune. And so—despite the absence of much enthusiasm on Bates's part to date, and in the hope that he will yet develop a fondness for the sport that we can share as he grows older—we go.

Some, like Paul Spiotta, have a stiffer backbone, though, and are resolute in their determination to be done with Major League Baseball.

10

Family Trip

Batavia Muckdogs at Niagara Power (June 17) and
Queen City at Batavia Muckdogs (June 18)

By mid-June, I'd begun to feel as if I was leading two parallel lives, one in Batavia and one back home outside Pittsburgh. So I thought the time was right to introduce the people who had heard about each other but never met. With that in mind, Marcy and I decided to take a family road trip to Buffalo and Batavia. As I struggled to jam everything we thought we needed to survive two nights away from home with two kids into the car, I marveled at how we were transporting more gear for a long weekend than I had deployed with to Iraq for a year. Our cargo included: the insanely expensive Snoo crib for Shea, ambient noise machines, baby chairs, strollers, Bates's scooter, not to mention wipes, diapers, snacks, a portable pharmacy of infant and child Motrin and Tylenol, an iPad, coloring books, and toys. Shocked that four people could somehow require this much for a short trip, we set sail north on Interstate 79 for a night outside Buffalo, where we hoped to take in a Muckdogs road game against the Niagara Power on Friday night, before heading to Batavia to watch the Muckdogs host Queen City on Saturday night.

As often happened when I traversed the highways connecting postindustrial middle American cities, I was struck by how many Americans were clearly struggling. On this journey we stopped at a Bob Evans outside Erie and were waited on by an older woman who had to have been in her seventies. She was remarkably kind, lavishing Bates and Shea with compliments and hustling to get our food out

quickly before, as I'd warned her, their behavior might begin to dete-
riorate. I couldn't help but imagine one of my grandmothers waking
up early, putting on a Bob Evans uniform, and spending a day waiting on strangers alongside the interstate at an age when they'd more
than earned some time to rest and relax with their families. When
she learned we were traveling from Pittsburgh, the woman told me
that her daughter lived near there and how she and her friends were
struggling to find formula for their babies. And so this grandma
would spend some of her off days buying formula in Erie and making the two-hour drive south to deliver it, a journey made even more
difficult by record-high gas prices. She volunteered this information matter-of-factly and didn't make herself out to be a martyr. As
we thanked her for her service, we were saddened that there wasn't
much we could do to give her a boost aside from offering encouraging smiles and a nice tip.

After checking in to a "boutique" hotel in Niagara, we were
greeted with the worrisome news that there would be a house band
performing on the outdoor patio outside our window, which triggered panicked thoughts of Shea being kept awake and screaming
until the wee hours of the morning. Setting those anxieties aside, we
made our way to Sal Maglie Stadium for the game. The ride there
was a sobering one as we drove past a postindustrial wasteland of
abandoned storefronts, discount tire stores, and partially boarded-up
buildings that may or may not have been inhabited, all to the mellifluous sounds of Shea screaming in the back seat. I had a sinking
feeling and kicked myself for dragging the entire family from a comfortable home on what had all the makings of an epic boondoggle. I
knew Marcy had to have been trying to reconcile the urban blight we
were passing, framed by a lifeless slate gray sky, with my enthusiastic
tales of Batavia's charm and lovely evenings at Dwyer Stadium.

We arrived at a rather drab concrete stadium, painted blue and
yellow and surrounded by a chain-link fence. There was no line at the
lonely booth where we bought our tickets, and as we emerged from
the concourse and entered the seating bowl, we saw what couldn't
have been more than fifty fans scattered about. I'd played in high
school games that had a more dynamic atmosphere. I was relieved to
spot Betsey and Ginny, though, who had made the short drive from
their homes in Buffalo, and I hoped that perhaps these friendly faces

could help rescue the outing from being a total disaster. After I introduced them to Marcy and Bates and Shea, who had stopped crying by now but looked cold and uncomfortable in Marcy's child-carrying backpack as a bracing wind gusted in from the outfield, Bates asked Ginny, "Do you wanna play with me?" She gamely agreed. After a game of tic-tac-toe, he then began to empty his backpack of his cherished *LEGO Star Wars* "minifigs," earnestly introducing Ginny to "Finn, a stormtrooper who turned from the dark side to the rebels." A foul ball landed with a clank in the nearby metal bleachers, followed by an announcement asking the fans to "please return foul balls to the concession stand for a piece of candy," which even the ever-polite and unfailingly upbeat Betsey said was "cheap."

Stocky five-foot-ten, 195-pound Nolan Sparks was on the hill for Batavia and looked sharp, throwing hard and with impressive control. Julian Pichardo sat behind home plate in the first row of the grandstands, charting pitches to help Coach Eaton better track the performance of his pitchers. The game quickly became a rout with the visiting Muckdogs jumping out to a 6–0 lead by the bottom of the third inning, taking advantage of eight hits to go along with three Niagara errors, including a clumsily dropped foul ball by the first baseman.

As Bates's bedtime came and went, I voiced my concern about his being too energized to fall asleep when we got back to the hotel, to which Ginny observed, "That's what Betsey always did with my kids . . . she'd get them all wound up at bedtime and then leave." Betsey responded with a smile that "that's what godmothers are supposed to do."

After Batavia scored nine runs in the top half of the fourth on a sloppy succession of walks, wild pitches, errors, and some hits, coupled with Bates and Shea needing to get to sleep, we knew it was time to make our exit. We said goodbye to Betsey and Ginny, but not before making plans to meet Betsey the following morning at the City of Tonawanda Public Library to join her for the LEGO Club she hosted. When we arrived at the hotel, we discovered that the band had mercifully wrapped up; we then somehow enjoyed a magical night in which both Bates and Shea slept wonderfully. The surprisingly easy night gave some credence to Marcy's frequent admonition that I shouldn't always "catastrophize" and expect the worst from every situation. I had to admit, I was certainly guilty of such pessimism, as I'd fully expected a sleepless night followed by an exhausting day shepherding two desperately overtired kids around Dwyer Stadium. But maybe we had a chance of a good day after all.

*   *   *

The next morning we packed up our platoon's worth of children's equipment and luggage and made our way to the library to meet Betsey for LEGO Club, an event Bates was far more excited by than any baseball game. We arrived at a nondescript gray building featuring sterile and uninspiring 1970s architecture. As we made our way to a small white-linoleum-tile-floored room, we discovered about half a dozen kids sifting through numerous large plastic containers full of LEGOs that Betsey had laid out on folding white tables. Bates immediately lost himself building.

The library was unremarkable in every way aside from what was occurring inside of it, where the children were enjoying a hobby that encouraged collaboration and imagination, and one that—remarkably in our era—didn't include any high-tech devices like iPads or iPhones, or even anything with batteries. As time expired on the session, Bates asked Betsey if the *Star Wars* "Troop Transport" he'd constructed could be included in the display of the "builds" the other kids had made in the library's Main Reading Room, and she kindly agreed.

Betsey then quietly slipped Bates two LEGO minifigs she'd smuggled from the bins as a small gift for visiting all the way from Pittsburgh.

*   *   *

As we made the forty-five-minute journey east to Batavia, I was impressed by how such a simple experience in a local library had delivered so much. We checked in to the La Quinta and made our way to the ballpark. It was "Blue Devil Night" in honor of the local Batavia High School Blue Devils, traditionally one of the biggest draws of the summer, and the evening would feature postgame fireworks. As we entered the front gate of Dwyer, Dave Fisher, the security guard, came over to greet us, patting Shea on her bald head affectionately and commenting on what a beautiful baby she was.

It was sunny and a brisk sixty-two degrees. After showing Marcy, Bates, and Shea to some seats in the third-base bleachers, I went to the front office in search of the owner Robbie Nichols. The front office was a bare-bones affair, two desks connected to an adjoining room that housed the ticket windows, piles of old merchandise, programs, and printed schedules covering much of the floor space. Behind cinder-block walls was Robbie's office, a picture of him in his old hockey gear taped to its door. I found him there, looking tired. It had already been a long weekend for him, as Friday night had been packed in Elmira, where he'd helped Nellie work the game for their Fireworks Night. He hadn't gotten to bed until after midnight before waking up early, fortifying himself with some Dunkin' coffee, and making the ninety-minute drive north to Batavia in his Chevy Silverado pickup.

Robbie had his shoes off, elevating his pained feet, his daughter recoiling in mock horror from his "nasty toenails," the result, he said—not without some pride—of a pro hockey career spent in skates. Nichols had spent over a decade suiting up in musty locker rooms from North Bay and Kitchener in Ontario to Kalamazoo, Michigan; Glens Falls, New York; San Diego; and Phoenix. He'd made it to within a hair of the NHL when he spent two seasons with the Detroit Red Wings' AHL minor league affiliate, the Adirondack Red Wings, where he mirrored his contemporary, the famed Red Wings enforcer Bob Probert, as someone who amassed massive numbers of penalty minutes by "dropping the gloves" without hesitation, while at the same time possessing enough skill to make meaningful offensive contributions in the form of goals and assists. As Robbie remembered it, "I was a middleweight, and got beat up sometimes, but I was a team guy. I didn't care if you were Paul Bunyan, if you messed with my teammates, I was gonna take you on." He had learned early in his career that "you can bring twelve thousand fans to their feet more easily by fighting than scoring a goal," an attitude that helped ensure he was always a fan favorite.

Unfortunately for Robbie, he'd been dealt a last-minute curveball this weekend, as he'd recently learned that the Canadian team his Pioneers and Muckdogs had been scheduled to play had withdrawn from the season, and so he'd been forced to scramble to find opponents for what would now amount to exhibition games for some of the biggest dates of the summer in Batavia and Elmira. He'd managed to land Queen City, a team from the Buffalo Municipal League, to stand in as tonight's opponent. Robbie was always hustling, and I knew there was no way he was going to lose one of the biggest gates of the season, even if it meant scrambling halfway to British Columbia to find someone to play.

Robbie's interest in the management side of sports, first expressed to his dad during that car ride to a youth hockey game as a child growing up in Ontario, had been kindled more deeply when he was twenty and playing for the Kalamazoo Wings, where the players' days were often a blur of practice, games, and visits to the local strip club. It didn't take Robbie long to conclude that it didn't seem like the makings for a "fulfilling life," and he developed a curiosity about what took place in the front office. He soon found himself taking on a side hustle of helping work on promotions, getting commissions assisting with group sales, and selling dasher board sponsorships (the advertisements placed along the boards separating the ice from the grandstands). He would eventually find himself serving in the dual role of assistant general manager in the front office and left wing on the ice for teams in Phoenix and Glens Falls, New York.

His tenacity as an entrepreneur would later be evidenced when he bought the Elmira Enforcers of the Federal Prospects Hockey League. When COVID lockdowns had shuttered First Arena in downtown Elmira, where they played, resulting in the loss of income from eight expected sellouts and a playoff run (as his team had been first in the league in attendance), Robbie had swallowed his pride and resorted to selling Trump and Biden flags under a tent he would erect on street corners. It was "devastating," he said of the season's cancellation.

For the night's game I'd volunteered Bates to serve as one of the "guest batboys," and so I brought him onto the field to introduce him to clubhouse manager Erik Moscicki, who oversaw the guest batboys and batgirls. Bates immediately took a liking to Erik and began regaling him with stories—most involving obscure *Star Wars* characters—as Erik dutifully tried to instruct him on his responsibilities. When I tried to inject myself into the conversation, Bates shushed me away, as if he was embarrassed by my presence, a reminder that he was indeed growing up. But just as I felt a little saddened by this recognition, I saw him trying to show off to the game's "Baseball Buddies," the kids from local Little Leagues who would join the Muckdogs for a pregame catch. "I'm gonna be the batboy for like one inning," he bragged to them, adding with pride, "This is my helmet." Like slightly older kids everywhere, they seemed unimpressed. Still, he was soon running alongside the posse of kids as they chased Dewey, the Muckdogs mascot, around foul territory, Bates tugging on Dewey's arm to earnestly ask, "Do you know Sfike [how he pronounced Spike] or Turtle-ey?," two of the stuffie mascots that he had back home. Maybe he wasn't so old yet after all, I thought with a smile.

Queen City was a motley assembly of adults. They played in a twenty-five-plus league, meaning that their youngest player was still older than Batavia's oldest. Their pitcher was a portly junkballer who was lucky to hit 80 with his fastball but still managed to keep Batavia's batters off balance through the early frames. Skip shouted to his players to "act like it's BP [batting practice] and stay back," since the Queen City hurler's fastballs were basically the same speed as batting practice pitches. Erik, meanwhile, was carefully shepherding Bates through his batboy duties, which he seemed to be taking seriously, sprinting out to home plate to retrieve discarded bats whenever there was a break in the action, returning to the dugout, oversized red helmet bouncing on his head and bat in hand, with a shy smile suggesting pride in his work. Marcy, who had settled in a seat alongside Betsey and Ginny, would later tell me that the women had cheered loudly for him, shouting "Yay, Bates" every time he'd retrieved a bat.

Somehow the municipal league team of older Buffalonians, a few of whom looked as if they knew their way around the city's famed wing joints a little too well, had scrapped their way back from a 4–0 deficit to tie the score in the top of the sixth. Public address announcer Paul Spiotta, meanwhile, had invited Bates to join him in the press box to introduce the Muckdogs batters as they approached home plate for an inning. This was something that Paul did every so often, as the crowd enjoyed listening to young kids make these announcements, sometimes butchering a few names in the process. Still, I was a tad nervous, as I had no idea what to expect from Bates. As Marcy and I looked on anxiously, Marcy cradling Shea in her lap wrapped in a soft blanket, Bates approached the microphone and proceeded to announce each batter with nearly perfect diction. I'm not sure who was prouder, him or his parents, and we thanked Paul for the opportunity before making our way back to our seats near Betsey and Ginny.

By now the ladies had broken out their large blanket to help insulate themselves from the chill that set in as soon as the sun dipped below the left-field fence. Ginny said they'd been "bursting with pride" as Bates announced the batters. Meanwhile, Bates, who was now running on fumes as his bedtime fast approached, continued to ask them to "play with me," to which they unfailingly responded with a yes and a smile—something I certainly didn't always do.

Longtime season ticket holder Russ Salway was standing at one of the high-top tables nearby. He and a small posse of diehards were almost always posted up at the table that had a laminated printout with his name affixed to it, denoting that he had rented it for the season. They were in good spirits, no doubt aided by the tallboy beers that the "beer girl" wearing a striped referee top kept them well supplied with. Everyone seemed to know the group, with various passersby stopping to say hello and offering to share their popcorn and other snacks. I always enjoyed catching up with the gang, though I confess to doing the best I could to avoid one of their occasional buddies—who Betsey, Ginny, and I took to calling "Mr. No-Sleeves" on account of his propensity for tank tops—as he invariably cornered me if he saw my notebook out, often shouting, "Hey, pal, whatcha writin'?" before forcefully offering unsolicited advice on what I "needed to put in the book."

Salway's commitment to the ball club over the years was evidenced not only by his serving on its board but also by his having offered up his basement "man cave" for minor leaguers in Batavia to live in as part of the "host family" program. Though it has been largely phased out today, for a long time local families putting up players in their homes for free, or for a modest cost-of-living stipend, had been a feature of life in the low minors. It was an effective way for MLB clubs to save money and to establish connections between players and their fans. Lasting friendships were sometimes forged. Salway proudly shared the story of how he'd hosted Daniel Descalso in his basement for a summer before he ultimately worked his way up to the St. Louis Cardinals. Years later, Descalso invited him and his son, Nick, to a game when the Cardinals visited Pittsburgh, treating them to tickets plus dinner at a nearby restaurant afterwards.

The host program also arguably helped ground the players who graduated from it to eventually become major league stars in the world of their working-class fans. It's hard to imagine Justin Verlander having anything in common with fans like Salway, for example, as he celebrated a two-year, nearly $87 million contract by bringing his actress wife, Kate Upton, to a $450,000-per-week villa in St. Barts. While many players no doubt came from working-class origins themselves, there was still something to be said for experiences like sleeping on a sofa bed, gazing up at Salway's basement vinyl collection and "Wall of Fame" featuring Buffalo sports greats. It can be beneficial to have some humbling experiences on one's journey to stardom. Fresh memories of pedaling around places like Batavia on a bike provided by a host family might help offset the sometimes corrosive influence of fabulous riches on celebrity ballplayers. This is not to say, of course, that minor leaguers shouldn't be paid a living wage, or should be forced to endure terrible living conditions—both of which used to occur too often—but rather that something is lost when more and more connections between player and fan are severed.

Gone are the days chronicled by Roger Kahn in his brilliant account of the 1950s-era Brooklyn Dodgers, *The Boys of Summer*. In it, Kahn recounts how he discovered two-time All Star, two-time World Series champion, and one-time National League batting champion Carl Furillo installing elevators at the World Trade Center after his playing days were over. Likewise, he found All-Star pitcher Preacher Roe, who compiled a 22-3 record with the 1951 Dodgers, running a small grocery store in West Plains, Missouri, population 12,184. Surely few would wish that today's players be forced to toil away in obscurity when their playing days are over—like Billy Cox of the Brooklyn Dodgers, whom Kahn observes tending bar in a Pennsylvania VFW, writing that "no one knew he was the most glorious glove on the most glorious team that ever played baseball in the sunlight of Brooklyn." But at the same time, our connection to the sport is deepened when we are reminded that our heroes are human.

Now, with more players graduating from elite college programs where they have grown accustomed to "white-glove" treatment, in the words of one longtime scout, and with teams showering a handful of top draft picks with ever-more-lucrative bonuses, there is less of an appetite from major league clubs to have these precious assets play catch with young kids in small backyards across rural America, as Descalso once did with Salway's son, Nick. Salway will never forget the morning when he and Nick, then around ten years old, drove a player they had hosted for the summer to the Buffalo airport shortly after the season ended. He noticed Nick had been abnormally quiet for the entire ride, and as they pulled out of the airport and merged onto Interstate 90 for the drive back to Batavia, he spied a single tear sliding down Nick's cheek.

As we chatted, a foul ball arced over us and landed on Denio Street, which ran parallel with the third-base line, skittering into a driveway and under a car parked outside a neatly kept tan house facing the ballpark. Kids scrambled to chase after it. The scene transported me back to playing Wiffle ball in my grandparents' backyard— I was lucky enough to grow up less than a mile from them—with my younger brother, Tad, when I would wallop one of his pitches over their house and into the front yard of the neighbor across the street. Looking back, I marveled at how Tad had always been such a good sport despite nearly always losing to me, as I was six years older. He may have gotten the last laugh, though, as my college baseball career had flamed out ignominiously, whereas years of competing with someone who was bigger and stronger (at least for a spell) probably contributed to his success as an athlete, as he would go on to an accomplished baseball career pitching for Division I Cornell.

Batavia had by now finally put a little distance between themselves and the scrappy club from Buffalo, extending their lead to 8–4 in the bottom of the seventh, though the inning was not without some drama, as outfielder Josh Leadem was called out on strikes after two very questionable calls by the umpire, prompting Skip Martinez to slam his helmet to the ground in the third-base coach's box before sprinting to home plate to confront the umpire with a spirited tirade. Skip, a natural showman who (despite having added some weight from his playing days) still moved with the smooth athleticism that had landed him a free agent contract to play in the Tigers organization, breathed some life into the crowd with his eruption.

One man remained remarkably serene even as the crowd around him was worked into a tizzy. Ernie Lawrence, bespectacled and balding, a Batavia season ticket holder since 1986, sat quietly focusing on the yellow beads in his lap that he was fashioning into a rosary with the help of a set of pliers he worked expertly in his hands. He would later tell me that "having been to thousands of ball games, I find rosary building a good way to keep my mind and hands busy during the game. Baseball is a game that is played at a quiet pace with moments of excitement. There is plenty of time to talk to friends or build a rosary without being distracted too much from the game."

Marcy had by now brought the kids back to the warmth of the La Quinta, and as the weather cooled and the game's outcome seemed decided, I found myself drawn to this older man and the calm he projected. Ernie told me he'd inherited a love of baseball from his father, an accomplished player in the small city of Oneida, where he had grown up, though his father had died when Ernie was still young. When he wasn't working in his family's neighborhood grocery store, Ernie recalled a boyhood spent playing pickup baseball and football, as well as in local youth leagues sponsored by the city. A lifelong fan of the minor leagues, he would take his kids, Andrew and Amanda, on one-hour trips to Rochester to watch future Oriole stars like Eddie Murray, Mike Flanagan, and Cal Ripken Jr. play nearly thirty games a summer. This was before he discovered Class A ball in Batavia, where he loved how safe the smaller ballpark felt for his young kids, who in turn enjoyed being so close to the players and being allowed to roam freely. Ernie soon became a season ticket holder and later volunteered to be an officer on the team's executive committee. Trying to reconcile the appeal of summer nights at Dwyer with his relative lack of interest in the major league product on TV, Ernie observed how "baseball is a lovely game played in a big, pretty space. I've never been able to enjoy the game on television. All you see is the pitcher throwing the ball, the batter swinging the bat, and the one fielder who is going to catch the ball and throw it to the first baseman. The beauty of the bigness of the game is lost."

As Ernie and I spoke, the Muckdogs closed out a 10–4 victory in front of the remaining stalwarts who had braved the cold in anticipation of the postgame fireworks. I couldn't quite share in the celebratory mood, though, as my nose was running, and the biting wind made me envious of Marcy and the kids tucked away back in our warm hotel room. Still, the victory and fireworks accompanied by a soundtrack of eighties hits seemed to have put a bounce in everyone's step as they made their way to the exit.

After grabbing a hot chocolate in the hotel lobby to help warm up, I crept into our hotel room, careful not to disturb the sleeping little ones. Everyone was tucked in snugly, a pleasant change from the empty rooms that usually greeted me after long days at the ballpark. After a night during which everyone slept shockingly well, we woke to a beautiful day in Batavia. I watched the kids play at a nearby playground while Marcy went on a short run, everyone delighting in the cloudless sky. Then we piled into the car for the four-hour drive home, a successful visit in the books. As we drove home, with Bates insisting on watching the iPhone recording of his at-bat announcements repeatedly, I was pleased that the two worlds I'd been inhabiting had at least been temporarily melded, and hopeful that some of the connections that had been established might even last beyond the end of the baseball season.

11

Niagara Power at
Batavia Muckdogs

June 20

Ed Dwyer, after whom the Muckdogs ballpark is named, was a humble man. He never drew attention to the fact that for the nearly half a century he served as the president of Batavia's minor league ballclub, he did more for professional baseball in the community than anyone before or since. The product of a hardscrabble childhood on a nearby farm, Dwyer was a "math whiz," according to his son, John, winning the prize for best math student at his high school before going on to graduate from what would become the Rochester Institute of Technology.

Shifting his focus in college from engineering to retail, Ed graduated and started working in a prominent Rochester shoe store before pooling money with a colleague to open their own shop, Thomas & Dwyer, on Main Street in Batavia, in what was at the time its thriving business district. Dwyer would leverage his math aptitude, business acumen, and untiring work ethic—John recalls his father working six days a week at the store, followed by long Sunday afternoon sessions quietly laboring at the kitchen table of their house a block away from the ballpark—to eventually own three stores that served the region for over thirty years. He was also a civic leader, serving on the Chamber of Commerce and active at St. Joseph's Catholic church. And of course there was always that passion for baseball. John jokes that his father had four loves: "God and the church, his family, the United States, and baseball . . . but I'm not sure in what order."

Dwyer would serve as the team's president from shortly after its 1939 inception until not long before his death at the age of ninety-two in 1995, earning the moniker of Batavia's "Mr. Baseball." Unbeknownst to most, including even his own wife—John laughs when he says "My mother died not knowing what portion of her bank account went to bats and balls"—Dwyer would quietly help subsidize the team, providing equipment and never asking to be reimbursed. For decades he was a rather unassuming fixture in his seats along the third-base line, sitting alongside friends, a local dentist and jeweler, though he did love to "chirp the umpires," according to Bill Kauffman, who had a bird's-eye view of the "short, white-haired old Irish guy" from his seats higher in the third-base grandstands.

Ed Dwyer was emblematic of an era when minor league clubs were owned and managed locally, an era that is increasingly under threat as teams continue to be swallowed up by outside private equity investors. A prominent example of this was the recent purchase of the Iowa Cubs by Diamond Baseball Holdings. Shortly after the deal was finalized, longtime owner Michael Gartner, who had served as editor of the *Des Moines Register*, gathered the club's employees together in the Cubs Club stadium restaurant. They assumed he was going to thank them and bid farewell. But he had a surprise.

According to team president and general manager Sam Bernabe—who had begun working for the club as an intern in 1983 before becoming general manager in 1986 and eventually joining the ownership group in 1999—after offering the assembled a "beverage of choice," Gartner shocked his twenty-three full-time staff members by handing each of them an envelope containing a check in the amount of $2,000 for every year they'd worked for the team. Gartner, who owned 70 percent of the team, Bernabe, and the team's other minority owners gave away a total of $600,000 from their sale, with one employee receiving a check for $70,000. This was life-changing money for some of the recipients, and they were overcome with emotion. It wasn't the first time Gartner had subordinated his own economic interest in order to do right by his employees. When COVID canceled the 2020 season, he didn't lay anyone off, instead continuing to pay his staff for the duration of the work stoppage.

This was not the only example of magnanimous local owners like Batavia's Ed Dwyer. Bill Burke and his sister, Sally McNamara, had

been longtime owners of the Portland Sea Dogs before also deciding to sell to Diamond Baseball Holdings. Bill Burke had been so
inspired by Michael Gartner's generosity in Iowa that he vowed to
do the same thing when his sale became official. He was true to
his word, as he and his sister shared profits from their sale with the
team's eighteen full-time employees. Also, like Gartner, they had
continued to pay their full-time staff (and even seasonal game-day
employees) during the season canceled to COVID, despite losing
game-day sales revenue from an entire summer. "We're already losing
our shirts," Burke would recall thinking; "let's at least go for it and
help them out."

Bill Burke's father, Dan, had established the franchise in Portland
in 1994. Bill grew a little emotional as he shared his best memory
of their time there together, recalling: "Sitting with Dad in our box,
as the sun set between innings, he said, 'People really have fun here,
don't they?'" Bill had his own little epiphany when, during one of the
first games following minor league baseball's return after the summer that was lost to COVID, he saw a "young dad with his daughter
on his shoulders, ice cream smeared on her face, both of them so
happy, and I thought to myself, *This is a great business.*"

When Bill and his sister decided it was time to make a "graceful
exit" from baseball ownership, they insisted to Diamond Baseball, the
buyer, that they keep their box seat at Hadlock Field, so they could
continue to enjoy summer sunsets beyond the "Maine Monster" replica of Fenway Park's Green Monster for years to come. In addition
to being owners, families like the Burkes, Gartners, and Dwyers were
fans—fans who recognized that something went on within the confines of their ballparks that transcended the sterile label "content and
entertainment" used to describe minor league baseball on the website
of Silver Lake (Diamond Baseball's owner).

Longtime Portland ticketholders and staff will surely enjoy running into the Burkes as they circulate through the ballpark, but
their continued presence as spectators won't change the reality that,
according to the Iowa Cubs' Sam Bernabe, "the business is moving
away from mom-and-pops. I was born and raised here and recognize the team's importance to this town. But the business of sport is
moving away from this. Mom and Pop aren't capable of hanging in
there ... You need deep pockets to keep up." A private equity boss

and former owner of a major pro sports team quoted in a *GQ* article by Tom Lamont entitled "So, You Want to Buy a Pro Sports Team? Here's How" echoes this, explaining, "It's not gonna stop. Once capitalism gets involved, there is no moderating it. We are going into corporatized ownership. It's an arms race. And it's just gonna keep going. Capitalism will find its way into the cracks."

The generosity of some of these local owners stood in marked contrast to MLB, where some clubs proved reluctant to pay their minor leaguers during the COVID shutdown, and furloughs and pay cuts of baseball operations personnel were common, despite franchise valuations in the billions of dollars. ESPN's Jeff Passan pointed out the stinginess of some MLB owners during COVID in a tweet: "Just some rough math. Say there are 200 players in a minor league system. Paying each $400/week for June, July, and August is $5,200 per player. To pay every minor leaguer would have cost the Oakland A's a hair over $1 million. Owner John Fisher is worth an estimated $2 billion." Holdouts like the A's would eventually reverse course and agree to pay their minor leaguers for the duration of the lost season, but not before alienating some of the minor leaguers in their system who were already facing the most tenuous financial circumstances.

It would be both easy and inaccurate to portray all of the "old-school" local family owners of minor league clubs as altruistic saints focused on serving their communities even at the expense of their bank accounts. There were some rotten ones who invested the bare minimum in their clubs, taking advantage of the free labor in the form of players who were paid by their major league parent organization and contributing little to improve the fan experience. Though contraction was hardly a scientific or purely meritocratic process, it is true that it eliminated some owners who had proven unworthy of having a minor league affiliate.

But the subsequent exodus of committed family owners like the Gartners and the Burkes may portend a more significant loss. Former president of Minor League Baseball Pat O'Conner would allude to this changing dynamic when he explained, "In the old model the owner would live in town, speak at the Kiwanis Club, and see neighbors at the bank and post office. Distant owners don't face the scrutiny of the social conscience of the community." It is unlikely that the decision-making calculus of distant equity investors will mirror that of the local family owners of old, many of whom were influenced—at least in part—by the employees and fans they'd slowly gotten to know over the course of countless summer nights at the ballpark. Referring to Diamond Baseball now owning 30 percent of minor league teams, a sports business professor with extensive knowledge of the business of minor league baseball said, "These teams should be a prized possession of someone in the town who loves baseball more than just about anything else. Now these local clubs are part of an enormous portfolio run by a private equity firm based out of Silicon Valley and New York City [Silver Lake], just another way to make money alongside ownership stakes in enterprise software, financial technology, and eCommerce. How sad is that?"

*   *   *

The Muckdogs season was now about a third of the way complete, and the team occupied sole possession of first place in the PGCBL's West Division. The season's progression was accompanied by the approach of the summer solstice, which, as usual, triggered conflicting emotions. On the one hand, I savored the long days and pleasant nights that marked summer in the Northeast, but I also hated the reminder that days would now begin to grow shorter. It had always been a weird psychological tic, and one that had been magnified living near Pittsburgh, where the winters are especially dark and gray. I'd rarely encountered anyone who shared this peculiar reaction to a day most considered an unalloyed good marking the onset of summer.

I should've known I could count on Bill Kauffman, though, to have another complicated, and probably overly intellectual, take on the summer solstice. Here was a man, after all, whose unairconditioned attic "office" was an oasis of erudition amid the surrounding agricultural mucklands, hundreds of books piled every which way alongside scattered baseball memorabilia he had accumulated as a lifelong fan. Among his more treasured items, stashed inside a drawer underneath the jumble of papers and manuscripts that overflowed his desk, was a stack of dozens of blue envelopes containing his longtime correspondence with famed author and public intellectual Gore Vidal. Bill's wife, Lucine, a native of Los Angeles who nonetheless had grown to enjoy the more pastoral existence of their Elba homestead, recoiled at the sight of her husband's sanctuary, insisting that at a minimum the avalanche of books didn't begin making its way downstairs.

Regarding the onset of summer, Bill, as only a bibliophile could, told me, "The beginning of summer always has a touch of melancholy for me now. Since our daughter, Gretel, was quite young, she and I would sit on the front porch on the summer solstice reading the opening chapters of Ray Bradbury's *Dandelion Wine*, the loveliest evocation of a childhood summer. She's been off into the wider world for a decade now, and so on June 21, I'll read it to myself, and it's not quite the same."

For her part, later in the summer, recalling the tradition and its place in her childhood in Elba, Gretel would say, "We read it outside since I was five years old. I loved the description of the small town waking up. Elba is a small town, and I enjoyed reading about the small town nostalgia. My dad instilled the sentimentality of place in me, and the idea that having a community is important. I'm a sucker for underdog, imperfect places."

She paused, and then laughed as she said, "Hopefully I'm not getting written out of the will for living in Idaho now."

*   *   *

Dusk was gradually setting in on the eve of the solstice as I took a seat at my small desk in the corner of what had been my office and was now Shea's nursery. It was a lovely Monday night, and looking out the second-story window I could see fireflies beginning to flicker in the backyard. I wanted to catch up on some work before we left on a short midsummer family vacation. By now more than a few Muckdogs fans had told me how they would stream games on the team's YouTube channel when they couldn't attend in person. Seeing as how I'd become invested in the team's success, and found myself missing my new friends from Dwyer, I was curious to see what the broadcasts were like. So I decided to tune in to the evening's game in Batavia, in which the Muckdogs would be hosting the Niagara Power.

It would be my first time listening to an entire broadcast by John Carubba, the twenty-nine-year-old Buffalo native who served as the play-by-play and color commentator for the Muckdogs home games streamed on YouTube. I'd overheard snippets of Carubba's narration while spending time in the press box with Paul Spiotta, which was adjacent to the broadcast nook Carubba inhabited. But I had never tuned in until that evening's game. Labatt's Blue Light in hand (I'd developed an affinity for the beer on my trips to western New York where it is ubiquitous) and grabbing a stack of paperwork to plow through while I watched, I turned on the broadcast. Batavia, which had begun the season with a scalding 8-2 record, was welcoming the middling Niagara Power, who entered with a 5-6 record.

A student from the New York State School for the Blind recited the national anthem. While this ceremony can feel pro forma at some events nowadays, it always felt meaningful at Dwyer, in keeping with what seemed to be a sincerely patriotic spirit in Batavia. This spirit wasn't manifested in loud displays of belligerent nationalism but rather in little things like how people would stop for the anthem when walking around the ballpark, or preface many of their initial meetings with me by thanking me for my service, many of them then sharing stories of relatives who had served or were serving. On this evening, following the anthem, the crowd unleashed one of its loudest cheers of the night for a blind student who threw out the game's ceremonial opening pitch. Paul Spiotta would later say that observing the scene had caused him to tear up.

*   *   *

Paul always kept his eyes open for opportunities to use the Muckdogs to bring some happiness into lives that needed it. Rick Ruhlman had been a special-education student on the autism spectrum who graduated from Batavia High School in 1976, a year after Paul and a year before Bill Kauffman. Though unathletic, Ruhlman had a remarkable memory when it came to sports statistics. In high school he served as team manager, scorekeeper, and waterboy, the beginning of four decades of doing everything from helping keep score and run the clock at Batavia High School football and basketball games to helping in the press box at Muckdogs games. "Rick is a great example of a guy who might have fallen through the cracks in a bigger place, but here he found a niche, a job, an identity," said Bill

Kauffman. Learning that Rick's Parkinson's had taken a bad turn in recent years, Paul and Bill worked with Muckdogs general manager Marc Witt to honor him at a game. Paul would introduce Ruhlman, seated awkwardly on his walker, wearing an old Bills jersey and cap, to the crowd as he received a standing ovation:

> Rick Ruhlman, BHS Class of 1976, is an essential and beloved figure in the history of Batavia sports. Whether on the sidelines, in the locker room, from the press box, or in the stands, Rick has enriched and encouraged Batavia athletes in countless ways over the past half century. For his labors of love, Rick was inducted into the Blue Devils Athletic Hall of Fame in 2007. Tonight, the Batavia Blue Devils and the Batavia Muckdogs would like to thank Rick Ruhlman for a lifetime of service. Rick, you have made Batavia a better place.

While the on-field ceremony served as a heartwarming recognition of Ruhlman's contributions to local sports, it wasn't until I found myself helping Bill get Ruhlman home that I had a fuller appreciation for the man's life, and the meaning he must have derived from the Muckdogs. He somehow had been delivered to the stadium for the evening's ceremony without a way home, and so Bill volunteered to help return him there. However, Bill would discover that he couldn't get Ruhlman to his car, since he didn't have a wheelchair and Rick was too tired to get there using his walker. So Bill enlisted my help for the mission. After we were eventually able to load Ruhlman into Bill's car—not before I was drenched in sweat from our labor—we made our way to his dilapidated house on Watson Street on one of Batavia's rougher blocks on the south side of town. We had another struggle getting him into the ramshackle home he shared with his eighty-nine-year-old, half-blind mother, as it didn't have any ramp for his walker. We had to carry him in, with the help of a younger man who happened to be walking by with an unleashed dog and offered to assist. Once inside, Ruhlman's mom suggested we set him in his "special chair," a recliner facing a TV tuned in to an old episode of *Everybody Loves Raymond*. By now Ruhlman seemed utterly exhausted by the evening's exertions. The curtains on the house were drawn, so none of the setting sunlight made its way into the dark living area. His mother began crying when Bill described the ceremony honoring Rick, telling us, "He's my little boy and God gave him this special burden." With tears of what seemed to be both gratitude and sadness, she continued, "He's such a good boy, always trying to help me." As I scanned the downstairs of their home, where it appeared both of them slept on nearby couches, a print of Jesus's Last Supper on the wall, I was simultaneously struck by a powerful sadness at the gloom that permeated the place tempered with a glimmer of hope that there were still people like Paul, Bill, and the countless well-wishers Ruhlman encountered at the stadium who went out of their way to bring a little light into a difficult life.

*   *   *

As I tuned in to the YouTube broadcast of the Muckdogs hosting Niagara, I quickly discovered that the only thing that could make it watchable would be John Carubba's narration, since the visual component was limited to a single motionless camera located behind home plate that made it tough to discern any of the action. In this regard, the experience more closely resembled listening to an old-fashioned radio broadcast than watching a game on TV.

The most immediately noticeable aspect of Carubba's style was his energy, giving the impression that he was perpetually hypercaffeinated, coupled with an unbridled boosterism of his Muckdogs. The enthusiasm Carubba brought to the broadcast was not merely the result of a strategic choice on how to be a successful announcer, though. There was more to it than that.

Carubba's fascination with sports broadcasting can be traced to a car accident when he was thirteen years old that left him in a wheelchair, in a great deal of pain, for nine years. For a while he feared he might never be able to walk again. It was during these long days convalescing in a hospital, and later bedridden and in pain in his Buffalo home, that he discovered Yankees games on the YES Network. He immediately fell in love with the ritual of tuning in to the games and soaking in the soothing cadences of Michael Kay's play-by-play call. He still remembers listening to an interview Kay did with fellow sports broadcaster Joe Buck in which, as Carubba recalls it, Buck said that his goal was to "put a smile on someone's face and help them forget their troubles for a few hours." It resonated deeply with him, as watching Yankee games temporarily transported him far beyond the drab confines of his hospital room to a sunnier place, featuring powerful ballplayers clad in legendary pinstripes, striding gracefully across lush green grass in "the House that Ruth Built." For Carubba, the temporary escape from his pain to this better place was nothing short of magical, "the only thing that could put a smile on my face."

From then on, Carubba never had any doubt that he wanted to be a sports broadcaster. As a student at North Carolina's High Point University, he broadcast soccer, baseball, and basketball games for the university. He then returned home to western New York and broadcast high school games on YouTube and a local cable network. While juggling broadcasting gigs and helping out part-time at his dad's music store, Carubba learned that Batavia was launching a team in the PGCBL following the loss of their professional team. He immediately emailed Robbie Nichols to see if they needed a broadcaster. They met at the Eli Fish brewery in March 2022, and Carubba was hired (though he wouldn't be paid—unsurprising, given Robbie's thrifty ways). Despite not getting paid, Carubba was encouraged by Robbie's pledge to help him find full-time paid work in sports broadcasting if he did a good job, pointing to former interns and staff members he'd helped break into the notoriously competitive profession.

Despite Carubba's best efforts on this night, the game did not include much drama, as Batavia continued its dominant start to the season, spreading five runs across eight innings before Skip Martinez turned to hard-throwing Tampa native Julian Pichardo to close it out in the top of the ninth. Pichardo's grandparents were tuned in to Carubba's broadcast in their Tampa living room, having resigned themselves to being unable to afford coming to watch Julian play in person "unless we win the lottery." His grandfather Mike Baluja delighted in how Julian and Muckdogs fans had bonded, saying, "It gave me goose bumps to learn about how some of the young kids love him and how he inspires them as a role model . . . As a father, it's a blessing to watch." Even though he was watching from a living room a thousand miles away, Mike said Dwyer was "magical" on summer nights, an "oasis where I got lost last summer, where I could feel the ghosts of baseball past, and when it ended, I didn't know what to do with myself."

While Julian enjoyed spending time with the kids who idolized him, he was also there to pitch well and advance his career. "Make no mistake about it," Mike would say of the grandson he and Cindy had raised, "his goal is to make it to the pros. I don't know where his journey will lead, but I do know that right now he is living the dream. His hopes are high, and his talents are nearly there."

Tonight I knew Mike would be all smiles as Julian, despite giving up two hits, closed out the game without surrendering any runs. John Carubba called the final out with characteristic enthusiasm, exclaiming, "Do you believe this? Another day, another home game, another Muckdog victory!"

The Muckdogs were now 9-2 on the season and undefeated at home.

Oddly enough, the experience of watching the game at home had made me feel almost as much a part of the Muckdogs community as my experiences at the games themselves. I was reminded of the Pub Coffee Hub's informal writer-in-residence Eric Zwieg's observation that "ritual often refers to religious practice, but it can also be something like a ball game." As I watched from home and imagined those I'd grown to know as they moved through this reassuring ritual—Betsey and Ginny enjoying each other's company as they made the drive from Buffalo, Ernie Lawrence quietly beading his rosary, Russ Salway enjoying some tallboy beers with his buddies, Dr. Fanara losing himself in the game as his great-grandkids played nearby, Cathy Preston keeping score, Bill Kauffman waxing poetic about the ghosts of Batavia's past, his parents, Joe and Sandra, retiring early to the warmth of their nearby house—I wished I was there.

12

Vacation Trip to Kannapolis Cannon Ballers Game

June 24

Feeling a bit guilty that I'd been gone for much of the summer, I loaded up our Kia Sorento and headed to South Carolina with Bates, where we would pick up Marcy and Shea the following day at the airport in Charleston before heading to the beach for a week. Driving with Bates while the girls flew would save us some money on flights and a rental car, while also avoiding a nearly twenty-four-hour round-trip drive with a three-month-old. En route, I thought it would be fun for me and Bates to stop in North Carolina to take in a Kannapolis Cannon Ballers Single-A game.

After a long day's drive from Pittsburgh, we quickly checked in to our hotel and headed to the glistening $52 million ballpark that had hosted the Cannon Ballers since the return of minor league baseball post-COVID. For Bates it was love at first sight, as he discovered an enormous splash pad and bouncy house shortly after we entered the stadium. I shared his enthusiasm, though for me it was the craft beers on tap and lush diamond on display that were especially alluring. When I ordered an IPA and Bates asked for a Gatorade, the nice lady manning the beer stand winked and gave it to him for free.

Looking out over the field, I was immediately struck by how much bigger and stronger the players were than their collegiate Batavia counterparts, men and not boys. The pitcher was hitting 95, seemingly without even really exerting himself. The scoreboard appeared to be state-of-the-art, the stadium modern and pristine.

The entire operation had a sleeker and more corporate feel than the truly homespun Muckdogs games, but one still felt the pulse of community, whether it was the friendly ushers greeting regulars by name, families converging at the bouncy house and talking amiably with each other, or kids playing tag on the grass berm beyond the left-field fence. Bates, meanwhile, had befriended a young boy in the row ahead of us, and they were busy running around nearby empty seats "battling zombies" as the boy's parents and grandparents sipped beers and watched the game, three generations enjoying each other's company for a few hours while happily welcoming a father and son visiting from Pittsburgh into the fold.

*　　*　　*

Kannapolis, North Carolina, is deep in the heart of NASCAR country and is proud to be the hometown of Dale Earnhardt, the iconic driver who still enjoys near-mythic status in the American South. In fact, for years Earnhardt owned a share of the local minor league club, which at the time was named the Intimidators, borrowing his nickname. This is noteworthy because more than one minor league baseball fan in the region told me that what MLB was doing to the minors mirrored decisions made by NASCAR in the early 2000s. A fascinating article in *The American Conservative* entitled "The Decline and Fall of NASCAR" explains how NASCAR's corporate leadership, reflecting a desire to expand beyond their traditional southeastern fan base:

> built new tracks in Miami, Chicago, Dallas, and Las Vegas. These were cookie-cutter tracks, all one and a half miles long, with luxury boxes and suites like you'd see in an NFL stadium. Formerly tracks had been individually distinctive with their own special quirks . . . NASCAR did not increase the number of races in its schedule, so it was a zero-sum tradeoff that resulted in many smaller tracks closing down. For small towns like North Wilkesboro and Rockingham, having a track was a draw that brought in revenue from tourism and hospitality. But for NASCAR, the revenue was just too small, especially compared to the potential of large markets like Miami and

Vegas . . . For some NASCAR fans, this marked a betrayal by the sport they loved . . . Such a pattern of change is familiar to NASCAR's base of working-class fans in the southeast. The suits came in and changed everything, leaving the old loyalists both bewildered and worse off. They had been dispossessed. Something dear had been taken from them.

The parallels to MLB's contraction of the minor leagues were striking; in each case corporate chieftains, placing what they perceived as a means toward an improved bottom line over the interests of some of their most devoted fans, alienated smaller communities in favor of major markets, all while making their product more homogenous and less colorful. In NASCAR's case, these decisions triggered over a decade of decline in both TV viewership and race day attendance. The impact of MLB's similar decisions on its already fading popularity remains to be seen.

*   *   *

Experiencing firsthand the enjoyment of a Cannon Ballers game highlighted once more the disconnect that existed between the intangible contributions these teams make to civic life and MLB's one-dimensional view of minor league baseball as existing solely to identify and cultivate talent for major league teams in big cities. More than one former minor league owner, as well as industry insiders, expressed fears that 2020's contraction of the minor leagues was just "phase one," with another possible round cutting the number of minor league teams from 120 to 90 on the horizon.

Several of these insiders suggested that MLB was envious of sports like football and basketball and wanted to move toward those models, where college, rather than minor leagues, served as the primary proving grounds for younger players (which of course did not require any investment from professional teams). One former owner suggested that the 2022 "unionization of the minor leagues increased the likelihood of contraction, as it drove up the cost of an affiliated team [according to their first-ever collective bargaining agreement with MLB minimum minor league salaries would increase from $4,800 to $19,800 a season for rookie ball; $11,000 to $27,300 at High Class A; $13,800 to $27,300 at Class AA; and $17,500 to $35,800 at Class AAA] . . . MLB clubs aren't going to increase their minor league budget, and so they may just decide to spread the same money on fewer players."

Resistance to the ongoing threat MLB poses to minor league baseball has been muted by the reality that those most impacted by it—current and former minor league owners—are the least eager to speak critically of the commissioner's office. "No one is banging on a garbage can [referencing the Astros practice during their sign-stealing scandal] describing this is how MLB operates and what they're doing to the minor leagues," said one former minor league owner. The reason for this is simple: no current owners want to upset the powers-that-be and find themselves on the list of future rounds of contraction, while some owners who already had their teams stamped out remain under the hope (or illusion) they may someday get an affiliated team back. I spoke to numerous current and former owners (some of whom had lost millions when their affiliated teams fell victim to contraction), and they were almost universally unwilling to go on the record with concerns or grievances.

Fans were far more willing to voice their anger. One longtime minor league fan whose team was extinguished wrote to me, "RIP minor league baseball. This team used to bring our community together from all demographics: police, mill workers, Latinos, the country club set. It wasn't stratified, there were no luxury suites. This marks the end of an era."

*   *   *

Many would contend that the modern "era" of minor league baseball's renaissance had been brought about by *Bull Durham*, the iconic 1988 film loosely based on writer-director Ron Shelton's experience as a minor league ballplayer, which is located near the top of most lists of the best sports movies of all time. Lines and nicknames from *Bull Durham* still populate the lexicon of baseball nearly forty years later. Generations of baseball fans are now familiar with the love triangle including hotshot rookie Ebby Calvin "Nuke" LaLoosh (Tim Robbins), his world-weary minor league veteran mentor "Crash" Davis (Kevin Costner), and their mutual love interest, Annie Savoy (Susan

Sarandon). Mention the movie to almost any baseball fan, and you will likely get a response that sheds light on their own relationship to baseball, or, in the case of Eric Zwieg, a pithy zinger at the expense of Bill Kauffman. When I mentioned to Zwieg that Bill was one of the few fans I'd spoken to who didn't enjoy the film, he responded, without missing a beat, "That's because Annie Savoy threatens Bill's manhood with her sexual and intellectual freedom."

Given the film's place in the pantheon of all-time great baseball movies, it's noteworthy that *Bull Durham*'s creator, Ron Shelton, said he was "outraged" at MLB's recent contraction, adding, "Manfred is the Antichrist, and you can quote me on that . . . For him it's like any another business, a tech company or auto company . . . There's no love for the game." MLB owners make more money than ever, he said, but "don't understand baseball's social importance and how it connects us. How can they pay some players $350 million and not have enough money for Bluefield, West Virginia [the town nestled in the Appalachian Mountains where Shelton once played in the minor leagues that recently lost its team to contraction]? It's greed. Rural America is falling apart, and a modest investment could help hold it together."

Shelton's outrage was echoed by countless fans in smaller communities whose minor league teams had been eliminated. Rich Schauf, the former Batavia cop and longtime minor league season ticket holder, said his "hatred" of MLB was such that not only will he not watch games anymore, but he grows angry every time he even surfs past the MLB station on television when flipping channels. David Horne, one of the most passionate baseball fans I knew, regularly communicated his simmering anger to me in the years after we first met as I researched my *Harper's* article on MLB's elimination of the Appalachian Rookie League. For decades he had been a season ticket holder to the Appalachian League's Burlington Royals, the AAA Durham Bulls, and Elon University's team, as well as a devoted fan of major league baseball. But more recently, explaining his decision to sever all connections with MLB, he wrote to me:

Will:
    In a world where the owners like Steve Cohen are literally over-paying millions of dollars on injury-ridden pitchers and

over-the-hill position players in an attempt to stroke their egos by winning a championship, it would cost relatively nothing to keep professional baseball in the small towns of America.

MLB is just so greedy and soulless. With every action, MLB makes my decision to distance myself from it more palatable.

It bothers me to my soul that I have walked away to such a degree.

I feel that I've abandoned a lifetime love, when in actuality it's obvious that it's the other way around.

Bull Durham's Ron Shelton noted the parallels between the winner-take-all nature of the baseball business and Hollywood, where "one actor can now command twenty-five million dollars while much of the rest of the crew can barely make a living wage."

The similarities between Hollywood and professional baseball were indeed striking and extended from the almost unimaginable disparities in pay to the evolving criteria for identifying and investing in "talent." As in baseball, where analytics have increasingly supplanted human intuition in the scouting process, Shelton said, "Algorithms are fucking everything up in Hollywood. *Bull Durham* would never get made now, since it doesn't conform to a proven formula. There's no big game, and by the end of the movie the two main characters aren't even on the team anymore. Yet it's not only okay, but deeply satisfying. The MBAs think they can do entertainment better than entertainment people, and they're ruining it."

Shelton went on to lament how "studios used to be some of the most creative places around, and now they are the least creative, replacing knowledge and instinct and intuition with numbers and algorithms and computers." Whereas in the "old days studios would take fliers" on films based on the informed judgment and experienced instinct of a studio executive, some of which would go on to become Oscar-winning Best Pictures, an increasing reliance on algorithms designed to predict the future based only on past performance results in far fewer opportunities for creative long shots to get a chance, he contended. The days of brilliant but unconventional film ideas being plucked from obscurity and going on to box office fame may be going the way of a sixty-second-round draft pick like Mike Piazza making the Hall of Fame. This new world may indeed be more efficient, which is why the MBAs managing these businesses are ushering it in, but we should at least be aware of what we stand to lose when human judgment is increasingly sidelined. Do we really want a world in which the possibility of a beautiful and transcendent surprise—be it artistic or athletic—is sacrificed in favor of a clinical world of boring quantitative precision?

*　　　*　　　*

Following a great time in Kannapolis at the Cannon Ballers game, Bates and I finally retired to a nearby Holiday Inn Express (way after his usual bedtime, as his mom would good-naturedly scold us), before making our way to Charleston to pick the girls up at the airport and onward to the beach the next morning. Unfortunately it rained nearly every day on our long-anticipated trip, our middling to nonexistent beach days interspersed with less-than-restorative nights of sleep, due to three-month-old Shea's frequent wake-ups. Still, we managed to sneak in at least a little beach time and a few visits to the Salty Dog for seafood, piña coladas, and root beers for Bates between cloudbursts.

While we managed to salvage some fun at the beach, it was the Cannon Ballers game that seemed to provide Bates with the most enduring memory from the trip. In keeping with our tradition when visiting small-town sporting events (a tradition made easier by the fact that one didn't have to spend a fortune just to get into the stadium), he'd gotten a small plush "stuffy" at the game, which he, unsurprisingly, named Cannon Baller. For the rest of the summer, when I tucked him in at night, he would be sure to have Cannon Baller at his side, often reminding me how much fun it had been to "stay up later than I ever had" that night in Kannapolis, before falling into the innocent sleep of the young (though, to be fully transparent, it was sometimes I who, lying beside him, fell asleep first).

13

Geneva Red Wings at Batavia Muckdogs

July 3

Though I had had a great time on the short vacation with Marcy and the kids, part of me was still eager to get back up to Batavia and reconnect with the team and its fans. After our long drive back to Pittsburgh from the beach (about twelve hours, versus Marcy and Shea's ninety-minute flight), I dropped Bates off at home and continued north to Batavia the next day. As I passed the mucklands outside town en route to nearby Elba to join Bill Kauffman for a late afternoon pregame beer, I drove by a semi-trailer parked outside town with a huge TRUMP 2020 mural painted on its side. It pulled me back from the bucolic reverie I had temporarily fallen into as I passed the lovely fields bathed in sunlight, the smell of manure powerful even with the windows up, and back into the turbulent world of hyperpolarized American political life.

Later on, I would see a rusty, souped-up pickup truck with an extremely loud muffler barreling down Main Street with enormous American and Confederate flags streaming above its bed (I suspect the odd contradiction therein may have escaped the truck driver's notice).

These episodes reminded me of Dwyer Stadium's resident contrarian Eric Zwieg's admonition—as only he could deliver one—not "to become a Batavia cheerleader and go on waxing nostalgic about everything," since, as he pointed out, the realities some are escaping at the ballpark may not be so wonderful. This was not the only time he would be critical of his adopted community, at another point remarking that "Batavia business is small-time, the arts are small-time, the baseball is small-time, and the restaurants are small-time." Perhaps anticipating the question of why, then, he had decided to settle down here, in the next breath he would comment on how grateful he was that the town had welcomed him as warmly as it had.

Eric would note that he'd seen "a lot of humanity" while traveling through poor swaths of the deep South in bands, implying that much of what he saw was not so much Norman Rockwell Americana as Cormac McCarthy dystopia. While I bristled at being lectured about rural America, seeing as how I had also spent plenty of time journeying those same byways, Eric's observations nonetheless made me think. Was I guilty of presenting a misleading Disney-like fantasy of the Batavia I wanted to discover as opposed to the Batavia of reality? It wasn't until I reflected on his observations during one of my drives back home to Pittsburgh that it occurred to me that the two things weren't mutually exclusive, but rather interconnected. There was obviously an uglier side to small town America, as there is to all places, but this helped make what happened on summer nights under the lights at places like Dwyer so special and important: baseball bringing the best out of people and strengthening the bonds that hold us together. The curmudgeonly Eric himself captured precisely that dynamic one time when he told me, "I've been embraced by people at the games, Bill Kauffman invited me to sit in his group, a community within a community, and I love that about it. The games take me back to my childhood in Jamestown, and I can take comfort in these rituals."

*   *   *

These were the sorts of thoughts I had when I pulled alongside the pleasant house that Bill and Lucine Kauffman had now lived in for over three decades after Bill convinced her to move to Batavia for a "one-year experiment" to see if she liked it. Something about Bill's rumpled, professorial demeanor, his wry wit and ready smile, the attic office overflowing with books, his ongoing refusal to possess an iPhone (in fact, I don't even recall seeing a television), and the beautiful surrounding countryside sometimes made me feel as if I had journeyed back in time and was visiting a rural man of letters from centuries prior. The entire ambiance served as a soothing antidote to the ever-accelerating whir of technology that sometimes felt like it was hijacking my life, as I noted my weekly iPhone usage readings reaching alarming levels.

It was in this house that in recent years a few dozen people would gather every fall to celebrate "John Gardner Night," an idea Bill and a local community college professor had come up with back in 1996 to commemorate the works of the novelist, Batavia's most prominent literary export. Recalling the origin of the event, Bill joked, "Gardner's probably not even one of my hundred favorite writers, but he's ours . . . and as his literary star wanes, it's up to us to keep him alive." The idea was simple: they would invite friends to the Pok-A-Dot restaurant to take turns reading aloud from Gardner's work. At the time they had no idea they were giving birth to a tradition that continues to endure over a quarter century later (though it has now moved to Bill's home, where he invites attendees—a number of friends from the Dwyer Stadium bleachers among them—to "get something to drink from cider, coffee, wine, or beer . . . especially if it's one of those long passages Gardner's editor should have nixed").

As we enjoyed the summer twilight, fresh IPAs in hand, Bill and I got to talking about Batavia baseball, and some of the more colorful fans Bill had gotten to know over the years. Bill launched into the tale of Don from Rochester. As Bill recounted, Don was a sixtyish-year-old bachelor who began coming to Muckdogs games back when they were an affiliated club, always wearing a train conductor's cap and carrying an orange, which he would methodically unwrap and eat as the game unspooled before him. At first, he would sidle into a seat about two or three rows away from Bill and his gang of third-base bleacher friends. As the season slowly progressed, he would sometimes make fleeting eye contact with Bill and smile, though he remained seated at a safe remove. As one summer bled into the next, Don inched ever so slightly closer, eventually ending up close enough for Bill to introduce himself. And then, gradually, what began as friendly, but brief, daily greetings evolved into actual discussions, to the point where Bill considered Don a friend.

Then one summer Don was no longer there. Bill would learn that he had passed away. Speaking affectionately of Don, Bill said, "This was his family now, and when he died, he was missed. He appeared by himself those first summers, but even then, he was not by himself and not alone. Simply by his presence, he became part of this."

*   *   *

In recent years there seems to have been a gradual rediscovery of the psychological benefit that can come from belonging to a community. This has stemmed in part from increased reporting that there is a "mental health crisis" of loneliness that threatens to overwhelm America—which was only accelerated by COVID. Surgeon General Vivek Murthy released an advisory "calling attention to the public health crisis of loneliness, isolation, and lack of connection in our country," laying out a framework to "advance social connection." In an accompanying guest essay he wrote for the *New York Times,* Dr. Murthy wrote:

> We need to acknowledge the loneliness and isolation that millions are experiencing and the grave consequences for our mental health, physical health and collective well-being ... Loneliness is more than just a bad feeling. When people are socially disconnected, their risk of anxiety and depression increases. So does their risk of heart disease (29 percent), dementia (50 percent), and stroke (32 percent). The increased risk of premature death associated with social disconnection is comparable to smoking daily—and may be even greater than the risk associated with obesity ... When we are less invested in one another, we are more susceptible to polarization and less able to pull together to face the challenges that we cannot solve alone ... Given these extraordinary costs, rebuilding social connection must be a top public health priority for our nation.

Obviously, the cure to the nation's loneliness epidemic and associated mental health woes is not as simple as going to baseball games in intimate ballparks. But my experience at Dwyer had clearly demonstrated the psychological benefits of taking in a beautiful sunset at the ballpark in the company of friends, building the "social connections" the surgeon general had identified as so critical to our health and happiness. And unlike the communal value of gathering to watch major professional sports—or blockbuster concerts by artists like Taylor Swift, Beyoncé, or Bruce Springsteen—that are logistically and financially difficult to attend with any real frequency, the sunsets and associated fellowship surrounding Muckdogs games were available to all at minimal cost for the entire summer.

Here was a place where you were welcomed, and where your absence would be noticed, unlike the dispiriting realization Bill Kauffman had had one night while living in DC when there was a fire nearby and it occurred to him that he didn't know any of his neighbors. He thought to himself, had he perished in the fire, "No one in the area would give a fuck."

Of course, rural areas don't have a monopoly on communal bonds, or on the historic role of baseball in fostering them. My Irish American grandfather loved sharing fond memories of playing stickball in the streets of the Washington Heights neighborhood of Manhattan where he grew up—and where there have been close-knit immigrant communities of various ethnicities for over a century. He shared stories with me—sixty years later—from when he served as a batboy during Negro League games with every bit of the nostalgic devotion Bill felt toward Batavia and the Muckdogs. In my grandfather's later years he took pride in watching the rise of future MLB great Manny Ramírez and noting that Manny had attended the same George Washington High School he had graduated from, in what was now a predominantly Dominican neighborhood.

Whether urban or rural, though, it is worth asking, will our kids today have the same sort of vivid memories of neighborhood sports, or will their memories be a blurry haze of childhoods spent staring at devices, accompanied perhaps by time spent crisscrossing the country in the highly organized—and expensive—corporate youth travel leagues that are increasingly rendering local rec leagues obsolete? The answer surely depends on several factors. But in many parts of America, the neighborly bonds that both my grandfather and Bill spoke of with such affection have been fraying. As national corporations assume dominance of realms that were once managed locally (like youth sports) and our economy continues to reward mobility over rootedness—not to mention as we increasingly retreat into digital realms—we disconnect from much of what once held us together.

*   *   *

If a doctor were to write a prescription for an uplifting night at the ballpark, the July 3 evening matchup against the Geneva Red Wings at Dwyer would've been it. Jerry Reinhart was tossing batting practice to his best friend on the team, catcher Mitch Fleming, who, at six feet three, 235 pounds, was an imposing presence but had nonetheless not yet found his footing at the plate. As the mustached Fleming worked through the mechanics of his swing, "Take Me Home Tonight" echoed through the still empty pregame bleachers. Both Reinhart and Fleming were returning for their second summer on the squad, having bonded over rounds of golf together at Batavia Country Club, whose staff they had befriended at the popular local watering hole T. F. Brown's Wednesday Wing Night.

I bumped into Assistant Coach Tom Eaton, who had already begun to monitor the league's playoff race, telling me that four teams would make the playoffs, two from the East Division and two from the West Division. Eaton, who carried himself with the military bearing of the former naval reservist he was, was a baseball lifer, a longtime coach and former scout. He said he would be "scoreboard watching" tonight—if there had been an out-of-town scoreboard to watch—and that if Utica lost, Batavia would take over first place in the West. Skip Martinez then told me that they were excited to have Division I Fairleigh Dickinson right-hander Josh Milleville on the mound, as he'd been having a strong season.

Dave Fisher, clad in his usual fluorescent yellow shirt that said SECURITY on it and ball cap denoting his status as Gulf War veteran, greeted me warmly and asked about my kids. He said he expected the usual mischief tonight—perhaps some high schoolers throwing things at each other or climbing atop the picnic tables—and complained of some grief he'd recently gotten from teenagers he was kicking out for causing trouble, joking, "How could I be guilty of favoring anyone? I hate everyone equally."

Nellie Nichols was busy preparing the food they would serve visiting families of the players as part of the team's midsummer Family Weekend. She looked polished and professional as always, sporting jewelry, hoop earrings, done-up hair, and makeup even while laboring near a hot grill in a crowded concession stand, reflecting her belief that "society makes superficial judgments based on appear-ance," a reality that she disapproved of but nonetheless suspected was true. She recalled a time when she'd been working outside the stadium in Elmira, dirty and wearing a backpack blower, when she met some people whose attitude toward her changed immediately from condescension to respect when they realized she owned the team. The experience had brought her back to her childhood in the Los Angeles foster system and sometimes feeling looked down on for being "that unkempt kid." She resolved as a foster mom to always make sure "my girls looked on point, were dressed nice and had their hair looking nice, since I knew they already had one strike against them as foster kids, and so it was important that they look nice, kept their heads up, and were polite so they didn't give people any more of a chance to hold something against them."

Nellie was almost always upbeat and enthused, which I suspected could also be attributed, at least in part, to her own tough upbring-ing. She said that since she never had parents who would bring her to games, she'd always been envious of kids who did. Recalling how as a child she'd searched for loose change "to buy a charm sucker," she now sometimes reflected in amazement at how she ran the concessions "and can get whatever I want . . . It's so weird how life works . . . God must be listening."

As fans continued to file into Dwyer and the opening pitch approached, kids from the nearby Orleans Little League swarmed Muckdogs players for autographs in the dugout as an honor guard from the Knights of Columbus assembled along the third-base line. Clubhouse manager Erik Moscicki tossed a ball with one of the Little Leaguers. Though Erik was not as well built as the Muck-dogs warming up near him, and his delivery less smooth, the young boy he was throwing to seemed no less delighted by the experience. Erik was using a pro-style catcher's mitt with the Phillies logo and his nickname, EBARRS, referring to a time the players had cheered him on as he participated in a "team freestyle rap," embroidered on it. The previous summer the players, at Jerry Reinhart's invitation, had pooled their money together to buy Erik the mitt. Pitcher Julian Pichardo was proud to take part in the small gesture benefiting the "hardest-working human I've ever met." The fact the team had made the effort to buy him the custom glove meant the world to Erik, who'd later say, "Being surprised by the way they did it and seeing the support from the community after I posted about it on Facebook was incredible. People would ask to hold the mitt at games, and players from other teams would ask about it. I realized how big a deal being part of the Muckdogs was."

The visiting Red Wings, wearing blue tops to go with gray uniform pants, entered the game at 11-9 while Batavia stood at 15-5 as the season approached the midway point. The game would be a crisper affair than some others had been, featuring sharp pitching with both offenses combining for only two runs over the course of the first six innings, after which the score remained deadlocked at 1–1. Paul welcomed his grandson, Gabe, who, like Bates, was five years old, into the press box to introduce some batters just as Bates had done a few weeks ago. I missed Bates as I watched Gabe swell with pride following each announcement. He told me about the Muckdogs jersey he got for Christmas and how his grandma had gone to a local store to have his favorite player Jerry Reinhart's number nine added to it. Gabe pointed to the Little League fields beyond the left-field fence and proudly told me he played there, running the same basepaths trod by generations of Batavia kids, from Ross Fanara to Bill Kauffman to Jerry Reinhart and now him.

Gabe was thrilled when Reinhart came up clutch with the score still tied 1–1 in the bottom of the seventh and singled with a runner on, moving the go-ahead run to second with two outs. Another local product, Gavin Schrader, a rising freshman at nearby Niagara University, who moved with the coiled gracefulness of a natural athlete, then drilled a double down the left-field line on a two-strike fastball. Batavia's Daniel Burroway scored from second followed by Reinhart, who barreled through third-base coach Skip Martinez's late stop sign and narrowly beat the throw from left field with a headfirst dive home. Skip wildly punched the air, any irritation at Reinhart for ignoring his stop sign outweighed by his excitement at Reinhart's being called safe at home. Play-by-play announcer John Carubba sounded as if he was about to hyperventilate as he described the sequence, with Batavia pulling ahead 3–1 and moving to within six outs of their sixteenth victory of the season.

Eric Zwieg, easy to spot in his Mets cap, happily informed me that they had just taken two of three in a series against the Rangers.

Winter at Dwyer Stadium

Pregame at Dunn Field, Elmira, NY

Batavia Muckdogs players signing autographs for the game's Little League "Baseball Buddies"

"The Gang"—Muckdog fans Joe and Sandra Kauffman, Bill Kauffman, Ginny Wagner, and Betsey Higgins

Northside Deli, Batavia, NY

Marcy and Shea Bardenwerper watching as Bates Bardenwerper announces the batters in the press box

Bates Bardenwerper serving as guest batboy for the Batavia Muckdogs

Author and longtime Muckdogs fan Bill Kauffman in his attic study

Muckdogs season ticket holder Betsey Higgins in her home library, Buffalo, NY

Foxprowl Collectables owner and local musician Bill Hume, Batavia, NY

Kelly's Holland Inn, Batavia, NY

Clubhouse manager Erik Moscicki
cleaning uniforms in the shower

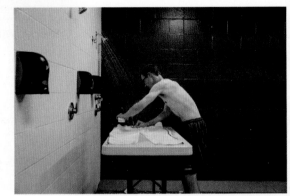

Public address announcer Paul Spiotta (left) in the Dwyer Stadium press box

Elmira Pioneers season ticket holder Herb Tipton, ninety-four, who has been sitting in the same seat at Dunn Field since 1973

"Popcorn Bob" Brinks, who has been making popcorn using a secret recipe at Dunn Field in Elmira for forty years

Nellie Nichols, who owns the Batavia Muckdogs and Elmira Pioneers with her husband, Robbie Nichols, working the concession stand at Dunn Field, Elmira, NY

Kids playing catch alongside the field, Dwyer Stadium, Batavia, NY

Dewey the Muckdogs mascot, Muckdogs dance team members, and a young fan

Charles Bennett, who shags foul balls outside Dunn Field in Elmira, NY

General manager Marc Witt's whiteboard, which tracks the logistical arrangements necessary for every home game

Robbie Nichols and some of the Muckdogs summer interns enjoy some pizza before tackling their postgame tasks.

Muckdogs manager Joey "Skip" Martinez celebrating a playoff-clinching victory with catcher Mitch Fleming

Muckdogs owner Robbie Nichols after being doused with ice water during a postgame celebration

Muckdogs season-ticket holder Ernie Lawrence quietly working on a rosary in the Dwyer Stadium grandstands

Muckdogs manager Joey "Skip" Martinez embracing clubhouse manager Erik Moscicki

His carefree and happy Mets fandom always reminded me of what I had lost. My inability to share in his enthusiasm, and explanation for why I had grown disenchanted with the direction MLB seemed headed, irked Eric. His defense of MLB leadership stemmed in part, I suspect, from his innate contrarianism (since the league's ruthlessly capitalistic business practices would have otherwise been at odds with what seemed to be a left-leaning political ideology), and in part from a genuine love of the Mets that he wanted to remain unspoiled by such concerns.

Our discussion turned to writing, as Eric had recently finished reading my first book and was working on a novel for his MFA, which he said had postmodern stylistic influences and was "writing itself now." He wanted to "let it steer itself so that it isn't too tight," continuing that he sometimes had a tough time with over-bearing instructors who tried to "steer him" when in fact sometimes his writing was "one step beyond their comprehension." He then volunteered, "Sometimes I hurt people's feelings by offering my opinion too strongly and telling people what they don't want to hear." I couldn't help but chuckle as I recalled one time when, discussing the difference between his fiction writing and my nonfiction work, he'd said, "I don't mean to demean what you do, but it's not art. You're not creating something from nothing."

Just as I began to again grow annoyed as I remembered that comment, I stole a glimpse of him as his attention was back on the diamond. While Eric was supremely adept at getting under my skin, as I watched him cheer on the Muckdogs, I couldn't help but feel my agitation dissipate, replaced by an awareness that despite (or, perhaps even because of) his eccentricities, he was still one of us, part of our little gang. All I could do was shake my head and think to myself, *Good ole Eric,* as Bill Kauffman had often said to me when recounting one of their idiosyncratic discussions.

Skip Martinez handed the ball to Carlos Rodriguez, the hardest thrower on the Muckdogs, with a fastball in the low 90s, to close out the night's game. The Red Wings players were on their feet in their dugout and talking a lot of trash for a team that was losing 3–1 and down to their final three outs. "The Final Countdown" played, and there was a palpable energy coursing through the Dwyer Stadium crowd.

The Geneva leadoff hitter reached on a single before Rodriguez, clad in knee-high socks the colors of the American flag, struck out the next batter with an explosive fastball. Next up was Geneva's six-foot-one, 250-pound Nick Serce, who had been establishing himself as one of the league's foremost power hitters, with four home runs already on the season. John Carubba was characteristically bullish on Rodriguez's chances, saying he was "locked in with sharp command and electric stuff." The left-handed-hitting Serce would prevail in the matchup of power versus power, though, launching a fastball that hooked over the right-field fence as the last traces of pink on the horizon gave way to dark blue, small holiday fireworks celebrations from neighboring communities visible in the distance. After pausing to admire his towering fly, Serce slowly made his way around the bases before being greeted by whooping teammates as he crossed home plate.

The game was now tied, 3–3, and Rodriguez appeared shaken. He hit the next batter to send the go-ahead run to first and then threw wildly to first on a failed pickoff attempt, allowing the Geneva runner to advance to second base. The mood in the Batavia dugout had transformed from electric to funereal. Kids leaned over the nearby fence separating the bleachers from the edge of the dugout begging for autographs, which they usually succeeded in getting from compliant players, but this time they were greeted with dismissive refusals from the grim bench. Rodriguez finally composed himself enough to retire two batters on strikeouts and escape further damage.

Nick Serce, who had just tied the game with his home run, came in to pitch the bottom of the ninth. He quickly retired the side in order, sending the game into extra innings.

The ordinarily voluble Skip Martinez sat alone in the dugout under a shelf of batting helmets with a pensive expression as Geneva came up to bat in the top of the tenth and proceeded to score two more runs and take a 5–3 lead into the bottom of the inning, a lead they would not surrender, going on to win 5–4.

As the postgame fireworks wound down with a Springsteen ballad playing, I saw the voice of the Muckdogs on YouTube, John Carubba, carefully using his cane to help navigate the steps down from the press box. I felt kind of sorry for him. Pale and carrying a few extra pounds, he'd missed a loop when putting his belt on and looked a little bedraggled following the close loss. He said, ruefully, "I finally got to call my first home run of the summer, but it wasn't the kind I'd been looking forward to." It was evident from both his words and his body language that the defeat stung.

The night's blown save would leave an indelible mark on Carlos Rodriguez, the flamethrowing closer that Jamestown assistant coach and longtime scout Barry Powell had said possessed the best arm in the league. A few weeks later I would catch up with Carlos before a game and immediately detected something was off as the usually affable player angrily slammed a ball into his glove. He told me that he'd just met with Skip Martinez and was leaving the team and returning home to Tampa. He was frustrated that he was in his early twenties and "not even in the minors," explaining that he wanted to go home and be a firefighter.

Skip would later tell me that Carlos had also quit the previous summer. "I gave him a second chance," Skip said, continuing, "First time shame on you, second time shame on me. Carlos let his teammates down and let me down. I gotta worry about our guys who are sacrificing and grinding and I'm not gonna waste my time on you if you're a cancer." He said this time he hadn't even tried to talk Carlos into staying.

*　　*　　*

The entire episode reinforced Barry Powell's observation on why it was important to have real-life scouts get to know players beyond the various metrics that could be gathered through technology. "If something looks too good to be true, you'd better investigate," he'd said. Unfortunately for baseball lifers like Powell, some are now suggesting that traditional scouting could be dead in five years. In their book *The MVP Machine: How Baseball's New Nonconformists Are Using Data to Build Better Players*, Ben Lindbergh and Travis Sawchik explain how the Astros are pioneering methods of replacing people with machines, culling their scouting department to fewer than twenty by 2019, so that it now totals less than half of MLB's next smallest scouting staff. Instead of having men like Barry Powell roaming the country, Houston found it more efficient to collect video and have it dissected in a central front office. This evolution corresponded with the rise of technocrats in running MLB. The authors describe how the number of MLB general managers who had once been minor leaguers in the 1980s was 67.6 percent and had dropped to 20.6 percent by 2010. Conversely, 40 percent of MLB general managers hired in the 2010s were Ivy Leaguers, as opposed to 3 percent from the 1970s to the 1990s.

Whereas at first some baseball lifers had fought this evolution, closing ranks around their plastic bottles filled with tobacco spit and handwritten scouting reports, by now they all knew that they'd have to adjust—quickly—or be rendered obsolete. And so knowledgeable baseball men like Barry Powell, who'd been studying players from behind home plate before many of today's general managers had been born, were now reduced to enrolling in online analytics courses, where various self-professed gurus charged up to $2,000 for eight-week tutorials with names like "How to Become a Baseball Analyst" and instruction modules featuring content like "Introduction to Solutions Used by MLB Teams: Rapsodo, Blast Motion, Motus, and Edgertronic."

There was something that struck me as profoundly sad about seeing these proud men being forced to seek the validation of online instructors (some of whom were likely snake-oil salesmen) in the hope they could convince a generation of young Harvard Business School–educated management consultant types of their continued utility. While Powell was humble enough to say these courses taught him "how much he didn't know," and optimistic enough to envision a continued role in the game, he was also perceptive enough to sense how this embrace of data and computer modeling could damage the sport. After nearly half a century in the game, he was still a romantic at heart about baseball and what it meant to America, saying, "Baseball has brought people in the country together through tough times—the baseball cap itself is symbolic of this—and I hope analytics doesn't take away from it."

Jeff Luhnow, one of the men who had embraced this brave new world of sophisticated computer modeling in baseball decision making most vigorously (and whose success with the Astros—before his role in their sign-stealing scandal cost him his job—prompted other baseball executives to follow suit), seemed unmoved by any romance left in the game, though. Reflecting on his time in baseball in a recent

Sports Illustrated profile, Luhnow said, "It was very opportunistic that I ended up in baseball. It could have been football, could have been basketball. I love baseball—it's always been one of my favorite sports. But I'm a *sports* fan; I'm a technology person; I'm a businessperson."

The contrast between Luhnow and Powell, and their respective attitudes toward baseball, is illustrative of the crossroads at which the sport found itself at the dawn of the *Moneyball* era in the early 2000s. To the dismay of some, and excitement of others, the sport's leaders chose a path, the path blazed by Luhnow and his like-minded, efficiency-driven "businesspersons." And, as was the case in so many contemporary American industries that have aggressively embraced rapid technologically driven change, there wasn't much thought given to the impact such a decision might have on those who had devoted their lives to the industry, nor to the opportunities available for those aspiring to enter it, much less the quality of the resulting product offered to its consumers.

I was conflicted about this evolution. One the one hand I was a former Ivy League baseball player and had been friends with some of the very guys (and the ones I knew were all guys) who were on the vanguard of this change. I didn't think they were bad people, or that they were setting out to destroy baseball. I'd also always harbored a bit of residual frustration with the stereotypical "old school" baseball scouts, who sometimes had struck me as a tribe of unimaginative lemmings at my high school and college games, whipping out their radar guns in unison when the one prospect they'd come to watch took the mound and then, almost theatrically, packing them up and taking off the moment that player exited the game.

Admittedly, on a personal level, I was probably jealous of those receiving this attention, but, more objectively, I'd also believed that there was sometimes real talent on the field that was being ignored. These experiences observing scouts had left a bad taste in my mouth, as well as an enduring distrust of their judgment and imagination.

That said, on the other hand, as I witnessed the transformation of baseball into a more bloodless exercise in which the human element was increasingly being excised in favor of technology, I found myself longing for those old days that, at the time, had always bugged me.

14

Fourth of July 5K in Batavia and Geneva Red Wings at Batavia Muckdogs

July 8

My wife, Marcy, has long been an avid runner, having completed eight marathons. She introduced me to holiday 5K runs, which I'd grown to really enjoy, especially those held in smaller communities. I noticed that Batavia would be hosting a Kiwanis Independence Day 5K on the Fourth of July, and so I signed up for it. Admittedly my prerace preparation—downing craft beers the night before with Bill Kauffman as we discussed everything from our mutual friend Eric's latest barbs to the dismal state of the world—was less than ideal.

Despite the late night and one too many IPAs, I was relieved to wake to a beautiful morning for a run. I headed to Centennial Park in the heart of Batavia's nicest neighborhood, where lovely century-old homes with graceful front porches faced streets lined with enormous trees that cast a welcome shade over the course. I spotted Paul Spiotta sharing some encouragement with his wife near the start line as she got ready to run. A quick prerace speech was made, the national anthem was played, and someone fired a starter's pistol. As I lumbered my way through the pleasant neighborhood and the sun rose over town, I felt as if I weighed about five hundred pounds and resolved to keep myself in better shape as my summer of book research and travel continued, vowing to cut back on the roadside McDonald's meals, as my new Dwyer Stadium friends Betsey and Ginny had often counseled me. I was both uplifted and inspired, though, to see families gathered on their front lawns to cheer us on, some handing out water and other goodies.

And, indeed, I would have to make a conscious effort to recall these simple acts of kindness and community spirit later that very day when news broke of yet another mass shooting, this one at an Independence Day parade outside of Chicago, in which seven people were killed and dozens wounded. Though I had long been of the opinion that a good citizen needed to remain informed, I was starting to move toward Nellie Nichols's philosophy of "no longer being a news watcher, no longer wanting that negativity in my brain." Was the desire to remain "informed" worth the psychological damage? Time and again, flickers of happiness—such as those inspired by the morning's race—were quickly and mercilessly extinguished by depressing news beamed into my phone from hundreds or thousands of miles away. I wondered if humans were built to withstand a nearly constant assault on their emotional equilibrium, an assault that was amplified by algorithms preying on our vulnerabilities. A hundred years ago, for example, one's happiness on a beautiful morning in Batavia couldn't be shattered numerous times a day—every day—by "Breaking News" reports breathlessly relaying tragedies from far-away states and countries, or transparently partisan political coverage designed to boost ratings while triggering outrage at the opposing party.

Maybe Bill Kauffman, who did a much better job than I of tuning this out, was right when he rhetorically asked, during a panel discussion at the University of Wisconsin, "What would be left?" if we spent less time consumed by this cacophony of distant discord, and then answered his own question: "The church down the street. The bar on the corner. The band playing in that bar. The baseball field. Books. Coffee shops. Neighbors chatting on front porches. Farm stands. The fields behind my house green every summer with cabbage or corn stalks. There would still be graves to tend. Dogs to walk. Beer to brew."

*　　　*　　　*

Tonight the 16-9 Muckdogs would be welcoming the 13-11 Geneva Red Wings, who had recently come from behind to top them in extra innings following Carlos Rodriguez's ninth-inning meltdown. I was disappointed to learn that neither Betsey nor Ginny would be at the game, as Ginny had been roped into cooking dinner for an extended family visit and Betsey hadn't been feeling well. Betsey told me she planned on tuning in to John Carubba's YouTube broadcast, which she found pleasant and relaxing.

Carubba loved his job, even if it was unpaid. He explained how he sometimes worried that he was too busy with the demands of broadcasting the games to fully appreciate the experience, at which point he forced himself to "look around between innings, take a deep breath, and soak it in . . . feel the cool breeze, look at the beautiful field and bustling grandstands, and reflect on how cool it is to be in the press box doing what I'm doing."

After a local Boy Scout troop presented the colors for the national anthem, Tyler Prospero took the mound and made short work of the Red Wings in the top of the first. The stadium appeared to be about 75 percent full, which meant there were about two thousand fans on hand, a solid Friday night midsummer crowd. Some blue was finally beginning to muscle the darker clouds out of the sky. Batavia was poised to jump out to an early lead off Geneva's soft-tossing lefty in the bottom of the first with a single followed by a hit batter before cleanup hitter Josh Leadem ended the threat by hitting into an inning-ending double play.

I saw Cathy Preston, notebook in hand, dutifully keeping score as always. When she saw me she fished around in her purse and produced a pack of *Star Wars* trading cards, insisting I take them home for Bates. She explained that they'd belonged to her first husband, Jonathan Colby, who had been killed in a car accident on April 20, 2011—ten days before their daughter Aurelia's seventh birthday—and that when she had heard me mention how much Bates loved *Star Wars,* she'd made a note to find some for him. I couldn't help but think about the fact that Bates was also six years old and how utterly shattering it must be to experience something like that as a young family.

Jonathan had been driving home from an overnight shift at a Lowe's in Buffalo, when, according to reporting in the *Batavian,* his vehicle "drifted over the center line . . . consistent with someone falling asleep" just before 7:30 a.m. on West Main Street, resulting in the head-on collision that ended his life. According to the paper, his last Facebook status update—posted four hours before the crash—read "Overnights really starting to hit me now."

Jonathan's death in April came just weeks before the family would ordinarily purchase Muckdogs season tickets for the upcoming summer, and in the agonizing days and weeks following the loss, Cathy was conflicted on whether to return to Dwyer Stadium. Jonathan, who was something of a renaissance man, taught a Latin class at Notre Dame High School and helped run the high school Scholastic Bowl tournament. He had been the one who taught Cathy to keep score. Baseball was "the big thing we came together to do as a family," said Cathy, and she knew it would be strange not having him there. But, at the same time, she thought it was important for them to accept the fact that "although the world stopped for him, it didn't for us . . . it was okay to grieve, but I knew we also needed to get on the horse and move forward, and trivia and baseball were what we did." And so she bought the season tickets, and when Muckdogs management, in an effort to deliver some happiness to the mourning family, invited her daughter, Aurelia, to throw out the first pitch on Opening Day a few weeks later, they accepted the invitation. Years later, Aurelia would recall how "at seven years old, I threw the first pitch . . . I can't imagine the ball went very far. It was a big moment for me—my picture was in the paper. Soon after, that picture was hanging on the fridge."

Being back at Dwyer Stadium, once again taking part in the daily rituals, was comforting to Cathy, with little things like texting Paul Spiotta if she had a question on how to mark a complicated play in her scorebook assuming an outsized significance. She found a measure of peace in the familiar rhythms of "pestering Bill Kauffman with trivia questions" and responding to Sandra Kauffman's maternal inquiries about Aurelia's childhood. She even developed an unlikely friendship with a curmudgeonly older man she affectionately nicknamed "Sir Grouch," who, between various gripes and heckles, helped her develop a deeper understanding of the game.

On this night I asked if Aurelia, now nearly grown up at eighteen years old, would be there, but Cathy said that she wouldn't, as she had to wake up the following morning at 5:00 a.m. for her McDonald's shift. Cathy then provided a small boost to my ego by tossing me a trivia softball, asking, "Which hedge fund billionaire bought an MLB team recently?" She knew I was a Mets fan and so would likely know the answer was Steve Cohen. It occurred to me that with her regular trivia questions, Cathy was—in her own small way (and though I surely wasn't suffering from a devastating personal loss like she'd experienced)—making me feel at home in this small community much as others had done for her when she needed it most.

After answering correctly, I thanked her again for the *Star Wars* cards before heading to the concession stand to grab an Italian sausage and nachos (my 5K promises to myself regarding my diet had been quickly forgotten).

*   *   *

As the fifth inning neared its end and dozens of kids, a few of them barefoot, gathered alongside the left-field fence awaiting the opportunity to do the nightly running of the bases, I was transported back to summer nights in the backyard of my grandparents' house, where, also sometimes barefoot, I would scamper around on the cool grass chasing fireflies. Sometimes we played a game my grandpa had first played on the streets of the Washington Heights neighborhood of Manhattan he'd grown up in. He would bounce a Nerf ball (it would have been a "Spaldeen" back in the New York City of his childhood) off the back stoop so it would ricochet into his backyard, where I would dart to try to catch it before it hit the ground. Even as an older man, I will never forget the grace and fluidity with which my grandfather moved, exhibiting the natural athleticism he always had, never even spilling a drop from the glass of Glenlivet he often cradled in his other hand.

Tyler Prospero turned in a strong performance before eventually being pulled by manager Skip Martinez in the top of the sixth inning with a 6–2 lead after giving up a single and a walk. He was replaced by Trey Bacon, the Tampa native whose smaller stature masked a powerful right arm capable of fastballs in the low 90s. Bacon must have inherited good baseball genes, as his older brother, Troy, had been a fourth-round draft pick of the Atlanta Braves and now played for their AA affiliate. One of the runners Bacon inherited would score before he escaped further damage, the Muckdogs holding on to a 6–3 lead heading into the seventh.

I saw Robbie limping around while munching on a pretzel, the evening's thinner crowd allowing him to take a rare break from working the register. I asked him about the overall health of the league, as it had occurred to me that, while his teams were drawing remarkably well (Elmira and Batavia typically finished atop the PGCBL in attendance), others were not. Perennial powers Amsterdam and Mohawk Valley thrived despite being in economically challenged areas, but laggards like Niagara were barely able to pull in one hundred fans a night. Robbie conceded he also worried about this, lamenting how some of the league owners seemed content to "charge the kids four thousand dollars for the summer to play and call it a day, happy to own a team and break even," while others would simply "give away one-dollar tickets, which is useless and won't put anyone in the seats if the ballpark experience is still shitty." The tough reality was that while Robbie had helped to rescue competitive baseball in Elmira and Batavia, he needed a league in which his teams could compete, and that required a critical mass of entrepreneurial owners committed to putting out a product that would draw enough fans to make baseball at this level a viable enterprise. In a business with notoriously thin margins, baseball's long-term survivability in these markets remained to be seen.

I found Ernie Lawrence, the rosary maker, in his usual spot down the third-base line "enjoying the beauty of this big outdoor space on a nice night." The comment prompted his wife, Sandy, who had joined him that night, to gently tease him for his unflagging positivity, saying, "He's color-blind, so things always look beautiful." Ernie told me he'd been a regular at Muckdogs games since 1984, missing only 2008, when he was doing volunteer church work in El Salvador and Guatemala. Like so many fans of the minor leagues, he took special pleasure in tracking players who began their professional careers in Batavia and ultimately made the majors, noting that there must have been nine players on the 2011 St. Louis Cardinals World Series–winning team that he'd watched play at Dwyer.

I was impressed by the sense of inner peace the sixty-eight-year-old Ernie projected. Part of me wondered if this wasn't partly attributable to the fact that he didn't carry a cell phone (between Ernie and Bill, I began to wonder if I had not in fact befriended two of the only remaining people in New York State not to even possess a flip phone). Like Bill, Ernie did say he grudgingly carried a flip phone at Sandy's insistence when traveling, but that he liked to be alone, and "with a cell phone you can't be . . . You may not hear from me for a few days, and people need to understand that." The more I observed the sense of calm Bill and Ernie radiated, the more I couldn't help but think that there was some real wisdom we could all be gleaning from them.

Though tonight Ernie was joined by his wife, he often came by himself. Like a number of the fans I'd gotten to know who came to games alone, he explained how he liked being surrounded by people but not feeling obligated to "dedicate attention to them." A folk musician, he said that he also went to forty to fifty concerts a year alone. In both instances, he appreciated experiencing the pleasure of solitude in the surrounding embrace of a larger group.

Somewhat incongruously for the contemplative rosary maker, I thought, Ernie explained that he'd been a "rock music nut" as a teenager, before gravitating to folk music. He loved Ramblin' Jack Elliott, Pete Seeger, Joni Mitchell, and James Taylor and began touring coffeehouses performing folk music in the 1970s. Eventually marriage and a job teaching special education for troubled learners and AP Physics led Ernie to settle down and stop performing on the road.

In 2006, though, Ernie's son, Andy, came—in Andy's words— "limping home with my tail between my legs . . . My life was in shambles," following a rough patch as a young man living in Cincinnati. Worried about his son, and a believer in the therapeutic value of music and performing (not to mention the value of time together), Ernie asked Andy if he wanted to play with him. Andy said yes, and they ended up performing over 250 shows over the course of the next few years. Playing music with his father would help Andy heal and find a better place physically and psychologically. Andy would eventually stop touring with his dad as his life stabilized with a new career and family, but Ernie kept performing, averaging nearly one hundred shows a year for eight more years. Ernie clearly treasured the time he'd spent onstage, but was quick to add that "a lot of my good fortune is sitting next to me," referring to his wife, Sandy.

Ernie reminded me of Robin Williams's character, Dr. Sean Maguire, in one of my favorite movies, *Good Will Hunting,* in that he was remarkably erudite and well-read—he always had a good book on hand to read during the downtime between innings—and seemed blessed with a sort of spiritual contentment that doesn't derive from material prosperity. He lived a frugal life, finding happiness in simple pleasures and seemingly fulfilled by an awareness that he was doing his part, however modest, to help make the world a better place.

As we chatted, it was time for the seventh-inning stretch, and I was heartened to hear a group of young teenagers near us singing "Take Me Out to the Ballgame" with what seemed to be a youthful innocence rather than the ironic detachment more often found in that demographic. They were "big kids," as Bates would have reverently referred to them, but not too cool to enjoy this ballpark ritual.

The Muckdogs bats, meanwhile, continued to sizzle. An offensive barrage from the heart of the order—Tyler Cannoe, Josh Leadem, and Daniel Burroway—led to three more runs in the bottom of the seventh, extending the Muckdogs lead to 12–3. And there it would stand, as Trey Bacon was lights out, shutting the door on the visiting Red Wings. When Bacon escaped a bases-loaded jam to record the final out, John Carubba breathlessly exclaimed, "Who says the twenty-seventh out doesn't have entertainment value . . . Your Muckdogs win in convincing fashion, now you can go out, celebrate, and enjoy your Friday night!"

After the game the players lingered to sign autographs for the kids assembled along the fence leading to their locker room, which was wedged between the outfield foul line and Denio Street. After the last of the kids left with an autograph and a smile, they retreated to their locker room, where they stripped off their uniform tops before loading plates with fried chicken and grabbing seats in the leather recliners. Skip came in and filled a plate. He appeared not to be going hungry this summer, showing off the physique of a former athlete who now enjoyed some of the creature comforts that came with coaching rather than playing.

Another familiar face in the postgame locker room was John Carubba. He would usually come ambling in after signing off from his broadcast and make his way to interview the "Player of the Game" for the podcast he'd taken the initiative to create. In it, he would include commentary on the game as well as postgame interviews, with game highlights spliced in. He would usually begin work on it earlier in the day before heading from his home in Buffalo to the ballpark at around 4:30 p.m. All told, it would tack on another two to three hours of labor to his already long day. He would spend the remainder of his pregame time preparing a "script" of sorts that he would refer to early in the game, color-coded in a red font for Batavia and the visitor's color for the opponent. He hoped this sort of additional information would make his broadcasts more insightful and colorful. Carubba did this extra work not only because he enjoyed it, but also, more importantly, because he thought it would make him more marketable to the AA or AAA teams he hoped to work for in the future.

Carubba worked hard at his craft. Just as some of the more dedicated Muckdogs players would arrive at the ballpark early to take extra batting and fielding practice, so too would Carubba spend some of his "off" time listening to the broadcasters he most admired, such as the Mets' Gary Cohen, the Nationals' Charlie Slowes, and the Yankees' Michael Kay. Unfortunately for him, the job market— never an easy one in sports broadcasting—had become even harder. Just as the Muckdogs players were competing for fewer draft spots— as the major league draft had been cut from forty rounds to twenty rounds beginning in 2021—so too was Carubba competing for fewer baseball broadcasting jobs in a fiercely competitive landscape that had been cut by 25 percent following the elimination of forty minor league affiliates.

For now, though, Carubba's mood matched the celebratory atmosphere of the Muckdogs clubhouse, as he was doing what he loved and had high hopes for the future. Since the Muckdogs were traveling this weekend, and Carubba did only home games, he looked forward to some time to catch up on producing his podcasts and hanging out with his family. It didn't seem as if he had much of a social life. I couldn't believe, for example, that a baseball fanatic like him had been to only two major league ballparks, and had never been to PNC Park, home of the Pirates, which was only three hours away and generally regarded as one of the most beautiful places to watch a game in the major leagues. I felt a little sorry for him, as he was such a genuinely nice guy, almost painfully earnest in an age where snark and cynicism sometimes seemed to reign supreme. In his own way, it seemed, Carubba was like several of the fans I'd gotten to know in the grandstands, people who were perhaps slightly out of step with society at large—often in ways that were commendable—and who found at Dwyer Stadium a welcoming cocoon in which they could insulate themselves from the more discordant elements of contemporary America.

15

Geneva Red Wings at
Batavia Muckdogs (Doubleheader)

July 14

Before an afternoon doubleheader, I made my way to the Pub Coffee Hub in the hope of running into Eric, the artist-in-residence (or so I thought of him), and perhaps Bill Kauffman and Paul Spiotta. As luck would have it, all three were there.

Eric was seated at his usual perch at the coffee bar, postmodern novel in hand. I told him I'd be heading to Jamestown with the team the next day, happily adding, "That's your hometown, right?" in an effort to establish a friendly rapport, since some of our odd interactions seemed to quickly take on an adversarial air.

"Rochester," he responded curtly. "I'm from Rochester."

"Oh," I sputtered, confused, as I was certain that he'd told me he'd grown up in Jamestown.

He clarified. It turns out that he was originally from Rochester but had moved to Jamestown when he was seven. He shared stories of childhood baseball and hockey games in Jamestown, before recommending a bar he used to like called the Puzzle Lounge. He then announced that he'd be at the Muckdogs game the following week when his Mets were off for the All-Star Break. Once he had corrected me on his biography and updated me on his schedule, he headed off with Bill for a walk in the cemetery across the street, but not before inviting me to bring my glove next time so we could enjoy a game of catch together. He truly was impossible to figure out.

I couldn't help but chuckle as I recalled Bill's wife, Lucine, telling me about a recent play that Eric had written, in which she had performed. Bill wrote a *Spectator* piece on the show in which he observed:

> I should mention that the play also featured a teenaged girl dressed as young Arthur Schopenhauer, reading passages of the doleful Danziger's impenetrable prose. One memorable line began, "Ontologically speaking . . ." Meanwhile, my wife wandered the coffee house stage, shaking her head vigorously and muttering "Poodles, poodles, poodles" . . . (With a few clicks of this infernal machine upon which I am typing, we learned that Schopenhauer said that he preferred the company of poodles to "common bipeds"; literary mystery solved.)

As we sat at their kitchen table one evening, Bill and I nursing beers after a Muckdogs game, Lucine read a portion of another of Eric's shows that reminded me a lot of the Beat poet Allen Ginsberg's poem "Howl," in that it featured the repetition of certain words over and over in almost hypnotic (if one is being generous) or nonsensical (if one is being harsh, or, I suppose, and as Eric would no doubt contend, one is simply a hopeless philistine) fashion. While her oration—coupled with the evening's IPAs—had triggered belly laughs from me and Bill, the play had earned a favorable review in the local *Daily News*. The paper had quoted Eric as saying, "Theater tends to be the same thing over and over again . . . The same successful shows—the shows that make a buck. To me that's a dead art. It's history."

Regardless of whether one found it thought-provoking or impenetrable, it was undoubtedly Eric, emblematic of his quest to deliver art to "Blah-tavia."

*   *   *

There was another person even more committed to delivering art to Batavia than Eric, and that was Gregory Hallock, the executive director of GO ART! Just as the Muckdogs brought baseball to the community, GO ART! was committed to improving its cultural life. It had funded many of the plays Eric had put on. Hallock, a gay man with a Puerto Rican daughter and African American/Dominican son, had by all accounts breathed considerable life into what had been a sleepy organization, having more than tripled the amount of state grant money they issued to local artists and creators in recent years. When he first moved to Batavia with his ex, who was Filipino, and interracial children, he was afraid that they wouldn't be accepted in the community that was deep red politically. He'd heard "horror stories of people being scared and leaving." And, in fact, there were some initial causes for concern, such as when a woman came up to him and said, "I wanted to let you know you're doing an amazing job, but I just don't think you should be allowed to be married and have kids." He was, however, ultimately relieved to discover the community made them all feel at home. He credited Robbie and Nellie with hosting a Pride event at Dwyer when it was the only local venue, since it was outdoors, that could accommodate a large gathering during COVID restrictions.

When I told Gregory about how games at Dwyer Stadium seemed to provide an important opportunity for people to come together and see each other as humans, he enthusiastically agreed, sharing the story of how one of his mom's friends asked him to dance at his wedding and explained to him how she initially didn't want to come but felt compelled, since she'd gone to his siblings' weddings. The woman then broke down crying and thanked him for "showing me what love is, since I never knew anyone like you, and so my opinion was only based on thoughts . . . It's different when you know someone."

Muckdogs fan, Landmark Society volunteer, and local arts patron Richard Beatty commented on how "Gregory's work has a totally different vibe in this conservative town, where it's been a flicker of light." Gregory even echoed some of Bill Kauffman's thoughts on the merits of small town life, saying that "in New York City someone like me would be a dime a dozen, but I'm the only person like me here, which allows me to do stuff I couldn't do somewhere else. I can make a bigger difference, since some of this stuff is already happening in big cities, but here I can create the wheel and be part of something amazing."

Beatty would tell me about a modern art exhibition GO ART! would host that served as a great example of this. The event, featuring impressive paintings, murals, and sculptures from local artists, was undeniably cool, reminding me of something one might have found shortly after the fall of the wall in East Berlin, gritty and with an undiscovered, underground feel. The exhibition occupied a small slice of the now largely vacant twenty-nine-acre Harvester Center industrial complex that had once been the beating heart of the city's economy, and represented Batavia's past, and what had been lost, but also, with its enthusiastic patrons gathering amid the handful of embryonic start-ups and small businesses that now called the Harvester Center home, suggested the possibility of a rebirth. Eli Fish owner Matt Gray even brewed a new beer for the exhibition, and Pub Coffee Hub owner Rob Credi got a special license to stay open late and sell it. These flickers of resurgence were in large part the result of the determined efforts of a handful of people—some of whose relationships had blossomed at Dwyer Stadium (Muckdogs regulars Richard Beatty, Cathy Preston, Bill Kauffman, Betsey Higgins, and Ginny Wagner were among the attendees)—not to give up on their community.

GO ART! inhabits what had been a "gentleman's club" of the historic variety, the old Batavia Club, which had been around since 1882 before finally closing its doors in 2001. GO ART! converted the old club's bar, an oak-paneled room that had once been the exclusive preserve of Batavia's most powerful men, into a "speakeasy" serving cocktails and craft beers a few nights a week, with local art available for sale adorning the walls. It almost felt subversive, a countercultural artistic outpost tucked away in a conservative area more commonly associated with farming and heavy industry.

GO ART!'s inviting confines reminded me of a similarly incongruous locale I had grown fond of while undergoing officer, and later infantry, training at Fort Benning, Georgia. There was a used bookstore in nearby Columbus called JudyBug's Books that housed a coffee shop in back. It was owned and managed by a charming book lover who may or may not have been gay. It didn't matter. JudyBug's was the first place I would head (admittedly, often on my way to one of the nearby bars) when granted weekend leave from the base, drawn to the oasis of intellectualism that stood in such contrast to the regimented culture that otherwise dominated my life. On these precious weekends, a friend of mine—a Yale graduate with similar interests I'd randomly met while assigned to clean the "latrine" in Basic Training—and I would usually split a hotel room near Columbus's main drag and hang out in the bookstore by day before transitioning to the adjacent bars by night, reveling in our brief tastes of freedom. Poking fun at the military's tendency to develop an acronym for everything, my friend even took to referring to such weekends as "EOTA"(environment other than Army).

Interestingly, I suspect my attraction to places like JudyBug's in Columbus, and GO ART! in Batavia, when coupled with my distaste for what can feel like a phony, corporate, and "enforced" liberalism prevalent in America's more affluent precincts, might suggest that I am every bit the contrarian that Eric Zwieg is, gravitating to that which feels threatened, and recoiling from that which feels unthinking and oppressive. It also highlights the fact that celebrating localism does not require returning to, or even necessarily preserving, the past, as GO ART! had actually replaced an institution that had been around for over a century and enjoyed a rich history. Even so, GO ART! served as a valuable addition to the community's cultural landscape, regardless of what had stood before in its place.

GO ART! was keeping one final surprise. I noticed that it housed the "Owen Library," a collection of books adorning a tastefully remodeled sitting room near the front entrance. I knew the name sounded familiar, and, sure enough, Gregory confirmed that the benefactor was in fact the same man who Bill Kauffman had joked was notorious for being the "cheapest man in Batavia." Stories of the lifelong bachelor's miserly ways were the stuff of local legend, a small sampling including: insisting to a date that they "go Dutch" to Bob Evans and then producing a buy one, get one free coupon for his share of the tab; the local country club to which he belonged having to put away the free razors and toiletries from the locker room after he would routinely pilfer them; and crashing local funerals only to stock up on the cold cuts available at the memorial lunch, which he would then duck out of early, satisfied to have secured free food for a week. Bill and others had long joked that when Owen died, it would be discovered that he'd secreted away a small fortune, and he would then be regarded as the most generous man in the county when he gave some of it away ... As it turned out, he had, as other local institutions would also soon reveal that they'd been the recipients of his posthumous largesse.

*   *   *

Arriving around 3:00 p.m. for the doubleheader's 5:00 p.m. start, I dropped into the locker room, where I found clubhouse manager Erik Moscicki diligently plugging away at his pregame tasks. While a summer working for the Muckdogs was, for many of the interns and entry-level employees, viewed as a stepping stone to gain the experience necessary to rise in the competitive world of sports business, for Erik it was the destination. Batavia held special meaning for him, as his hometown that he was proud of and fiercely loyal to. He would later tell me that his devotion to the team resulted from a desire to "give to the community I'm from, grew up in, and will probably continue to live . . . It's a small community, a far cry from Pittsburgh [referring to where I live], and close-knit—the kind of place where you want to see the best in each other."

Erik continued to work inside the windowless locker room while outside the crack of the bat echoed through the still-empty ballpark as the Muckdogs took batting practice under a bright sky. As I savored the sun's warmth, I feared that I was developing an unhealthy obsession with this delightful summer weather. As sometimes happened when left alone with my thoughts at Dwyer, my mind turned to Bill Kauffman, someone with whom I could commiserate about my meteorological hang-ups and find an empathetic ear. That, or he felt bad for me and had been humoring me when he'd explained how his mother, Sandra, always "sighed on July Fourth and lamented how the summer was almost over." He had even confessed to also sharing a bit of the "early summer melancholy, sometimes mourning the end of things (like baseball season) before they've begun," adding "there must be a word (probably German) for this."

I'd begun to notice that the atmosphere surrounding the team had grown a bit more serious as the season approached its final few weeks. While Skip still seemed to be a "players' manager" who allowed the college kids to play by "big boy rules" under his watch, there was now a sense of purpose—to make the playoffs, which they had missed out on by one game the previous summer—that was more palpable than during the carefree days of early June. Skip had already begun to manage his pitchers with an eye toward the postseason, trying to simultaneously rely on the anchors of his rotation to win and secure a postseason berth and not overtax them to the point that they would need to sit out the playoffs, as several had come with an innings limit requested by their college coaches.

John Carubba was making his final pregame preparations in the press box. He appeared a little nervous about the Muckdogs' chances, even though they would be starting ace Nolan Sparks, who had been dominant all season, in the first game of the doubleheader. But that was just John. He invested as much—or more—of himself into the outcome of these games than the players.

Carubba's pregame concerns proved to be without merit, as Batavia would cruise to an easy 8–1 win in the first game of the double-header behind another strong outing from Sparks, who threw 5⅔ innings, allowing only four hits and no earned runs. Sparks carried himself with a self-confidence bordering on cockiness, but stalwart fan Ginny Wagner loved it, saying, "I love his swagger and scowl—like 'I'm kicking ass' and I know it."

I spent much of the game chatting with Arron Brown and his young son, Nolan. Arron was a thirty-nine-year-old sixth-grade teacher from Pembroke Intermediate School, about fifteen miles to the west of Batavia, whom I had first met a few weeks prior when he'd been honored as "Teacher of the Game." Arron had been especially thrilled to be chosen, as he and Nolan were baseball fanatics. During the summer of 2020, when minor league baseball had been canceled due to fears over COVID, Arron would wake up at 4:30 a.m. to watch ESPN broadcasts of Korean professional baseball, going so far as to adopt the Samsung Lions as his team so he could enjoy a fun rivalry with a good friend who chose a different team. He'd been teaching from home, and those dark predawn mornings watching Korean baseball while eating cereal and texting his friend remain a treasured memory from an otherwise difficult time.

Baseball had always occupied an important part of Arron's life. He'd been "devastated when the Muckdogs left—it was like losing part of yourself." Like other locals, though, he'd rallied behind Robbie and the collegiate Muckdogs, relieved to at least have some form of competitive baseball preserved in the area. As a teacher with students from diverse backgrounds, he'd always valued social harmony and the institutions that helped to foster it. To Arron, Dwyer Stadium was one of these places. "I know people in the stands have different views on the world and political and social issues, but when someone turns a double play, all that goes out the window," he said.

I'd noticed this in my own interactions, both online and in the real world. I had something of an epiphany one afternoon walking home from the Bridgeside Market, the deli a few blocks from my home where I liked to grab lunch, when I read someone's comment "Go Fuck Yourself" in response to what I had thought had been a fairly innocuous article I posted on Twitter. Before I knew it I'd been dragged into an impassioned and blood-pressure-spiking argument with an unnamed Twitter account out there in the ether. *This is insane,* I thought to myself; *who knows if this is even a real person.* Meanwhile, in the terrestrial rather than digital world, at various times I found myself cringing at Guy Allegretto's political observations when they parroted some of FOX News's more outlandish stories, and also Richard Beatty when he volunteered an offhand putdown of the right that could have come straight from MSNBC. It was too much, from both directions. But the great thing about Muckdogs games was that it didn't matter. We had a common bond that transcended the toxic tribal loyalties that our society seemed so intent on imposing. It was similar to how my military friends and I tolerated political disagreements with each other far better than we would with strangers, since we were connected by something outside of politics. In both cases we were able to see each other as multidimensional humans and not simply avatars of a political ideology.

As we watched a game that featured a handful of errors and noticeable lack of offensive power, Arron acknowledged that the quality of play was down from Batavia's days hosting a minor league team. He applauded the team's outreach to the community and general manager Marc Witt's providing free tickets to the Pembroke schoolchildren, though, saying, "Yeah, it's only a college league, but it's a big deal for these kids who get to go out on the field and play catch before the games." Pembroke was not an affluent area, he said, and some of the kids had rough home lives. "This is the Super Bowl and the World Series" for the singers and band members who got to perform on the field before the game, he said, adding how proud he was that "little Pembroke got to show off this amazing talent."

General manager Marc Witt worked the phones all winter trying to organize local school districts like Pembroke's (the students would be given free tickets) and community organizations to participate in as many home games as possible. To accomplish this required extensive logistical planning, since every game ideally included a pregame color guard, a school band and cheerleaders, someone to throw out the first pitch, Little Leaguers to be "baseball buddies" and join the players on the field to play catch before the game, a Teacher of the Game, a Veteran of the Game, and a group to host a 50-50 charity raffle. A huge whiteboard hung on a wall in the front office to help track the status of these elements for each home game. Providing children from these groups with free tickets to a game was not purely an act of charity, though. It was also an astute business decision. The theory was that each child would be accompanied by at least one parent, who would purchase a ticket and most likely some concessions. Groups like these were valued, as they often spent more money per game than season ticket holders, since they were more likely to buy souvenirs on a rare visit to the ballpark than someone who went every night. Furthermore, if the kids had fun, they'd ask their parents to come back, and Muckdogs management had just created more fans. In this Marc adhered to an enduring principle of minor league sports; namely, above all else, get people to the games, whether by hook or by crook. No one benefits from empty seats.

Arron recalled with fondness how excited his son, Nolan, had been to play catch with a shortstop from Pepperdine the previous summer. Not only did Nolan keep the ball, as well as a signed Muckdogs poster (which he hung next to framed posters of legendary Bills Bruce Smith, Thurman Thomas, and Jim Kelly), but he also begged Arron to engage in a bidding war for the shortstop's signed jersey after the game, when Robbie auctioned them off. While Arron's wife wasn't thrilled at how much he'd spent on a jersey from "a college kid," Arron was convinced that things like this helped grow Nolan's love of baseball.

Sitting in the near-empty bleachers on a midweek afternoon in shorts, a tank top, and a ball cap—as if he had just come from the beach—Arron was a picture of contentment. This was partly because as a teacher he was free to spend an afternoon at the ballpark during the summer, but also because he seemed to genuinely derive satisfaction from "playing a role in shaping young lives and having an impact on the future."

"It sounds cheesy," he said, "but Pembroke is small and thrives on being a tight-knit community, a place where people take pride in being there for each other and helping each other." By now I'd heard this sentiment echoed by so many that it had begun to sound like a talking point some PR guru had handed them. It was also not the first, nor would it be the last, time that I noticed a sort of spiritual contentment that seemed to take hold in some who were making valuable contributions to their communities, even for jobs, like teaching, that paid criminally little relative to their value to society. I also couldn't help but contrast this with the remarkable sums of money some of my old college friends were making holding financial jobs that were of dubious societal value, yet for whom one still sometimes got a sense that something was missing. As I reflected on this, I was also sensitive to the risk of romanticizing economic challenges, which can of course lead to considerable stress, sleepless nights, and sometimes more serious problems. These were the sorts of places my brain would meander as the game unfolded before me, the sorts of detours that wouldn't be permitted by the breakneck action at basketball or hockey games, or the fever pitch of emotion that characterized football games.

Later on, during the second game of the twin bill, Ernie Lawrence, the resident rosary maker, flagged me down to tell me that he'd finished my book on Saddam and the young American soldiers tasked with guarding him in the months preceding his execution. Unlike Eric Zwieg, Batavia's avant-garde playwright who'd told me what I did wasn't art, Ernie had kind words for the book, saying it "was a good story well told." Coming from someone who was never without a quality book in his hand, I appreciated his assessment. He'd clearly given the book considerable thought, telling me he'd struggled with one of its central questions; namely, the extent to which Saddam's surprising relationships with the soldiers were genuine or the result of his manipulating them.

Ernie's son, Andy, would have been unsurprised by his father's reflections on my book. Andy marveled at his father's blend of religious faith and omnivorous intellectual curiosity, telling me, "His faith is central to who he is, but his mind is so wide-ranging. Dad has the rare combination of devout faith and open-mindedness. He's well-versed in an insane variety of topics. Lots of worldly people scoff at faith, and vice versa. Not many people are able to maintain devotion to both things with so little conflict. I was a lucky kid."

Meanwhile on the field, the Muckdogs, now 22-10 after their victory in the doubleheader's first game, continued to play well in the nightcap. Josh Leadem led off the bottom of the first with a single, followed by two stolen bases. I'd grown to really enjoy Skip's aggressiveness and took notice of how stolen-base attempts led to more action than in MLB games, where a focus on home runs (and avoiding outs on the basepaths) had led to a nearly 40 percent decline in stolen-base attempts over the past decade (though, to give credit where credit is due, MLB rules changes entering the 2023 season, such as limiting the number of pick-off attempts and increasing the size of the bases, seemed to be sparking a rediscovery of this dying art). Leadem's leadoff single was followed by two more hits and a fielder's choice, and then topped off by a bases-loaded double off the bat of Columbia University's Kyle Corso, staking Batavia a 3–0 lead.

In the second inning the teams continued to show off the sort of "small ball" that had fallen out of favor in the big leagues, with Geneva bunting runners over from first and second to second and third, manufacturing a run that scored on a subsequent infield single. By now the grandstands were about half full, and shadows from the light poles beyond the left-field fence were approaching the infield dirt as the sun set over Dwyer. I decided to make my way over to join Betsey and Ginny for an inning or two to enjoy the sunset with them, as I knew it was Betsey's favorite part of the game, and I enjoyed seeing her take such pleasure from it.

Tonight, though, was one of the unfortunate nights when their enjoyment was impaired by the man they'd dubbed "the screamer" who would occasionally sit in front of them, swill twenty-four-ounce beers, and grow louder and louder as the game went on. It was even more uncomfortable when he brought his young son. He was a rather large man, and every time he stood up to shout his pants would slide down and reveal his ample rear, which added to the unfortunate nature of the entire spectacle. To add to Betsey and Ginny's consternation, Batavia left the bases loaded when cleanup hitter Daniel Burroway struck out looking to end the inning, prompting the ordinarily serene Betsey to jump to her feet and shout, "You need to go to the eye doctor" to the ump. The only thing I enjoyed more than her quiet contemplation of Dwyer Stadium sunsets was when she lobbed G-rated insults at the umpire in moments like this.

Joe and Sandra Kauffman were preparing to leave by the bottom of the third due to the chill in the air. One of the benefits of $99 season tickets—which worked out to less than $5 per home game (single-game tickets cost $9 for general admission or $11 for VIP seats)—and living two blocks away was the ability to leave after a few innings and not feel guilty about it. I was always sorry to see them take off, as I enjoyed the portal into Batavia's past their stories provided. Joe, eighty-seven now, clearly recalled the various times during which Dwyer Stadium (formerly known as MacArthur Park) sometimes found itself thrust into service resulting from hostilities overseas. Joe described how he would accompany his father to a small cupola atop a building beyond the right-field fence that served as a civil defense lookout tower to scan the skies for enemy planes during World War II. He explained that army units had conducted training at MacArthur Park, where he and his friends would collect the spent brass shell casings from soldiers' M1 carbines off the grass. Though too young to have served in the war himself, he took visible pride in safeguarding the "shadow boxes" displaying the medals earned by local veterans who had passed away and whose families had chosen to get rid of them. One even hauntingly included a Japanese flag with handwritten script on it that had been taken from the helmet of a Japanese soldier who had been killed.

It was obvious that enjoying the company of friends at Dwyer—even if only for a few innings a night—contributed to Joe and Sandra's vitality and happiness. The relaxed good humor with which they could almost always be found in their usual seats near the top row of the bleachers suggested that there was something therapeutic in spending time with their bleacher neighbors. Maybe, I thought, before we embrace virtual reality and robotic pets for companionship in old age, there was a time-tested antidote to loneliness right before our eyes.

While the Muckdogs continued to enjoy strong attendance on

the season, with just over 1,600 eventually flowing in after work for the second game of this doubleheader, I was reminded by an email I'd just received of how MLB's attendance numbers had been trending downward for the better part of twenty years, with the generally woeful Pirates a consistent laggard. It was from the Princeton Alumni Association of Western Pennsylvania (PAAWP) and read:

> When we brought back the PAAWP Pirate game this summer after a two-year hiatus, we assumed the same level of pre-pandemic demand and bought our usual 20 tickets. Unfortunately, three years of futility by the Bucs and mounting disgust with the Pirate ownership have clearly taken a toll, and we're stunned to report that not a single ticket has been ordered by an alum. Consequently, the PAAWP Board has voted to give the tickets away on a first-come first-served basis, so they won't go to waste.

Bill and I joked that the poor Pirates were getting perilously close to literally not being able to give tickets away.

*   *   *

Though clearly MLB was not thrilled with declining attendance, they may not have been as concerned as one would imagine, according to some who study the business of professional sports. For starters, franchise values remain high despite flagging attendance, for several reasons. One is that the league benefits from the fact that even though the population (and therefore number of possible customers) is growing, the supply of MLB teams remains the same as a result of the monopoly status the league enjoys by virtue of its antitrust exemption. Furthermore, and perhaps even more importantly, there are only thirty teams, and there are a lot more than thirty billionaires who would enjoy the prestige and social capital (not to mention virtually guaranteed franchise appreciation) that comes from owning a team. The *GQ* article "So, You Want to Buy a Pro Sports Team? Here's How" captures this dynamic, quoting a lawyer who advises on sports acquisitions as saying, "You might have the biggest boat, biggest house, biggest jet—but there's only one Yankees, only one Cowboys. They're collector's items."

Additionally, Andrew Zimbalist, a professor of economics at Smith College who has written extensively on professional baseball, explains that even with declining attendance MLB is making money, since ticket prices are higher, there are more high-revenue-producing luxury suites, and in-stadium advertising is more profitable due to a higher-income fan demographic. On top of this, the explosion of sports betting is unlocking even more money for owners. This may partly explain why A's owner John Fisher—an Exeter, Princeton, and Stanford business school graduate and heir to the Gap fortune, whose net worth is estimated to be $2.8 billion—decided to ditch Oakland and move the A's to Las Vegas. In addition to the team's receiving $380 million in public funding from the state of Nevada, Stanford economics professor Roger Noll suggested to the *San Francisco Chronicle* that the franchise value of the A's could double, as "they'd be able to integrate a gambling casino into the stadium. People in the sports industry believe that is going to be the next major source of profitability. Zero costs, and it could be a billion dollars in profits."

Of course, in order to facilitate the move, Fisher didn't hesitate to take tanking to a new level, gutting a team that won nearly one hundred games in both 2018 and 2019 and allowing the Oakland Coliseum to crumble (while doubling season ticket prices prior to the 2022 season), in what surely appeared to be an effort to drive down attendance and bolster his case that Oakland wasn't worthy to host his franchise. Never mind the team's colorful fifty-five-year history in Oakland, highlighted by the legendary 1989 "Battle of the Bay" World Series against the San Francisco Giants, featuring stars like Jose Canseco, Mark McGwire, and Rickey Henderson and interrupted by the Loma Prieta earthquake, or the fact that loyal fans had come out to the dumpy Coliseum in respectable numbers during the A's successful campaigns. In the end, none of that mattered. MLB abandoned the gritty blue-collar fan base that called the Coliseum's cheap seats home in favor of generous public financing and a new ballpark in Vegas that will cater to gamblers and out-of-town visitors to the Strip.

Kevin Reichard, founder and publisher of Ballpark Digest and a knowledgeable observer of the business of baseball from MLB all the way down to collegiate summer leagues, echoes Zimbalist's thoughts about attendance. Reichard says, "Attendance is the most misleading metric when evaluating the success of an MLB team. Per capita spending, not total attendance, is more important, and this has been rising steadily. This also explains why they are now building smaller, thirty-eight-thousand-seat ballparks, as the model is fewer fans spending more." Of course, while MLB may remain sanguine about its short-term economic prospects despite flagging attendance, that doesn't necessarily mean that the long-term health of the sport will similarly benefit from this economic model.

Ginny Wagner, expressing the naivete of the fan not yet jaded by an understanding of the sport's more Machiavellian business leaders, wondered why MLB games cost so much to attend "if they need fans?" Her friend Betsey Higgins was likewise perplexed by "why billionaires have to charge so much." They suggested how popular it would be if MLB clubs created a "special family section" that featured $20 tickets and would result in fans "going berserk with happiness and helping to grow the sport." By this point I knew enough about the behavior of the owners to understand that they charged as much as they did because they could, yet I still couldn't help but wonder why we never saw even one renegade owner make a decision that may have cost an inconsequential number of dollars relative to his overall fortune, but contributed to the long-term health of the sport and benefited working-class fans in a meaningful way.

Additionally, the aggressive move toward promoting in-game online betting through sites like DraftKings and FanDuel, while lucrative for owners, will encourage fans to spend more time placing and monitoring bets on their iPhones and—too often—losing money at the expense of enjoying time with their friends and family, let alone actually deriving pleasure from the experience of watching the game. How can you discuss life's eternal questions with people like Betsey Higgins and Bill Kauffman, after all, or even explain the game to your children, if you're glued to an iPhone, placing bets and sweating out the results?

* * *

As the game entered its seventh—and final (since it was a doubleheader)—inning, Skip Martinez pulled starter Tyler Prospero, who had done well, allowing only three runs on eight hits. As he took a seat on the bench and enjoyed the well wishes of his teammates, I hustled toward the concession stand to grab a sausage before it closed. Before I could get there, I was flagged down by Dr. Ross Fanara, in his usual seat just behind the on-deck circle alongside his wife, Shirley, and the great-grandsons they raised, Kamdyn, who was in preschool, and Kartier, who had just finished kindergarten.

The Fanaras' seats were about the same distance from the field as, but a world apart from, those inhabited by the patrons of the new "Cadillac Club" at Citi Field in New York, the membership-only speakeasy where, for $24,999 a season, a member will be provided an "in-stadium concierge" to access "a private bar with field views, lounge seats, flat-screen televisions, in-seat storage and personal beverage coolers." Despite his lack of access to a flat-screen television or concierge, Ross was in great spirits, proudly telling me that it was his eighty-first birthday. His eyes lit up and he broke into a wide smile as a number of passersby stopped to congratulate him.

One of them was Sherri Wahr, whose son, Myles, fifteen, was Dewey the Muckdog for the summer, and whose daughter, Lydia, twenty, was on the Muckdogs dance team and acted like an older sister to Kartier. Sherri said that before discovering the Muckdogs, "I'd never been into baseball before, it wasn't exciting for me. It seemed so long and boring, but now I can't imagine summer any other way. We spend the entire summer here, and it's so much more than baseball."

*   *   *

Ross and Shirley Fanara's affection for each other was never far from the surface, evidenced often by Shirley's gentle teases of her husband. They still laugh at the story of their first date. Shirley was seventeen and a senior in high school at the time, while Ross was in his first year of graduate school. Ross was on his way home from playing in a Sylvania Factory League baseball game in Batavia and saw a cute girl sitting on her front porch. He shouted to her, asking if she wanted to join him for dinner, and she nodded yes. He brought her to the Your Host Family Restaurant, a popular western New York twenty-four-hour diner chain that had jukeboxes in the booths. They both ordered hamburgers with cherry Cokes, topped off with a Mexican ice cream sundae. The bill came out to around $6, at which point Ross discovered that he had no money, as he'd forgotten his wallet, having left it in his uniform. Today, Shirley delights in reminding him that he pulled the "old I-forgot-my-wallet trick," while Ross responds with a sly grin, "She paid, and I've been paying ever since."

They corresponded for a few years while Shirley went to nursing school and Ross finished his medical studies before getting married. As the years went by, elements of their origin story would fade away. Sylvania, sponsor of the baseball team Ross had played on when they met, shuttered its Batavia television manufacturing and assembly plant in 1976, relocating to North Carolina, ostensibly to remain competitive with Japanese manufacturers. The resulting layoffs by one of Batavia's largest employers compounded the community's struggle with an unemployment rate that was already at 10 percent. Meanwhile, Your Host restaurants would file for bankruptcy in 1993, no longer able to compete with fast-food chains. Their closure marked the end of an era that had begun with a humble hot dog stand in Buffalo forty-nine years earlier.

The Fanaras' marriage, though, would survive and flourish.

"She's been right by my side for sixty years," said Ross, before adding, "and we both love baseball."

Ross was also a man of quiet, but strong, faith, and would begin every day watching mass on television and then praying the rosary, crediting his bout with polio as having brought him closer to God. Still, Ross's life had not been without spiritual turbulence. He recalled a particularly tough time as a younger man when he was especially "low" and "asked the Blessed Mother for a sign, something to reassure me things would be okay." That same night he was heading home to Batavia from a podiatry conference in Buffalo on the interstate when a snowstorm hit and reduced visibility to near zero. He hit a patch of ice that sent him sailing off the highway and up a roadside berm, his car launched airborne, then spinning around after it crashed back to earth, finally coming to a stop back on the highway pointed in the same direction he had been traveling. He was unharmed and continued his drive home. He believes it was a miracle in response to his troubled prayers, and he has carried a rosary with him ever since.

*   *   *

With the exception of Shirley and perhaps a few close friends, no one in Dwyer Stadium would have known the dramatic highs and lows of Dr. Fanara's life. Sitting in his seat wrapped in a warm jacket, with a soft smile spread across his face, Ross looked like any number of the older men remaining to watch Batavia go on to a 7–4 victory, completing the doubleheader sweep of the Geneva Red Wings. Yet there was a remarkably rich history residing underneath his placid exterior. I was reminded of Bill Kauffman's comment that "each person is their own novel, we just don't read most of them."

A few of the more knowledgeable fans in the crowd discussed how Utica had just lost a key home game to Watertown, which helped Batavia in the battle to make the postseason and secure a first-round home game. I ducked into Robbie's cinder-block office, where I noticed a few cracks in his usually stoic exterior as he told me that his foot had been hurting even more than usual all night, before continuing, "But there's only thirteen days and twenty-two hours left in the regular season. Not that anyone's counting."

16

Batavia Muckdogs at Jamestown Tarp Skunks

July 15

I was in the midst of a busy stretch of games that had begun with Thursday night's doubleheader with Geneva and would soon take me to Jamestown, where the Muckdogs were scheduled to take on the Tarp Skunks on Friday night before they headed to Elmira to face the Pioneers on Saturday. I figured I'd better squeeze in my trip to Foxprowl Collectables before I forgot to grab the "special treat" Bates now expected every time I returned home, especially after a recent blunder where I'd proudly produced an Emperor Palpatine *Star Wars* figure only for him to glumly inform me that he already had it. I'd also grown to enjoy my chats with Bill Hume, the charmingly eccentric owner.

Arriving at Foxprowl and noticing a concert schedule for a classic-rock cover band named Red Creek on the counter, I asked if they were any good. Bill told me that they were good, and he should know, as he played bass guitar for them and was the "new guy" in the band despite having joined it eighteen years ago. He said the band was formed in 1972 and played covers of Skynyrd, AC/DC, and Metallica at local bars and places like "the beer tent at the carnival after the tractor pull." It dawned on me that one of the reasons I enjoyed dropping into Bill's shop was his seemingly perpetual good humor. He volunteered to me that whenever he was asked, "How you doing?" he'd answer, "I play music and sell toys for a living. How do you think I'm doing?"

He admitted that, like everyone, he had his own share of tough days, but added, "Even if I'm in a bad mood and don't want to interact, I want this to be a happy place, a safe place, a welcoming place, where you are amongst friends—nerdy friends—but friends—and we can geek out together." Much of what Bill sold could, after all, be found on Amazon, perhaps some for a little more, some for a little less. But Amazon couldn't deliver the smiles that stemmed from conversation with, and recommendations from, this cargo-shorts-and-tank-top-wearing bass player with crazy hair and a crazier personality.

I made sure to get to Dwyer on time, as I was going to ride the bus with the team to Jamestown, about two hours to the southwest. This was a favorite road trip for the Muckdogs players, as Jamestown played in a beautiful historic old ballpark and usually drew strong crowds. As soon as I boarded the bus I was reminded of how little had changed since my days of riding team buses nearly thirty years ago, with the coaches up front, the quieter and more cerebral players next, and the goofballs and cool kids near the back, where their shenanigans could better go unnoticed. True to form, Trey Bacon and Kyle Corso—both of whom struck me as among the more introverted players—sat near the front, while Batavia's hometown son Jerry Reinhart, charismatic clubhouse leader Mitch Fleming, and power hitter Tyler Cannoe held court near the back.

The mood was relatively quiet this afternoon, though, as the bus began to sail west on the New York State Thruway. Skip Martinez FaceTimed with his son back home in Tampa while Coach Eaton quickly pulled a blanket over his head, resting on an oversized pillow, and fell asleep. He always reminded me of the NCOs I'd known in the army, quick with lifestyle hacks to maximize comfort in uncomfortable situations. Most players behind him sat one to a pair of seats, some trying to steal some sleep with shades on and earphones in, while others talked quietly. I suspected that the grind of a summer featuring games nearly every day—following long college seasons that had begun over the winter—was beginning to take its toll, one day blurring into the next, a baseball version of the movie *Groundhog Day*. Somehow I found myself squeezed behind Skip Martinez, who had his seat fully reclined and jamming into my legs, with a garbage can in the seat next to me. Meanwhile the young batboy across the aisle from me was sprawled comfortably over two seats.

As you approach Jamestown from the north, following a patch-work of country roads through pretty, rolling countryside and farmland, it doesn't seem possible that you're in the same state as Manhattan. There were advertisements for the "longest running PRCA rodeo east of the Mississippi," and "Fuck Biden" signs were prominently displayed from more than one farmhouse.

Downtown Jamestown had the same sort of hollowed-out, aban-doned feel as Elmira. A beat-up old car with cardboard in place of a window was stopped at a nearby red light. The few people who were out sucked forlornly on cigarettes as they sagged against boarded-up storefronts. Billboards with the message "Combat Addiction" were everywhere, providing helplines for those in crisis. Just about the only "draw"—if one can call it that—was the Lucille Ball Desi Arnaz Museum, celebrating the actress who had grown up nearby, which hosted famous comics on occasion. It was hard to reconcile what one saw in struggling communities like this—of which there seemed to be so many—with the throwaway line so ubiquitous dur-ing campaign seasons that America was the "greatest country on the face of the Earth."

As the bus pulled into the lot outside Russell E. Diethrick Jr. Park, though, the postindustrial blight had receded into the rearview mirror, and we were welcomed into a sun-soaked old ballpark that seemed as enchanting now as it must have been when it opened in 1941. It had gone on to host minor league games for over seventy years until 2014, when the Jamestown Jammers (New York–Penn League affiliate of the Pittsburgh Pirates) left for Morgantown, West Virginia, at which point a collegiate summer league team took up residence.

The Muckdogs quickly unpacked their uniforms and gear in the spartan cinder-block visiting team locker room and took the field in their shorts and red Muckdogs short-sleeve hoodies for batting practice, as a soundtrack of rap music played over the PA system. Fluffy white clouds floated overhead, and batters sprayed line drives for teammates—augmented by clubhouse manager Erik Moscicki—to shag on the beautifully maintained field.

Tonight was Rotary Buyout Night, meaning that the local Rotary Club had purchased all the tickets and therefore admission was free for everyone. As the Muckdogs took batting practice, there was a reception for the Chautauqua Sports Hall of Fame, a nonprofit honoring "Chautauqua County Sports Celebrities." The president of the organization, Randy Anderson, a jovial balding man wearing a Tarp Skunks jersey, khaki shorts, and flip-flops, welcomed the attendees before delivering some remarks highlighting the history of the local Hall of Fame and the Tarp Skunks. He noted how MLB greats like Randy Johnson, Giancarlo Stanton, Dave Roberts, and Nellie Fox had once played on this field.

The career of Nellie Fox, a diminutive second baseman, is representative of so many of the changes that have taken place both on and off the field since his nearly twenty years in the major leagues ended in 1965. Fox played in fifteen All-Star Games and won an American League Most Valuable Player Award in 1959. Unbelievably, in today's era where players strike out in over 20 percent of their at-bats and some sluggers strike out over 200 times in a single season, Fox fanned just 216 times in his entire career, or once in every 42.7 at-bats. In his post-baseball life, Fox co-owned and managed Nellie Fox Bowl, a bowling alley in Chambersburg, Pennsylvania, near where he grew up. I tried to imagine Bryce Harper spending his retirement days handing out bowling shoes.

Randy Anderson explained to me how, after losing their minor league team and then having a collegiate team fold, a handful of local sports insiders and community leaders rallied to salvage baseball in Jamestown. They managed to recruit a consortium of about forty local investors, each of whom ponied up about $10,000 for a share in the ball club, to stand up a community-owned team and enter it into the PGCBL. After the 2020 season was canceled due to COVID, the Jamestown Tarp Skunks reintroduced competitive baseball to Diethrick Park in 2021.

The city council was supportive of the team, recognizing that it made Jamestown a more attractive place to live, and cut deals discounting the team's lease payments on the city-owned stadium in exchange for having the team's mascot and players appear in community events. A local family prepared meals for both the home and visiting teams and delivered them to Diethrick Park on game days. The team generated modest revenue from advertisements in its programs and on the outfield fence, local business sponsorships, fees paid by the players to play for the summer, concessions, and ticket sales. But with money required to rent nearby college dorms to house the players, make lease payments (even if discounted), pay the head coach, assistant coach, and staff, as well as provide uniforms and equipment, the team was lucky to break even. This summer was especially tough with record-breaking gas prices resulting in hundreds of additional dollars required to finance each road trip on the team bus. And of course, lurking on the horizon was the unanswered question of what would happen after the initial seed money from the investors ran out.

For now, though, these existential questions about baseball's long-term viability in these smaller communities were far from most people's minds. There was a game to enjoy. The smell of the field's freshly cut grass wafting into the slowly filling grandstands brought me back once again to my childhood summer evenings. I suspected it was the "Proust effect" at play, as I had often mowed my grandfather's lawn before playing baseball there, and that smell would sometimes transport me back to those carefree twilight hours. The rolling hills beyond the pine trees ringing the outfield fence and covered blue grandstands enveloping the infield contributed to an intimate feel, and a sense that we were insulated from whatever may be transpiring elsewhere in the struggling community on this beautiful night.

The Muckdogs entered the game playing good baseball, and after their sweep of Geneva in the previous day's twin bill, they found themselves in sole possession of first place in the league's Western Division, with a few weeks left in the regular season. Their momentum would continue as they jumped all over Jamestown's starting pitcher, who looked eerily similar in quality to those I remember facing in high school, with slow fastballs and curves that didn't curve. Before the game, Batavia's Kyle Corso had commented on how the league had some "good arms, and some not-so-good arms." The top of the first inning was ugly, with three walks, three wild pitches, and an error by Jamestown helping Batavia stake an early 4–0 lead, which they would only build on as the game went on.

Meanwhile, as I explored the lovely ballpark, I discovered that Jamestown's most peculiar claim to fame (in a small town baseball ecosystem featuring no shortage of bizarre attractions) was its so-called Best Seat in the House. Occupying a strategic perch right behind home plate and dead center of the press box was an enclosed plywood toilet stall featuring a panoramic, open-air view of the entire field. There was even a plaque on its door featuring the words of well-known "veteran ballpark traveler" Ben Hill, whose hundreds of visits to minor league parks were featured on MILB.com: "The best press box toilet in all Minor League Baseball . . . Where else could one answer nature's call while enjoying such a beautiful view?"

One of the regulars in the press box was Scott Kindberg, sports editor of the Jamestown *Post-Journal,* which had been covering local news for nearly two hundred years. None other than Eric Zwieg, who had spent much of his childhood in Jamestown (though—as he had been quick to point out—he was *from* Rochester), had suggested I reach out to Kindberg. Eric said he'd been teammates with Kindberg on the 1972 Jamestown Container Little League team. Kindberg had gone on to start working for the paper in 1983. Forty years later, he was still there, a "dinosaur," as he put it, when so many others had moved on over the years.

Kindberg credits his father with laying the foundation for his becoming a newspaperman, fondly recalling how his dad would take him to games and show him the press box. He said that as a kid, it was the "biggest deal ever to hang out in the press box" and that he sometimes still marveled at the fact he now covered games there. Like so many newspapers serving smaller communities, the *Post-Journal* was on life support, its daily print run having dropped from twenty-eight thousand in 1983 to under nine thousand now. The *Journal* was owned by none other than Pirates owner Bob Nutting, and, though Kindberg would not speak ill of his employer, I knew that Nutting was notorious for presiding over papers that were shells of their former selves, through no fault of their hardworking, yet skeletal, staffs. I was reminded of how, in both the newspaper industry and baseball, small and midsized communities were at greatest risk of losing civic assets that had been around for over a century, as private equity vultures circled those fighting to survive.

Kindberg explained how Jamestown had once been renowned for furniture making, claiming to be the "Furniture Capital of the World," but had been playing "catch-up" since the exodus of many of its manufacturing jobs in the 1990s and early 2000s. He recalled stories of how in the 1950s a cop would need to direct traffic in the bustling downtown, whereas today a business was as likely to be boarded up as it was to be busy. He applauded the efforts of the local government to resuscitate the city, but admitted he wasn't sure they could ever totally recover. Still, he was an optimist and said he wouldn't have spent his life there if he didn't like it, praising downtown's Lucille Ball Desi Arnaz Museum, which opened in 2018, as a newer attraction that was "phenomenal, and makes you feel like you're in LA or New York City."

Kindberg followed the game as closely as one can follow a game that had turned into a 15–4 rout by the fifth inning, with a Jamestown reliever giving up ten earned runs on seven hits and six walks. He would be filing a story on it in the next day's paper, a brief respite from the high school sports coverage that kept him stretched thin throughout the school year. He was bullish on the team's immediate future, noting that while some fans had been reluctant to embrace the collegiate league, many had come around, as they enjoyed the focus on winning (as opposed to just developing talent), affordable prices (the previous night had featured $2 tickets, hot dogs, and sodas), and fun promotions. He also pointed out how the aggressive style of play, as evidenced by a recent game with ten stolen bases, was entertaining.

Kindberg, a lifelong baseball fan who said he was "in heaven" when his grandfather bought him a season ticket when he was nine, told me he would sometimes sit alone as a kid keeping score at Diethrick Park for an entire game. But he was not sanguine about the long-term health of major league baseball. "Are my grandkids going to care?" he asked, before answering his own question, "MLB has lost its charm, and I'm not sure they are."

Even the self-professed optimist Kindberg couldn't help but grimace, though, as Jamestown continued to implode in just about every facet of this game, ultimately losing 16–4 when the mercy rule was invoked to end the lopsided contest after the seventh inning. The scoreboard didn't even do justice to how uneven the game had been, as it didn't capture the 12 walks and countless wild pitches Jamestown's motley assortment of pitchers were responsible for.

I couldn't help but feel bad for Jamestown's assistant coach, Barry Powell, who spent hours in the bullpen on off days and before games mentoring his young pitchers, patiently offering suggestions on their mechanics after each fastball missed its mark or curveball ended up in the dirt, but had been forced to cobble together a rotation from a bullpen that had been losing a war of attrition all summer. Before the game, Powell had commiserated with his old friend and fellow baseball lifer Batavia assistant coach Tom Eaton. Between the two of them resided nearly a century of accumulated baseball wisdom, gathered traversing hundreds of thousands of miles across the country while coaching and evaluating young baseball players. As they spoke, they quickly fell into that baseball vernacular—referring to "that lefty in Guilford who Boras is representing, so you know he's good"—in which they were fluent. They reminded me of two old veterans bellied up at the local VFW, trading war stories, proud of their time in the trenches and a little suspicious of outsiders. There were frequent references to "the good Lord," as both were religious men, as well as corny jokes, like Powell's reference to eighth grade "being the best three years of my life." They commented on how in today's major league game, "size and power are everything, and if you can run, hit, or field, that's a bonus . . . If you strike out a hundred times a year, that's fine." Of course, it was noteworthy that the two attributes most valued by big-league clubs—size and power—were the two in shortest supply in this league, which helped to explain why Powell was doubtful any of this year's crop would be drafted in MLB's reduced twenty-round draft.

And, like coaches from time immemorial, Powell and Eaton lamented some of the challenges that came with this "new generation" of players, especially those who had in recent weeks begun offering excuses for why they had to quit and go home. Attrition was a problem that—so far at least—Skip Martinez had done a reasonably good job avoiding, whereas Jamestown's roster was now down to a skeletal seventeen players. "Remember our twelve-hour bus rides to Jacksonville with no AC?" Eaton asked. "These days the guys complain about everything."

"They sure do," Powell responded. "Nowadays they'll complain about a perfectly nice hotel room."

*   *   *

Barry Powell grew up in rural South Boston, Virginia, located not far from the North Carolina state line, with a population of just over eight thousand. As for most boys growing up there at the time, hard work was expected at a young age, with six-year-old Barry tasked with milking cows twice a day, at 3:30 a.m. and 3:30 p.m., as well as pulling tobacco, and, a few years later, pumping gas at his uncle's corner store. Baseball, then, was a real treat for him and boys like him, as it offered a break from exhausting manual labor. He relished any opportunity to play catch with his mom, who introduced him to the game (as well as football and basketball), as she'd been a talented athlete herself.

Powell's account of his childhood and the role of sports in it reminded me of the classic baseball book *The Glory of Their Times,* in which some of the greatest baseball players from the early years of the twentieth century looked back as older men on their careers, sharing colorful stories of baseball's past in the form of first-person reminiscences. One of them, Stanley Coveleski, recalled working in the coal mines for seventy-two hours a week as a twelve-year-old, for a nickel an hour, joking that he never knew the sun came up except on Sundays, when he was off. His baseball practice entailed throwing stones at a tin can after he got off work. He would go on to lead Cleveland to win the 1920 World Series, pitching three complete-game victories, in a career that would land him in the Hall of Fame. Following his retirement from baseball, Coveleski settled down in South Bend, Indiana, where he ran a service station and offered free pitching lessons to kids in the field behind his garage.

I mentioned to Powell how I sometimes found myself bribing Bates to go to hockey practice with a McFlurry from McDonald's or a Pokémon card. Even I, who had enjoyed a far easier childhood than Powell, sometimes couldn't help but step back and contemplate the absurdity of offering rewards for a young kid to play a game. But for children today, when the alternative too often is sitting on a couch watching a device or playing video games, sports practice can seem like an onerous imposition.

*   *   *

After the game, the Muckdogs retreated to the cinder-block visiting locker room and wolfed down plates of pasta a local family had prepared for them. Then they boarded the bus and began the roughly two-hour drive back to Batavia. Skip checked the score of the Utica game, as the Muckdogs were now jockeying to get into the playoffs and hopefully earn a good seed so that they could play their first playoff game at home. This was also important to Robbie, who knew that additional home games meant more revenue, whereas a playoff road trip would actually cost him money, as he would need to pay for the bus while earning nothing. The competitive, but ordinarily upbeat and gracious, Skip flashed some real anger when it came to Utica, where he had briefly coached and experienced a bad breakup, leading to his defection to Batavia. "Fuck those guys," he said; "I can't stand that coach or their owner." He was thrilled to see them mired in a losing streak as the season approached its end.

The bus was quiet as it rolled northeast on Interstate 90, the illuminated screens of a few portable devices glowing in the darkness. It finally docked outside the clubhouse in Batavia at around 11:30 p.m., disgorging its sleepy passengers from its womb-like darkness into the disconcertingly bright locker room, where the players quickly dumped their gear, stripped off their dirty uniforms, threw on casual clothes, and took off for the nearby dorms where they were spending the summer.

On the one hand, it was the end of a night indistinguishable from so many others over the course of the season. On the other, for these young Muckdogs—who will wake up one day and, like generations of ballplayers before them, be shocked to discover that decades have somehow passed since they last took the field under the lights on a summer night—I suspect it will help form part of a kaleidoscopic memory they will always treasure. Jerry Reinhart would later say that these bus rides were his most treasured memories from the summer, observing, "You don't really notice how special those moments are when you're in them, but looking back you think 'Wow, that was awesome.'"

In a funny way, the same went for me as spectator to the comforting rhythm of these summer days and nights at the ballpark, though, at age forty-five and predisposed to a nostalgia that could sometimes verge on melancholy, I was already too aware of just how fleeting the experience actually was.

17

Batavia Muckdogs at Elmira Pioneers

July 16

The Muckdogs were headed to Elmira for a Saturday night showdown between Robbie and Nellie's two teams, so that morning I set off on the two-hour drive from Batavia for the evening's game. On my way I made a short detour to check out the farm a few miles outside Batavia where some of the most memorable scenes in the iconic baseball film *The Natural* had been filmed. Nearly every baseball fan, for example, remembers the tree that was struck by lightning and from which a young Robert Redford would carve the bat he would name Wonderboy. One night, over beers at his customary high top on the third base side at Dwyer, Russ Salway had told me much of the movie had been shot nearby. I'd been surprised, as I'd always imagined the pastoral scenes of Redford's childhood on a farm had been filmed in Iowa or Nebraska. Then again, not many people outside of this swath of western New York realize just how important agriculture is to the region.

The movie had always been a favorite of mine. Excited to see where much of it had been filmed, I stepped out of my Jeep on a dirt road near what had been Redford's childhood farmhouse in the film. There was a gentle breeze rolling across the nearby sun-dappled farmland. Memories of Robert Redford playing catch with his son in the film, alongside this same cornfield where his father had once taught him the game, flooded my head. The experience of actually being there, and the memories it evoked, was spiritually revitalizing in a way I never would have expected. There was a crisp purity to this radiant summer afternoon—and the sweet nostalgia it triggered—that couldn't help but make me feel a little better about the world.

Not long after leaving to continue making my way to Elmira, I drove past a father pitching baseballs from a bucket to his young son at a local park outside the charming town of Leicester. It was striking—I couldn't remember the last time I'd seen a parent and child playing catch outside of an organized team practice. James-town coach and longtime scout Barry Powell had recently told me he'd noticed the same thing, remarking, "Kids don't throw anymore. In the old days when you drove into a neighborhood you knew the house with no grass was where the kids gathered to play ... When my son was growing up, it was our house ... I told people, 'I'm not raising grass, I'm raising ballplayers.'"

Powell had identified the symptom of an enormous trend that continues to accelerate; namely, the corporatization of youth sports—especially baseball. Sandlot and local Little League games are increasingly giving way to an enormous, for-profit monstrosity: the $19.2 billion youth sports business. As journalist and admitted baseball fanatic John Miller wrote in the article "How America Sold Out Little League Baseball," the percentage of American kids who play baseball dropped from 16.5 percent in 2008 to 12.2 percent in 2020. Baseball's struggle to appeal to young people today is also evi-denced by the fact that the average age of a person watching a base-ball game on TV now is fifty-seven. There are myriad reasons for the sport's decline in popularity among children, but one is simply how expensive it has become to compete at the top levels. Miller, who coached a youth "travel team" near Pittsburgh (travel teams are essentially private club teams that can be quite expensive and compete regionally or even nationally, as opposed to far less expen-sive local programs like Little League), described a system where "in Florida, some high-level programs now cost over $10,000 per season," and where some families mortgage their homes so their kids can play. Private lessons costing over $100 an hour are not uncom-mon. Savvy businesses prey on the parental fear of missing out on instruction that they have been led to believe is necessary for their children to keep up with other young ballplayers. As a result, baseball (and other youth sports) continue to morph into an often toxic arms race to get kids into more "elite" leagues at ever-younger ages.

Needless to say, this would have all been unimaginable to parents whose kids played baseball back in the 1930s and '40s. Batavia native Bill Dougherty remembered a different version of childhood from this earlier era in his self-published history *Batavia Baseball: A View from the Bleachers:* "Our neighborhood played pickup games at the corner of Franklin and Pearl Streets. For the most part the neighbors put up with the noise and errant baseballs. Mrs. Glendening was the exception, often calling the police to disperse us when shouting became more than she could bear. It didn't help that her front porch was in left field. The boys didn't show any ill will toward her and always returned to their games the next day."

Gone too were the days when Ernie Lawrence ran the Little League in nearby Perry, where kids could play for $15 a year, and if a child didn't have enough money, the league would make up the difference. Decades later, men like Dr. Ross Fanara would still sometimes identify friends they'd lost touch with by the Little League team they'd once played on.

Even more recently, my mom had shuttled both of my younger brothers down to Police Boys Club #8 in Washington, DC, to attend practices presided over by a retired Capitol policeman (and former semipro ballplayer), Kenneth Burkhead (known to all as Coach Buddy). It was a decidedly low-budget, informal affair—there was no paperwork or fees, the lessons spread by word of mouth and were offered on an overgrown patch of grass alongside a football field— but the results were remarkable. Alums of the sessions stood out for their polished mechanics (if occasional bruised ego from the eccentric coach who was not known for his bedside manner) and often went on to high school and even college success.

Nowadays, travel ball families pay big bucks shuttling their kids to far-flung locales instead of to the local field, where neighborhood games were once played, the kinds of games that defined childhoods and would be remembered fondly for lifetimes, and where local legends like Coach Buddy once provided free mentorship. What remains is a more competitive, more expensive, albeit less fun and less communal, ecosystem.

It is also a lot whiter. According to Miller, the high price tags associated with youth baseball's privatization have contributed to baseball in America "becoming a mostly white country club sport for upper-class families to consume, like a snorkeling vacation or a round of golf."

The decline of American-born Black major leaguers is another area in which MLB is aware of a problem but has had little success reversing its momentum. The percentage of American-born Black players had dropped to 6.1 percent of Opening Day rosters in 2023 from 18 percent as recently as 1991.

MLB's decision to eliminate 25 percent of its minor league system, and cut the draft in half from forty to twenty rounds, will, according to many scouts and experts, compound this problem, as there will be more of a premium on "polished" players who have graduated from expensive travel teams, private instruction, and dominant college programs as opposed to taking chances on raw athletes who were not able to access this exclusive ecosystem. Organizations adhering to the gospel of efficiency, with half as many total picks, will naturally be less inclined to "take a flier" on someone with potential upside, but substantial risk, than in previous years, when they could afford to choose a lesser-known commodity in the later rounds of a larger draft and then patiently evaluate the prospect's maturation in a robust minor league system.

According to an MLB front-office analyst Miller quoted in his article, "The way it's going, all pro players are going to be rich, white kids from the suburbs, or Dominican or Venezuelan."

*　　　*　　　*

The season was now over two-thirds complete, and while the Muckdogs had cooled off a little from their torrid start, they still possessed an impressive 23-10 record when they visited the 15-17 Elmira Pioneers on Saturday night. I'd looked forward to getting back to Dunn Field, which, although literally falling apart in some places, still possessed a historic charm that was absent from the more modern Dwyer Stadium in Batavia. Nellie Nichols would describe walking the concrete corridors by herself in the postgame quiet and sometimes being "grabbed" by the black-and-white photographs lining the walls that depicted another era of baseball. She'd wonder what it was like back then, the crowd clad in suits and dresses. Sometimes, she said, almost as if summoning her inner Bill Kauffman, the darkened stadium could even feel otherworldly late at night, as if "the baseball spirits were sending their love and pushing me to not let baseball in Elmira die."

Before heading to the stadium, I made a short stop at Mark Twain's gravesite in Elmira's Woodlawn Cemetery, where Twain was buried next to his wife, Olivia, a native of Elmira, and their children. The family had spent many summers on a pleasant farm on the outskirts of town—which Twain would call the "quietest of all quiet places"—and where he would write some of his best work. My drive from the cemetery to Dunn Field brought me through Elmira's downtown. I had hoped it would somehow seem less depressing than it had been on my first visit on Opening Day, but alas it remained a sobering reminder of how these cities occupying New York's Southern Tier had been ravaged by a manufacturing economy that had been hollowing out for decades. The prison industry still survived, though, in the form of the maximum-security Elmira Correctional Facility (though the nearby "supermax" Southport Correctional Facility had been shuttered in March 2022). Otherwise, vacant buildings and empty streets signified yet another postindustrial city that felt left behind. I couldn't help but imagine all the individual dreams and hard work that had once gone into the small businesses that had been abandoned; too many boarded-up storefronts to count were the only thing left bearing witness to those more prosperous times. Elmira seemed to be lacking even the flickers of resurgence that could be found in Batavia, in places like the Pub Coffee Hub and the Eli Fish Brewing Company. Marc Witt, who served as general manager of both Batavia and Elmira, chuckled when recalling how the previous summer the Elmira play-by-play announcer had mentioned "fireworks" in the distance, which Marc informed him were in fact gunshots.

Elmira's economic struggles were compounded by its geographic isolation, marooned far from any larger cities, whereas Batavia was located along a heavily trafficked interstate less than an hour from Buffalo to the west and Rochester to the east. Marc marveled when he met an Elmira local who referred to a trip to Niagara Falls as if it were as exotic and distant as Paris. "Dude, it's in the same state," he thought. Another spoke longingly of how he'd always wanted to go to a minor league hockey game in Binghamton, as if it were an unattainable dream. Marc was confused, as Binghamton was only an hour to the east, until he learned that the man had no car. The community took pride in the Pioneers, though, something they could still call their own. Aside from the Pioneers, Marc noted, "there's a bowling alley and Mark Twain's grave."

As I approached the stadium, I made a quick pit stop into Kahuna's, a bare-bones bar tucked into the neighborhood of modest homes surrounding the ballpark. It was quiet on this Saturday afternoon. The only patrons were a handful of middle-aged men who looked to be in their fifties, wearing shorts and T-shirts, spaced about five feet away from each other on bar stools, making small talk with the tattooed female bartender. "Freebird" played on the jukebox. If Twain's grave had provided a brief glimpse of the transcendent, this spot was the perfect counterpoint, as salt-of-the-earth as a place could be. The concrete-floored bar had an Elmira Pioneers schedule on the wall, with baseball on one TV, the British Open on another, and President Biden speaking about the economy on a news channel. I braced myself for the reflexive anti-Biden sentiment common in this region, but none came. Instead, one of the men described his surprise to discover $12 beers and $4 waters on a recent visit to Yankee Stadium, four hours away. His tone was one of resignation more than anger. The bar was the kind of place where no one asked—or likely even wondered—why you came by yourself to suck down a Bud Light and then leave, which was nice, as that was precisely what I planned to do.

After finishing the beer, I headed the remaining few blocks to Dunn Field. Marc Witt greeted me with a smile and his customary enthusiasm, buoyed by the previous night's crowd of over three thousand and expecting another strong one; the Saturday night games featuring postgame fireworks were always a big draw. Marc had begun his career working for Robbie in group sales for the Elmira Jackals minor league hockey team before spending three years working as a sales rep for the NHL's Columbus Blue Jackets. Robbie, though, had smartly noticed the seemingly inexhaustible energy that had driven Marc to be the top sales rep for the Blue Jackets and convinced him to return to western New York to serve as general manager for the Pioneers (and later for the Batavia Muckdogs as well). Marc would also meet and later marry Nellie's daughter (and Robbie's stepdaughter), Tabbatha, who also worked for the Pioneers. Tonight Marc told me he had "something cool planned" and to make sure I was near the field to see it prior to the opening pitch.

Even though the opening pitch was still hours away, Marc and the rest of the staff, led by Nellie, had been hard at work all day. It was a family affair, as Nellie's son (and Robbie's stepson), Kane, served as groundskeeper, while Tabbatha ran the beer tent, and granddaughter Ava managed the upstairs concession stand. Nellie would often make an early morning run to Sam's Club for supplies before arriving at Dunn Field by 9:00 a.m. to check the locker rooms, make sure the tables and bathrooms were clean ("I can't stand dirty bathrooms," she would often say), stock the fridges, and begin prepping some of the food. By midafternoon the game day staff of fifteen to twenty people, many of them teenage summer hires, would begin to filter in.

The first fan to arrive at Dunn—at 4:50 p.m., an hour before the gates officially opened—was Herb Tipton, who was still proudly carrying a card he'd gotten at his ninety-fourth birthday celebration earlier that afternoon at the local Holiday Inn. He was clad in a navy blue Korean War Veteran ball cap, khaki pants, and a gray Pioneers jersey. The gates most certainly opened for Herb. A few of the staff shouted out, "Howya doin', Herbie?" as they went about their game day preparations at the concession stand. Marc Witt ducked into the merchandise tent to grab a seat cushion with Herb's name scrawled on it that they held for him at the stadium. "Not gonna get this kind of customer service at Yankee Stadium," Marc said as he emerged with the cushion and handed it to Herb. Next Herb went to the still-closed concession stand, where he got his usual Diet Coke from Nellie. That afternoon he'd forgotten to bring exact change like he usually did, so he pledged to pay for it later once they opened and the credit card machine was working.

Herb appreciated the lengths to which Robbie and Nellie went to make him feel welcome, saying, "They're number one. They always talk to me, and never blow me off. If a game is canceled, they'll even call to tell me." To thank them, he would sometimes make special treats for the entire staff, such as the "chocolate lasagna"—Oreos over chocolate pudding—he'd learned to make from a recipe his sister shared with him.

The Muckdogs were stretching and playing catch along the third-base line before the game. Skip Martinez called them in and delivered a short pep talk, the gist of which was not to get complacent, as he knew the relentless schedule of games could become numbing and gradually sap players' enthusiasm and commitment to winning. Most of these players had been practicing or playing nearly every day for six months, coming straight from their college seasons.

As a large crowd began to fill the stadium, I recognized the pro wrestler John Cena's "entrance music" coming on over the PA system and remembered Marc's hint that he had something special cooked up as part of the pregame entertainment. Instead of John Cena, though, a local wrestler introduced as Keebu Harris approached home plate, holding some sort of championship belt up in the air. He confronted an intern dressed up in a Muckdogs jersey who had been talking trash about Elmira as part of the pregame skit. The intern then attacked the wrestler with a folding chair, knocking him to the ground. By now both teams were on their feet watching the scripted melee, as were the fans in the grandstands. Harris struggled to his feet, working the crowd, before delivering the "Twist of Fate" to the intrepid intern. The wrestler would later tell me this was his "finishing move," inspired by his favorite WWE wrestlers, the Hardy Boyz. The Elmira "clubbie," dressed up as a ref, then sprinted onto the field and counted to three as Harris pinned the intern and the crowd erupted.

These moments before a game started were Nellie's favorite time of the workday, as she enjoyed watching kids laughing with their parents and grandparents as they streamed in the entrance to Dunn Field. "Family means a lot to me," she'd say; "we try to make this a happy place for people, since they're making memories here whether they know it or not." She was grateful for everyone who paid to come to a Pioneers game. Her modest upbringing made it easy for her to relate to the tough economic times many of the fans were experiencing. "I know what it's like to go to the grocery store these days," she said. "I don't even buy bacon without a coupon. Some people can either feed their family or go to a baseball game, and I'm grateful to anyone who chooses to come." And indeed, the fans converging on

Nellie's concession stand were overwhelmingly dressed in the tank tops, jean shorts, and camouflage hunting caps more commonly seen in an aisle at Dollar General than at big-city professional sporting events. "Lots of fans in Elmira don't have a lot of money, they're never going to Disney, so this is it for them . . . To a little kid, this is a big park, and their eyes get big when they see it, so we want to make it a special experience for them," Nellie said.

Nellie's reference to Disney World was illuminating, as Disney's amusement parks occupy an exalted place in Americana, much like major league baseball, and they too have grown more out of reach for ordinary Americans to afford. Nellie tried to instill in her children an appreciation for the sacrifices necessary to embark on a trip like that, explaining to them how "most people can't just 'go' to Disney without saving." And indeed, she was right, as an article in the business newsletter *The Hustle* explained how for today's minimum wage–earning parents, a one-day family trip to Disneyland would require nearly two weeks of pay. Aware of harsh realities like this, Nellie didn't want her children to take their opportunities for granted when they were young, and so she used family vacations to try to help them develop the virtue of frugality. She would have them save coins and periodically roll them up to deposit in the bank, where they could monitor their special vacation balance.

*   *   *

Back on the Dunn Field diamond, there was a ball game being played that was still reasonably priced. Batavia broke the game open in the top of the second, the scoring punctuated by a bases-loaded double off the bat of Kyle Corso as Batavia batted around the order, scoring six runs and jumping out to an 8–3 lead.

I went outside to see if Charles Bennett, the colorful foul-ball shagger I'd enjoyed chatting with on previous visits to Dunn Field, was there. I quickly spotted him in his usual spot adjacent to the grandstands on the first-base side, the best place to snag a long foul ball from the predominantly right-handed Batavia lineup. He was clad in the same outfit as last time, a Pioneers jersey with jean shorts and an Elmira cap. He immediately offered me a soda from a cooler in the back of his car. As we sipped our drinks and scanned the horizon for any incoming balls, he lamented how the city of Elmira was headed in the wrong direction, showing me a picture of a bag of needles he'd discovered in a nearby fence line as he was searching for balls. He'd lost a number of friends to fentanyl, observing that Elmira's location along a heavily trafficked transit corridor between New York City and Buffalo led to lots of guns and drugs being introduced to the area. Additionally, he pointed out that it was less than ideal that its prison was one of the larger sources of out-of-town visitors. This was not great for Elmira, as some friends and family of the inmates chose to relocate rather than make long visits every weekend and were themselves mixed up in crime, introducing further stressors into a social fabric that was already fraying. While fifteen years ago he could sleep with the door open and windows unlocked, he'd recently told his buddy, a cop, that if someone broke into his house, "You're gonna get one of two calls: someone was shot or is running down the street with an arrow in his ass," referring to the guns and archery weapons he hunted with.

Charles didn't seem as upbeat as he'd been the last time we'd spoken, and it soon became clear why. His mom was dying of cancer and had asked him to get estimates for crematoriums, bluntly instructing him to "put me in the burner, fry me up, put my ashes in a bag, and put me in the ground" when she died. Between his mother's slow death and the financial stress that came with trying to provide for his foster son after Dollar Tree had reduced his hours, I was amazed that Charles was capable of even the degree of equanimity he had. Despite, or perhaps because of, the tough times, he felt a certain comfort surrounded by the members of his small tribe in the grass parking lot on this overcast night outside Dunn Field, the familiar oversized posters of Larrupin' Lou and Bustin' Babe looking down on them. Despite all his worries, when a ball came arcing over the Dunn Field grandstands toward the grassy parking area, and Charles and his boy darted off to where they expected it to land, all was—for a brief but not insignificant moment—right in their world.

A little later, when I told Charles I was getting hungry and needed to head back inside the ballpark, he beckoned for me to come over to his aging sedan, where he rifled through his trunk for the "spare balls I always keep for the little ones so they can leave happy," before retrieving one and presenting it to me to bring home to Bates. I thanked him, and as I turned and began to head back inside, Charles shouted at me to bring my glove next time and join him shagging balls for a few innings.

As I reentered Dunn Field in the bottom of the seventh, the Pioneers were trying to claw their way back into the game, narrowing the Batavia lead to 8–5 before a fly ball to center field ended the rally. I went to the concession stand to grab a popcorn from "Popcorn Bob." Things had quieted down and so we chatted briefly, during which time I learned that not only did he take pride in his tasty popcorn, but was also a talented furniture maker, constructing high-end products out of oak or mahogany that he sold online and at flea markets. "If a piece of furniture I'm building won't last a generation, I'm not interested in making it," he said. I even detected a touch of frustration that some people had reduced him to a one-dimensional caricature—a persona he of course contributed to by literally wearing a "Popcorn Bob" T-shirt—and didn't recognize his highly refined skills in craftsmanship. "Popcorn and beer, that's not me, they're just some of the things I like to do," he said. As Bob scrolled through his phone showing me pictures of the beautifully handcrafted furniture he'd constructed, I marveled. I wondered how many people would have imagined that this sweaty guy—with unkempt graying hair shooting out from under a ball cap, tending to a popcorn machine in the bowels of a crumbling old ballpark—was capable of such artistry?

Entering the grandstands from the concession area, I spotted Korean War veteran Herb Tipton sitting in the same seat he'd occupied for decades of summer nights just like this. I took a seat next to him as he shouted, "Get over that wall," before a long Elmira fly ball landed harmlessly in a Muckdogs glove. Though he still had a contented smile on his face, he explained that he was frustrated that the Elmira manager always failed to "settle the pitchers down when they're struggling," and often left them in too long. On this night, at least, he had a point, as the Elmira starter wasn't given the hook until he'd surrendered eight runs, seven of them earned. When asked what his favorite part of the game was, he immediately responded, "Winning."

Learning that I was also a veteran, Herb commented on how much he appreciated it when kids would notice his Korean War veteran cap and stop and say "Thank you for your service"—recounting how one child even extended his hand as if he wanted something, only for a surprised Herb to discover that all he wanted was to shake his hand and thank him. I asked Herb what his service in Korea entailed and was unprepared—as I had been and would be several times that summer—for one of those abrupt detours from relaxed baseball talk to discussions of more cosmic significance.

*   *   *

Herb told me he was "very blessed" to be here, as the night he was supposed to return home from his six-month combat deployment to Korea, a 155mm howitzer shell had exploded near his foxhole outside Pusan, sending him diving on top of another soldier. Somehow, Herb said, the shrapnel entered the soldier he was covering while Herb emerged shaken but unharmed. Herb pointed to the left-field fence and told me that was how close the attacking Chinese soldiers had been, so close that he could see them, which he said he'd never forget. *Get me out of here,* was all he could remember thinking at the time. Luckily, he did manage to soon escape the fighting and head home.

"It makes you really appreciate this place," Herb said as he gazed out at the field. It was unclear whether he meant the United States, Dunn Field, or perhaps both.

I nodded in agreement, as that had been exactly how I felt upon returning to American soil. Though not wanting to equate my wartime service to his, I did feel compelled to share a memory that his story had sparked. As he described the near miss that had occurred on the eve of his exit from Korea, I was reminded of one of my unit's last nights in Iraq's Anbar Province in 2006. Soldiers were queued up outside our battalion headquarters waiting for darkened helicopters, flown by pilots with night vision goggles, to pick them up and begin their long journey home. I was attending an evening meeting with the incoming unit's leadership, when we heard and felt the concussive explosions of mortar rounds striking nearby. Our hope that perhaps no one had been injured was dashed seconds later when we heard the screams of the wounded.

It turns out the mortars had landed near the line of troops waiting to board the incoming choppers. As we scrambled around trying to find and help treat the wounded, I swear I heard the distinct whistle of another round sail close by and clenched my teeth, bracing for the worst, only to be greeted with silence. I will never know what that was—perhaps a dud. As the wounded were consolidated and prepared for a medevac, we were relieved to discover that no one had been killed.

The memory of this night had always stuck with me, as I couldn't help but imagine what a tragic waste it would have been had someone been killed just seconds before lifting off, ready to watch the flickering lights of that violent place recede behind them into the desert sky.

Herb seemed to enjoy speaking to someone who listened to his stories of Korea. I'd never bought into the cliché that most veterans "didn't like to talk about" their wartime experiences, because many of the ones I'd known seemed glad to, provided you listened carefully and respectfully. He seemed to appreciate hearing about my experience as well, nodding quietly as I shared it. When it felt as if the conversation threatened to cast too big a cloud on the pleasure of the moment, we returned to discussing the game. Herb told me that he looked forward to throwing out the first pitch the following night, which was "Military Appreciation Night." While I was glad to see him being honored, I was saddened to think about how few, if any, of the fans—preoccupied as we all are at games with the myriad distractions of food, drink, conversation, taking photos, and now iPhones—would ever really know what the old man tossing the ball to home plate had gone through as a young twenty-four-year-old desperately seeking cover on a distant field thousands of miles from home.

*   *   *

As Herb looked on, his ordinarily affable demeanor tinged with a trace of frustration at Elmira's subpar effort on this night, Skip Martinez gave the nod to Muckdogs right-hander Trey Bacon to close out the game. Bacon looked to be in command and, despite giving up a run, shut the door on the Pioneers for an 8–6 victory in front of a paid crowd of nearly three thousand. With the win, Batavia moved to 24-10 on the season.

As I waited to take in the postgame fireworks, I ran into Nellie, who was just beginning the long list of tasks that needed to be completed before she could head home and unwind for a few minutes with some marshmallows beside her backyard fire pit. Never one for self-aggrandizement, she was quick to point out that her stamina was nothing compared to Robbie's, who she said had begun crying with happiness the other day when he moved his toes for the first time since fearing "they'd been dead" following the onset of his ailment.

As the final notes of Toby Keith's "Courtesy of the Red, White and Blue" played and the last of the postgame fireworks dissipated into the night sky, I passed Keebu Harris, the local wrestler who'd performed in the skit before the game, on my way to the exit. He was quietly gathering up a small display of mementos from the folding table he'd been sitting at waiting for autograph seekers, of whom there seemed to be few, during the game. I felt bad for him and asked to look at some of his memorabilia. He immediately pulled out a photograph of what he said was his "first championship" that looked as if it had been taken in a ring constructed in someone's backyard. He appeared proud, though, undeterred by what seemed to have been a rather lonely vigil at his table. In this he was like the thousands of ballplayers and performers who toil in anonymity, unwilling to let go of big dreams in small towns across America.

18

Elmira Pioneers at Batavia Muckdogs

July 21

Ginny Wagner, her husband, Charlie, and their two sons live in the pleasant Park Meadow neighborhood in North Buffalo. Their house is a block from where a small monument marks the location of where President McKinley was shot by an anarchist on the grounds of the Pan-American Exposition in 1901.

Ginny grew up nearby and recalls how riding her bike to nearby Delaware Park—designed by Frederick Law Olmsted—marked a childhood milestone. It was in many ways a wonderful place to live, though that spring Ginny—a Black woman—had been shaken by the mass shooting targeting Black residents at a local supermarket a few miles from her home. One of the fallen was an eighty-six-year-old woman who was the mother of Ginny's next-door neighbor. Her neighbor, a retired Buffalo fire commissioner, had raced to the scene to help, only to discover his mother was one of the victims. The killing shocked and scared Wagner. She said that she sometimes asked herself why she stood for the national anthem at Batavia Muckdogs games when her country could seem enveloped in darkness, but that she then reminded herself that she was surrounded at the games by so many "friendly people like Bill Kauffman," which gave her "hope as an American." She strove to find a balance between an awareness of some of the terrible things going on in the world and becoming paralyzed by sadness or anger.

"I'm more determined to surround myself with happiness," she said, in light of so much heartbreak.

An important source of that happiness was going to Muckdogs games with Betsey. Ginny's husband, Charlie, said he was "amused" by her newfound interest in the Muckdogs, as "she'd never been a sports fan." He suspected that she loved the trips to watch baseball in Batavia for many reasons, perhaps most importantly, "It's her thing with Betsey. When at the ball game, she isn't anyone's mom, wife, or employee. She's just doing something fun and outside . . . Betsey's more into the baseball. Ginny never watches major league baseball on TV, though she will tune in to the Muckdogs on YouTube and watch as she does things around the house."

Charlie had actually been a minor league baseball fan long before Betsey introduced Ginny to the Muckdogs and had enjoyed going to Buffalo's old War Memorial Stadium when he was younger. He loved the carnival atmosphere and how the game felt less corporate than its major league counterpart. Charlie lamented how at the highest levels of pro sports the focus now seemed to be only on money and control, with teams too often "acting like corporations screwing the little guy . . . Sure, it may be more efficient and streamlined, but the uniqueness is lost."

Charlie pointed to the irony of MLB pushing the "Save America's Pastime Act" through Congress in 2018 in an effort supposedly intended to save baseball in small towns by exempting minor league baseball players from federal minimum wage requirements (thereby reducing the expenses required to maintain these teams), and then proceeding two years later to "destroy it in forty-two cities like Batavia."

"If someone says, 'It's just business,' that means they have no morals. It's not. Usually that means they just want to make more money no matter what, which to me is unconscionable," said Charlie. He was right to wonder whether, in a place like Batavia—where the cost of a minor league team to its major league parent was about the equivalent of one major league minimum salary ($700,000 in 2022)—the paltry savings was really what baseball needed. Something didn't add up.

In just the 2022–2023 offseason, superagent Scott Boras negotiated more than $1.24 billion in MLB contracts, including those of Carlos Correa (six years, $200 million), Xander Bogaerts (eleven years, $280 million), Carlos Rodón (six years, $162 million) and Brandon Nimmo (eight years, $162 million). In 2020, sixty-five players would make over $100,000 per game. So the question bears repeating: Did $700,000 in savings justify eliminating Batavia's team and those in forty-one other cities and towns across America?

Absurdities like this contributed to sentiments such as those shared with me by one former minor league owner who told me how he found himself "literally asking, 'Does [MLB commissioner] Manfred even like baseball?'"

Whether Manfred liked the sport or not, MLB owners were one constituency who clearly approved of his conduct. And, for Manfred, the most important one, as in July 2023 they offered him a four-year extension to continue serving as commissioner. While the terms of the deal weren't disclosed, he was likely offered a raise from the estimated $25 million (including bonuses) he'd been making annually. This came despite mixed signals as to the health of the game. While attendance in 2023 enjoyed a modest rebound from recent lows, the last four World Series have been the four least watched on record. And then there was Manfred's seemingly endless succession of tone-deaf comments sure to alienate fans, perhaps most notoriously following the Astros cheating scandal and their resulting 2017 World Series victory when, in rejecting calls for MLB to nullify the tainted victory, he dismissively referred to the World Series trophy —named the Commissioner's Trophy (in some remarkable irony)—as a "piece of metal."

Charlie, it turned out, had his own reasons to be suspicious of the motives of big business. He'd worked at a local TV station for twenty years, during which time the phone often woke him up in the middle of freezing Buffalo nights as he was called upon to drive the news truck to the scene of an emergency to facilitate live feeds for the local news. About ten years ago private equity bought the station, "sucked every dollar out of the business, spent a fortune on consulting fees," and the next thing Charlie knew, he and his crew were out of work.

Charlie has now been driving a city bus for ten years, a job he was qualified for by virtue of the commercial license he had from his time on the news team. This is sad, said Ginny, as his old job "was a good one, and he was good at it . . . He'd gone to school for it, and he loved it." Corporate ownership by a remote group with deep pockets, Charlie had seen, was far from a guarantee of a long and fruitful relationship.

*   *   *

Betsey Higgins told her boss at the library that she needed to leave at 5:30 p.m.—which he already knew, responding, "Must be Muck-dog season" before she'd even gotten the words out of her mouth. Yet Betsey was still running a little behind when her best friend, Ginny, arrived at her Elmwood Village home, about five minutes from Ginny's, to pick her up for the drive to the evening's game against Elmira.

"C'mon, let's go, Higgins!" Ginny shouted good-naturedly as she waited in the living room. Betsey soon emerged from the kitchen clad in her Muckdogs cap and jeans, carrying a container of snacks she'd bought from her favorite co-op that afternoon. "I go there almost every day," she said, adding with a laugh, "I'm a single chick—that's what we do."

The entire first floor of Betsey's house was lined with enormous bookshelves containing hundreds of books (arranged alphabetically; she is a librarian after all), many of them antiquarian and collected from independent booksellers around the world. The cozy living room, with its huge fireplace and stacks of books, seemed like the perfect place to spend a stormy midwinter Buffalo day, sitting in the easy chair, fireplace crackling, book in hand, perhaps a glass of wine on the side table. On a few occasions, when she was in a more reflective mood, Betsey would confide in me that she wished she'd had children. And yet, the contrast between the serenity of her living room and the sea of plastic toys and general chaos that defined my home, one that houses two kids under the age of six, made me think that her lifestyle was not without its appeal.

Thomas Hardy was Betsey's favorite author, and such was her fandom that she'd spent a few summers at Oxford auditing courses on him. She was particularly drawn to *Jude the Obscure*, recalling how, when she first read it, she'd been struck by the "anxiety, sadness, grief, and misery." Whereas many would shy away from a book described in those terms, Betsey was hooked. *This man can write,* she thought; *I gotta read more of him.*

Betsey and Ginny pulled up to Dwyer Stadium and hustled to the front gate with a few minutes to spare before the first pitch. They were greeted warmly with a hug by Dave Fisher, the Desert Storm veteran working security. They were a delightfully incongruous threesome. While Ginny's home displayed a Black Lives Matter sign, and Betsey had recently missed a game to attend a Pride march, Dave's Jeep included a bumper sticker with a bullet on it that read "Faster than Dialing 911."

As Betsey and Ginny made their way to their regular seating section along the third-base line, waving to familiar faces along the way, the first-place Muckdogs jogged onto the field to take on the Elmira Pioneers five days after their last matchup, this time back in Batavia. It was "Thirsty Thursday," and with cheap beer advertised, I was surprised to discover the ballpark only about two-thirds full.

When I approached the Eli Fish beer tent, I discovered why the $2 beer promotion may not have filled the stands, as they weren't serving craft beers, but rather cheap beers in small plastic cups that couldn't have contained more than eight ounces. I should've known that the ever-frugal Robbie would never have served up pricey sixteen-ounce craft beers for $2! Still, eight-ounce beers and all, it was surprising that a pleasant eighty-degree evening with only a few clouds passing lazily overhead hadn't resulted in better attendance.

The Muckdogs exploded for five runs in the bottom of the first on a collection of five hits, an Elmira error, and a flurry of walks and wild pitches from the Elmira starter. Cathy Preston, recognizable with her scorebook and pencil in hand, greeted me with a trivia question, though this one was a little tougher than usual: What major league team first put numbers on the backs of their jerseys? The answer, which I failed to guess, was the 1929 Yankees. She also noted that Freddie Prinze Jr., at the end of the 2001 romantic comedy *Summer Catch*, announced that he was "going to Batavia," even putting on a Muckdogs cap, after the successful summer playing in the Cape Cod League depicted in the film. It was the sort of observation that denizens of minor league ballparks often made—fans of teams in the Carolinas enjoyed telling me about brief scenes from *Bull Durham* that had taken place in their ballpark—as they took pride in their local team's inclusion, however modest, in the game's broader tapestry.

Cathy, who could see the stadium lights from her bedroom, had performed the same game day ritual for nearly twenty years, ever since her late husband, Jonathan, had introduced her to the Muck-dogs. She would leave her nearby home at around 6:30 p.m. to walk over to the ballpark. Keeping score had "become an obsession" for her, and she would head to a whiteboard near the entrance where the lineup was posted so she could copy it into her scorebook. Now the whiteboard with the daily lineups posted on it was gone, its unexplained removal a rare gripe Cathy had with Robbie's ownership, and so she'd duck into the press box to get the lineup from public address announcer (and fellow trivia buff) Paul Spiotta.

Cathy marveled at how many friends she'd made "through the Muckdogs, getting exposed to circles of people who would otherwise never come together." She explained how her daughter, Aurelia, learned to walk by toddling up the bleacher steps every evening to see an elderly couple who sat together and who "grew to adore her like another grandchild."

It's hard to imagine this sort of relationship blossoming at major league games, where most families are lucky to squeeze alongside tens of thousands of strangers a few times a summer. A Chicago-based sports business firm, Team Marketing Report, has for years been producing an annual "MLB Fan Index," reflecting how much it costs for "four adult non-premium tickets, single-car parking, two draft beers, four soft drinks, four hot dogs and two adult-sized adjustable hats" in each MLB stadium. The 2022 average was $256. Of course, owners will tell you these prices are necessary to pay the salaries of players like Bryce Harper of the Philadelphia Phillies, who will make roughly $1,000 for every minute he is on the field, and $63,000 per at bat, over the course of his 162-game season.

Though there would be no towering Bryce Harper home runs to admire on the field at Dwyer, childhood summers defined by Muck-dogs games still made a lasting impact on Cathy's daughter, Aurelia. Aurelia had once written a school essay saying:

> There isn't one summer I haven't spent time at the Muckdogs'
> Stadium. My parents have had season tickets for longer than

18 years. It was and still is a "safe place" for my mom. She loses herself in the game, infatuated with keeping score. Before I was even able to walk, it became a safe place for me too. My parents always sat on the third base side in the bleachers. My favorite part of going to the games was the routine. As a child afraid of change, it was comfortable. As soon as we walked through the gates, I would feel a peace within me. Although you would think baseball games would be boring for a child, I loved it there. I would make friends with adults, other children, and even the employees. I liked the fact that I was known and people looked forward to seeing me. I don't remember a time where I wasn't obsessing over being wanted. Through the other seasons of the year when baseball season is no longer, I drive past the stadium and feel a longing towards it. I don't always realize it, but the countdown to the start of the season is always in the back of my head.

The daily acts of kindness and the welcoming embrace of her neighbors that Aurelia captured in her essay would also provide her a measure of reassuring peace following the sudden death of her father.

Tonight, after their five-run first inning, nothing would go the Muckdogs' way, a night of futility punctuated by a disastrous fifth inning in which Elmira would bat around their entire order, plating seven runs on six hits to open up an 11–5 lead over their hosts. In the press box, Paul Spiotta, whose dispassionate cadences over the PA system belied a fierce desire for the Muckdogs to do well, simply shook his head and said, "I knew this was gonna be a long one from the moment it started."

I made my way to Joe and Sandra Kauffman's usual perch near the top row of the grandstands, hoping to find them before they left. I always enjoyed Joe's tales of the Dwyer Stadium (formerly MacArthur Park) of old, having told me about everything from when it had hosted stock car races—to include one night when a car crashed through the outfield fence—to professional wrestling, recalling how he and his buddies were hired to construct the ring that Gorgeous George would wrestle in. At the time, George had been one of the most famous wrestlers in America, and Joe even remembered his trademark "gold hairpins."

I discovered Joe and Sandra already bundled up in their jackets, and so I knew they were getting ready to go. Still, they greeted me with friendly smiles, and Sandra, as she always did, asked how Bates and Shea were doing. Joe, a kind man, nonetheless didn't seem like someone you'd want to mess with, despite being well into his eighties. After working as a surveyor for the New York Central Railroad, he joined a Batavia-based company that made front-end loaders. His employer, Trojan Industries, had operated one of the biggest factories in Batavia and been a sponsor of Batavia baseball. The minor league team was called the Batavia Trojans from 1966 until 1987.

In the late 1970s, though, the Trojan factory came under the control of a German company, and soon rumors of layoffs began to spread through the workforce. Joe half-jokingly tried to reassure himself that his job was safe by thinking, *They'd never lay off a good German like Kauffman* before soon discovering his name among the hundreds who had been terminated, some of whom had been discarded just before becoming eligible for their pensions. According to Joe, it was essentially a tax dodge by the German manufacturer, as they would send over loaders almost completely constructed overseas, save for putting on the tires and bucket, which required only a skeleton staff in the United States to complete. This allowed the company to escape the tariff that accompanied an import of vehicles that were built overseas. It amounted to a "screw job for the USA," said Joe, adding, "Outside owners don't care," his tone suggesting that he wasn't expecting sympathy, but rather just telling it like it is. I suspect that witnessing this as a child helped plant the seed of his son Bill's enduring distrust of large outside corporations and their impact on local economies.

Joe and Sandra soon made their exit and didn't miss much in the way of drama on the field, as the game's outcome was never in doubt. With Elmira up 13–5 at the beginning of the seventh, and a biting wind coming in from left field, Betsey and Ginny also decided to take off. They waved goodbye and made their way to the warmth of their car and the drive back to Buffalo. While they usually spent the pregame ride to Batavia catching up on how their days had gone, as they headed back west on the Thruway at night they often just listened to music, anything and everything, ranging from Bob Marley to Genesis to Lady Gaga.

The game had begun with a smaller-than-expected crowd listed at 1,127, and by the final uncomfortable innings, only a few hundred die-hards remained scattered throughout the grandstands, many of them in winter hats and huddled under Buffalo Bills blankets. One of them was Bill Kauffman.

As the temperature continued to drop, and the game slowed to a crawl, I'd begun to fantasize about grabbing a cup of hot chocolate from the lobby of the La Quinta and retiring to the warmth of my hotel room. Not Bill, though. Even as the teams turned to the bottom of their bullpen barrels, with pitchers struggling to throw strikes (Paul Spiotta would later tell me that the game featured a whopping seventeen full counts), Bill was just settling into his psychic happy place. As "Sweet Emotion" played between the eighth and ninth innings of this 13–5 yawner, Bill happily announced, "I kind of wish the game could go on forever . . . I love this." Though I'm a baseball fan, we were freezing our asses off and watching a sloppy game that was devoid of drama. I didn't get it. When I told Bill this, he just nodded sagely, clearly not agreeing, but also not wanting to spoil the moment with an argument.

*   *   *

After the game finally drew to a close, more than three hours after the opening pitch had been tossed, the handful of remaining fans made their way to the exit and spilled onto Bank Street, where all but a few night owls had turned off their lights and gone to bed.

I dropped into the front office, where I found Robbie, shoes off to relieve some of the pressure on his swollen feet, guiding assembled interns through their postgame responsibilities. Skip Martinez, still in uniform, Bud Light in hand, dropped in to chat with Robbie, upset with the result but not deflated, explaining that he'd expected it could be a rough game. Few of his top pitchers had been available, a challenge that had been compounded by "inconsistent umpiring." Skip said he expected the next day's game at Auburn to be more competitive, as he'd be starting his ace, Nolan Sparks.

Soon the interns would leave, followed by Robbie, who would make the short two-block walk to the small house he crashed at during the season, his neighbors Joe and Sandra Kauffman having tuned in to the end of the game on John Carubba's YouTube broadcast before going to sleep hours earlier.

As usual, that left only one person still working at Dwyer as Thursday night dissolved into Friday morning: Erik Moscicki. Alone in the shower, stripped down to his shorts, he was using water from the shower jets to help scrub the infield clay out of the Muckdogs uniforms by hand over a folding table, as dirty brown water pooled at his feet.

19

Jamestown Tarp Skunks at Batavia Muckdogs

July 23

Saturday morning featured what had become an annual tradition, the "Challenger" baseball game at Dwyer Stadium for kids with physical and mental disabilities. I was excited to have my father and Bates visit me for it. Robbie and Nellie had made this one of the most important events of the summer and found in Skip Martinez a more-than-willing partner in delivering some smiles to local kids. Shelley Falitico, who helped organize the event for Arc of Genesee-Livingston-Orleans-Wyoming Counties, credited Robbie with breathing life into the game, which, she said, "had been hit and miss over the years before he arrived."

At around 10:00 a.m. a dozen or so children who had developmental issues of varying severity, from autism to fetal alcohol complications, took the field, where they joined Robbie, Skip Martinez, and the Muckdogs. When I learned of the event, I'd worried that perhaps the players—who by this point in the summer were borderline nocturnal—would be a bit lethargic at this relatively early hour after the previous night's game. Skip, who had participated in the game the previous summer and seen firsthand the impact it had on the kids and their families, made sure the players would take it seriously, though, telling them beforehand, "This is gonna touch you, seeing what we take for granted . . . We have what they would give anything for." He didn't even think the pep talk was necessary, though, as he was also confident that once they showed up, "Humanity takes over."

He was right. Shelley first introduced the assembled Muckdogs to the eager kids, telling them, "You're gonna play with the pros," and soon enough a scrimmage had begun, complete with beeping baseballs for kids with vision problems. One of the youngsters, Isaiah Cook, wandered off toward the warning track with Muckdogs catcher Mitch Fleming in tow. The mustached, six-foot-three Fleming towered over the young boy, but both were all smiles as they talked to each other. Another young boy, who had Cornelia de Lange syndrome, a rare genetic condition that affects growth and development, had been chanting "Muckdogs" all the way to the ballpark that morning, according to his mom. She added that he was a "ham who loves people and interaction." Sure enough, the little guy was soon talking trash to the players, who laughed admiringly at his bold willingness to tease them during the scrimmage.

Skip and the players had fun goofing up to make sure it was a close game, Skip fumbling a catch at home plate as a young girl crossed the plate with a huge smile on her face. When one of the youngsters threw a pitch that almost clipped Skip, he dropped his bat and shouted, "Have you ever seen anyone charge the mound?" in mock anger. Everyone laughed. "Seeing them smile is everything," he'd later say, his voice cracking with emotion. Said one of the moms, "To us something like this may not seem like a huge deal, but this is the World Series for these kids. My son's been talking about it since last year's game." As pitcher Julian Pichardo helped a girl who had been in a wheelchair step across home plate, general manager Marc Witt said simply, "There's so much shit going on in the world, but at least we can do some good like this."

By now some tears were welling up in my eyes as well. It was beautiful to see how much of an effect this little game in an obscure corner of western New York was having on everyone involved. By contrast, it occurred to me that just a few hundred miles to the southeast, the New York Yankees' Gerrit Cole would soon go to work to earn his $36 million annual salary. On this day he would give up nine hits and four runs in a 6–3 loss to the Baltimore Orioles. Cole had signed a nine-year, $324 million contract, which falls short of the mark set more recently by the Dodgers' Shohei Ohtani, the recipient of the largest-ever MLB contract, $700 million over ten years. If Ohtani played every single regular-season game for those ten years, he would earn $432,000 for each of the 1,620 games.

I wasn't trying to be insufferable or pessimistic. I *wanted* to continue being a fan of MLB, and took no pleasure in being infected by these thoughts. But how could we understand these hundreds of millions of dollars sloshing around between MLB owners and players while the staffers from Arc GLOW and YMCA, doing the unglamorous work of giving these children one of the best days of their lives, were each trying to get by on less than $50,000 a year?

I'd expressed this sentiment to enough people to know that many—including plenty of folks earning modest incomes themselves—were not particularly troubled by the discrepancy, justifying it on all sorts of different grounds, most rooted in recognition of rare talent and well-established market principles. Some, meanwhile, just wanted to be entertained and weren't especially interested in whether these salaries were "deserved" or good for society. Yet, when I observed the selflessness displayed by the professional and volunteer caretakers, the kindness of Skip and the players, and the joy radiating from the kids and their parents at this Challenger baseball game, I was more convinced than ever that the extreme economic inequality personified by Major League Baseball (and all professional sports) was corrosive to a healthy society—and, for me at least, it was becoming an almost insurmountable obstacle to my desire to remain a fan.

*   *   *

I spent the afternoon working while my dad explored Batavia with Bates, including *two* separate visits to Foxprowl Collectables (not sure how Bates finagled his grandpa into this). They enjoyed talking to the owner, Bill Hume, whom my father found every bit as friendly and engaging as I always did. Of particular interest to both Bates and my dad was how some Pokémon cards were selling for 50 cents while others—contained in special cases—commanded over $1,000. (To be honest, to this day, despite countless hours canvassing obscure collectibles stores in search of Bates's favorite cards, I'm not sure I totally understand the answer.) While there they ran into some *Ghostbusters* cosplayers from Buffalo whom Bill had arranged to appear on the field before the night's Muckdogs game at general manager Marc Witt's request. One ghostbuster said he'd fallen in love with the movie as a kid, explaining, "I just couldn't outgrow this . . . though when I'm not chasing ghosts I work in heating, plumbing, and refrigeration."

We swung by the Eli Fish brewery for some good food and a beer and then over to Dwyer for the night's game against the visiting Jamestown Tarp Skunks. I looked forward to catching up with Barry Powell, their assistant coach, whose homespun wisdom and tales of life on the road were always a delight. Before the game started, there were the usual pregame festivities, this time featuring the participants from the morning's Challenger game accompanying the Muckdogs onto the field for the ceremonial opening pitch, which one of them threw out. Then the *Ghostbusters* theme song began playing over the PA system and the cosplayers from Buffalo drove onto the field in their replica "Ectomobile." Bates and the other kids, of course, were thrilled.

While these sorts of goofy promotions were popular—especially with children—and have long been a feature of the minor league experience, not everyone embraced them. There were some long-time fans of teams that had lost their professional affiliates, whom I would characterize as being of the "old-school" variety, who felt as if they'd been robbed of superior baseball, only to find it replaced by a "carnival-like atmosphere." These are the words of Rich Schauf, who had attended nearly thirty minor league Muckdogs games a year for twenty years but no longer frequented Dwyer to watch the college ballplayers. Schauf lamented how now there was no connection to whether a player will make it to the big leagues. "I wasn't a fan of the money and greed of MLB, but there was a meaning in being connected to something bigger. Now you just know that behind the scenes it's a money grab, using gimmicks to get people there," Schauf said. He disapprovingly recalled a Muckdogs game where a helicopter flew over during the fourth inning, and the game was halted for the hovering chopper to drop candy for kids to chase down on the field. He said that was the day the new team "lost me" by demonstrating that baseball was taking a back seat to zany hijinks. Schauf wasn't alone. In the eyes of fans like him, drafted professionals fighting to make the big time had been replaced by middling college players, the vast majority of whom would never play professional baseball, while games now featured an endless succession of silly stunts between innings.

There was some truth to the gripes of fans like Rich. That said, it seemed impossible to deny that the Muckdogs under the ownership of Robbie and Nellie were certainly better than no baseball. Furthermore, minor league baseball had never been a stodgy affair geared only to attract baseball purists. If anything, the opposite was true, as it had a long and rich history of leveraging goofy antics and fan-friendly promotions to get people in the gate, with the ballpark experience having always been as much about entertaining families and casual fans as it had been about pleasing traditionalists.

Bates and I went to thank Cathy Preston, devoted fan, trivia buff, and scorekeeper, for the *Star Wars* cards she'd given him a few weeks ago. She told me that she'd been cramming for a big regional team trivia tournament the following day at Batavia Downs, reading the World Almanac she carried in her purse during her free time to prepare, hoping to avenge coming up three points short in her effort to make "nationals" the previous year. Cathy was almost always upbeat and enthusiastic, remarkable for someone who had to overcome so many challenges in life, from a childhood bout with cancer to the loss of her husband in a car crash. She enjoyed her life surrounded by friends in Batavia and within her pleasant century-old home, just three blocks from the stadium. The blue three-bedroom Craftsman was surrounded by flowers, with one room bursting with her treasured jigsaw puzzles, over five hundred board games, and nearly a thousand books (nonfiction arranged by subject, fiction alphabetically by author's name—"my mom was a librarian," she said with a smile).

As Cathy looked on, scorekeeping pencil methodically doing its work, Jamestown drew first blood, jumping out to a 1–0 lead in the top of the first inning with a double, followed by a single and a wild pitch before Batavia starter Joe Tobia stopped the bleeding with a strikeout and a groundout. The Jamestown starter got out of the first smoothly, allowing one hit and no runs. This must have come as a relief to Barry Powell, as he had lamented his team's hemorrhaging of players as the season neared its end, telling me that his strategy for the night was to "use the only two pitchers we have available and then pray for rain." Despite Powell saying they barely had enough players to shag batting practice, the Tarp Skunks were still in the playoff hunt with only a week left in the season. Batavia was no less motivated to win. General manager Marc Witt said a Muckdogs victory would be huge, helping both of his teams, Elmira and Batavia, in their pursuit of playoff berths and postseason seeds that would guarantee home playoff games.

Batavia tied the game 1–1 in the bottom of the second when Daniel Burroway scored on a single off the bat of Jerry Reinhart, who'd been scuffling at the plate for much of the summer, with a .222 batting average. His frustration had even boiled over in the form of some outbursts toward umpires that had gotten him tossed from a few games. Some speculated about the pressure that was weighing on him, knowing this was his last opportunity to catch the eye of professional scouts or land an independent-league contract.

Nonetheless, Reinhart's timely RBI delighted the crowd, which tonight included Russ Salway's son, Nick, now twenty-five and living in Rochester. Nick had begun going to Muckdogs games when Russ pushed him there in a stroller and continued until he left home for college. To Russ it seemed like just yesterday that Nick was a young boy eagerly asking him, "Who are we getting this year?" referring to their annual participation in the "host family" program for Muckdogs players. Pointing to the kids playing various pickup baseball games in their usual spot near the Jamestown bullpen, Nick said that the scene was nearly identical to when he was a boy and got together with his friends for games of "wall ball," where someone would throw the ball against the wall of the visitors' clubhouse while the others scrambled to field it. I played the same game as a child, sometimes even by myself, throwing the ball against the wall of a nearby school and fielding it, imagining the empty blacktop to be Baltimore's Memorial Stadium, and myself to be Cal Ripken Jr., my childhood hero.

Though some kids continued to play these games, as I took a look at Bates, who fidgeted nearby between requests to use an iPad, and often seemed ambivalent about games of catch, I wondered how much longer the appeal of these simple ball games would endure. With a time in which kids can lose themselves in exotic virtual real-

ity worlds nearly at hand, I couldn't help but doubt the lasting appeal
of throwing a ball against a brick wall. While I wrestled with these
discomfiting thoughts, Russ managed to snag a foul ball, which he
gave to Bates. Bates did at least say thank you, but I suspected I was
more impressed by Russ's gesture than he was.

*   *   *

Ernie Lawrence was sitting in the third-base grandstand a few rows
behind Russ's high-top table. I'd recently listened to a CD of him
and his son performing and teased him about the fact that there were
a few songs that almost sounded like outlaw country, with tales of
violence I didn't expect from a man who made rosaries as a hobby.
He let out a deep laugh and explained to me that "murder ballads are
a big deal in folk music," before telling me how his "appreciation of
the beauty of language as a songwriter" was influenced by Faulkner
and Steinbeck. I noticed Ernie was sitting next to a younger man,
who he would later tell me had been a special-education student he'd
gotten to know as a teacher. As a child, the young man had had a
difficult time reading, and so Ernie would read baseball books aloud
to him, the two of them especially enjoying *The Glory of Their Times*,
those colorful tales of baseball in the early part of the twentieth century. Their after-school reading sessions had cultivated in the young
man an enduring love of the game, and one that continued to this
day, as he would join Ernie in the grandstands for a few nights every
summer. Ernie's obvious affection for him—and Ernie's experience
teaching others with special needs over the years—likely explains
why he was so happy when I described the morning's Challenger
game and recounted the impact it had made on special-needs kids
from the community and their families.

Ernie then volunteered to me, in an almost offhand way, that he'd
already lost one kidney to cancer and that his remaining kidney was
now functioning at under 10 percent, which meant that dialysis was
necessary. He seemed accepting of this diagnosis and, while not cav-
alier or dismissive of its seriousness, didn't seem dejected or desirous
of sympathy. The only wish he did express was that the dialysis could
wait until October so that he could enjoy the rest of the baseball

season and "a nice autumn in western New York before I have to change my life."

The fact that he was able to maintain his equanimity despite this sobering medical assessment may have also been attributable to another part of his life that he only now revealed to me. Until recently, before his blood work had indicated a worsening in his kidney, he had volunteered regularly at a nearby hospice. He said he was driven to do so, in part, by the influence of a passage from the Gospel of Matthew that reads, "For I was hungry and you gave me something to eat, I was thirsty and you gave me something to drink, I was a stranger and you invited me in, I needed clothes and you clothed me, I was sick and you looked after me, I was in prison and you came to visit me."

His work in the hospice was not glamorous. He would help clean up after, and sometimes change the clothes of, the terminally ill— sometimes those with just days left to live. He also served as an unofficial chaplain. Ernie said the work came naturally to him, though, as he "had always been around death . . . My dad was dying when I was born and passed away when I was eight." The experience of sharing the final days with the dying had imbued him with "a clearer sense of death, and a recognition that it wasn't the end of life, but rather a transition." This reinforced the spiritual strength he derived from his faith, while also leading to a heightened appreciation of life and the finite time we have to enjoy it here on Earth. Even his son, Andy, was amazed by his father's ability to "deal with his struggles as well as he does while fending off despair and maintaining peace."

"I think I've had a happy life," Ernie would tell me, the simplicity of his words belying their significance.

Ernie was quick to deflect praise for his hospice work, observing that he was "inspired by the other volunteers who often didn't have a pot to piss in and no money to give, but gave of their time. They were simple people, without a lot of special training, the sort of people who are otherwise invisible in the community." Ernie's modesty aside, it takes a certain kind of person to "see" the sorts of people who labor every day in obscurity to make our communities better places. Maybe they are the ones who greet our children with a smile each morning at day care, or those who take care of elderly family members at nursing homes. I credit Ernie with helping kindle in me the desire to identify them in my life and try my best—in whatever small way I can—to recognize them for their efforts. And I credit Muckdogs games with providing the setting that sparked chain reactions of positivity like this.

*   *   *

The top of the fifth inning delivered an odd sight as the Jamestown pitcher stepped off the mound and began vomiting into the grass behind it. Barry Powell made his way out to check on him, as did the catcher, and they huddled together for a few minutes. Most everyone in Dwyer expected the young pitcher to be taken out of the game, and so it came as a surprise when Powell patted him on the backside and returned to the dugout, leaving him on the mound. The decision made sense, though, when one recalled Powell's pregame comments about how few pitchers he had. The Tarp Skunks simply didn't have a bullpen to turn to, especially when the starting pitcher—whatever stomach issues he may have been battling—had thus far been dominant, allowing only one run.

Powell's decision would pay off, as the Jamestown starter managed to get through two more innings without allowing a run, before Powell eventually pulled him following six strong innings in which he allowed only one run on four hits. The pitcher's gutsy performance was a good example of how "video doesn't tell you everything," as Powell had explained, referring to the risk of becoming overly reliant on dissecting video when assessing prospects. Powell rattled off the sort of intangibles that can be missed with too narrow a focus on quantitative metrics like velocity and spin rate, things like how the pitcher does when it's cold and windy or when he isn't feeling well. These sorts of real-life variables can sometimes remain invisible on an Excel spreadsheet but rather require "the feel you get in your gut when you see something with your eyes" to detect, Powell would say.

*   *   *

This role of the "gut" and "intuition"—born of years of experience—was increasingly considered suspect by devotees of baseball's analytics revolution, however. Sig Mejdal is in many ways the embodiment of this new breed, though his genial manner and candor stand in contrast to the more sharp-elbowed and abrasive personalities of some of his peers like Jeff Luhnow, for whom he worked in Houston. Mejdal graduated from UC Davis with bachelor's degrees in mechanical and aeronautical engineering, and later earned master's degrees in operations research and cognitive psychology before going on to work for NASA as a researcher focused on, among other things, how to best manage sleep schedules for astronauts. His interest in identifying ever-more-sophisticated ways to analyze data to make baseball decisions had been recreational at first, taking the form of highly competitive fantasy baseball, until the book *Moneyball* inspired a career change. He then began his improbable journey into the top echelons of the baseball world, a path that began with a job in Jeff Luhnow's analytics department with the St. Louis Cardinals. Mejdal would follow Luhnow to the Astros, before jumping to the Baltimore Orioles to work for their new general manager, Mike Elias, a Yale graduate and fellow alum of the Cardinals and Astros organizations.

While some baseball lifers like Hall of Fame manager Jim Leyland, who spent eighteen years playing and coaching in the minors before another twenty-two managing four major league teams, remain leery of the need to quantify everything—"a baseball person can tell you when a ball jumps off the bat, you don't really need analytics to tell you about swing speed and exit velocity, you can stand by the cage and see it"—the new generation personified by Mejdal has a virtually insatiable appetite for numbers. In an interview with *Baltimore* magazine, Mejdal gave voice to the new way of seeing things, explaining: "What you see as an exceptional slider, or a wonderful fastball, can be quantified. Instead of saying, 'He just has good stuff,' we're able to describe the stuff to three decimal points and begin to see the specific idiosyncratic behaviors of the different hitters, and how they succeed or struggle against pitches that aren't just called 'a slider,' but instead a pitch of 83 miles per hour with 18 inches of horizontal movement, and 1.5 inches of depth."

Though Mejdal, and indeed most of the acolytes of this new way of thinking, claim that the best decisions will generally result from combining analytical firepower with human wisdom, when one digs deeper it sure seems that data is trumping experience. Mejdal recommended the book *Super Crunchers: Why Thinking-by-Numbers Is the New Way to Be Smart,* and while he didn't claim to subscribe to everything in it, if it is to be seen as illustrative of his line of thinking, it does not bode well for the human side of the decision-making equation.

In fact, the book cites studies that suggest decisions based on experience plus data actually perform worse than those based purely on data. "Humans too often wave off the machine predictions and cling to their personal convictions," the author, Ian Ayres, contends. He also approvingly cites another academic who said, "Intuition can be your worst enemy," in what Ayres describes as "the struggle of intuition, personal experience, and philosophical inclination waging war against the brute force of numbers." Frighteningly, though, the logical extension of this would seem to be a sport in which computers eventually are entrusted with just about every decision, from which players to draft, how to evaluate and compensate them, all the way down to lineup choices and in-game strategy. Can we imagine managers disappearing altogether, replaced by a dugout robot signaling the batter to bunt on the next pitch?

Perhaps this would in fact be the "most efficient" and successful way to manage an organization, but it's hard not to see the game being diminished as it begins to resemble a chessboard on which two Deep Blue supercomputers (the first computer to beat a world chess champion) square off. We've already seen the extent to which these quantitative models tend to produce similar outputs, which serves to homogenize the game by elevating the same skills and strategies. Barry Powell noted how quickly organizational uniqueness can disappear, the days of "Earl Weaver loving the long ball, the aggressiveness of Billy-Ball, and St. Louis embracing small ball with squeezes and hit and runs and steals" giving way to a more boring sport where power trumps just about everything, and all teams begin to look the same.

Near the end of his book, Ayres succinctly articulates the essence of his philosophy, which, I think one can safely say, is shared by most of baseball's ruling class today: "A broader quest for a life untouched by Super Crunching is both infeasible and ill-advised. Instead of a Luddite rejection of this powerful new technology, it is better to become a knowledgeable participant in the revolution."

For those whose sole objective is wins and losses, it can be hard to argue this logic. After a decade of mediocrity, the Astros, for example, rode their analytic prowess to become a near-constant post-season contender beginning in 2015, to include four World Series appearances, winning it twice (although their success was marred by their entanglement in sign-stealing scandals). And the Orioles, under Mike Elias and Mejdal, have bounced back from losing over 100 games in each of the 2018, 2019, and 2021 seasons (the 2020 season was abbreviated by COVID) to building a foundation of talent that appears ready to contend in the fiercely competitive AL East for years to come (that is, *if* the team's ownership proves willing to pay enough to keep some their blossoming young stars).

But the impact of a brutally efficient governing philosophy that subordinates man to machine on the game's appeal is more complicated. One can argue that the general managers who continue to push the sport in this direction are simply doing their job—which is to win—to the best of their ability. But doesn't the MLB commissioner, as the supposed steward of the game, have an obligation to do what's best for its long-term health, and perhaps even take into consideration the preferences of the fans on whose money the game depends to survive?

Perhaps there is at least a dawning awareness of this tension; in 2021, MLB hired Theo Epstein—whose shrewd front-office leadership had helped both the Boston Red Sox and Chicago Cubs overcome epic championship droughts to win World Series titles—to study ways in which to combat the deleterious impact of an over-reliance on analytics on the game. When he stepped down from his post in Chicago he had said, "The executives, like me, who have spent a lot of time using analytics and other measures to try to optimize individual and team performance have unwittingly had a negative impact on the aesthetic value of the game and the entertainment value of the game in some respects." Or, as Bill Kauffman puts it a little more forcefully, "These people are turning professional baseball into a rationalized, computerized, standardized monstrosity without heart or soul, and I for one hope MLB collapses. Baseball—the real thing, the game and the community it brings together—will still be there. Thank God."

The rule changes MLB implemented prior to the 2023 season—most importantly the pitch clock, limiting pickoff attempts, eliminating the shift, and increasing the size of the bases—have in fact improved the fan experience, shortening game times by nearly half an hour, from over three hours to just a notch above two and a half. Stolen bases have also been brought back from the dead, returning more action to the game. While these changes were welcome indications that the sport was aware it had a problem, the battle is far from over. Batting averages are still near historic lows, and too few balls are put in play. Moreover, tuning in to a game on television today can be disorienting to anyone who grew up when there was still a touch of poetry to the broadcast. Today statistics often substitute for evocative descriptions, as on-field action is broken down into component numbers, with spin rates, exit velocities, and launch angles replacing an artful turn of phrase. Can't we take even a moment to admire the majesty of a home run as it arcs into the sunset before being peppered with sophisticated computer-generated graphics? Or, as Muckdogs fan Ginny Wagner even more succinctly said with exasperation in response to this obsession with data, "Just show me green grass and the sky!"

*   *   *

Dwyer Stadium, thankfully, was still such a simple and sustaining place. As the game against the Tarp Skunks entered the seventh inning, Batavia's offense remained stagnant, having plated only one run and now trailing 3–1. Betsey and I were discussing her favorite author, Thomas Hardy, and *Two on a Tower,* her favorite story of his. It was another tale of doomed love—in this case an unhappily married woman who falls in love with a younger man—of the sort that appealed to Betsey. I sometimes wondered what it was about these stories of unrequited love that Betsey—who remained single in her fifties—so enjoyed, but I felt uncomfortable asking, though I suspected she had some stories to tell. I did know that Betsey was a devoted godmother to Ginny's boys, Thomas and James, whose photographs could be found throughout her book-lined house. When

Ginny underwent a brutal fifty-two-hour labor with Thomas, due to the umbilical cord getting wrapped around his neck, it was Betsey whom her husband, Charlie, turned to for help. She was there in no time, something Charlie, who was nearing physical and emotional exhaustion himself, will never forget.

Turning from Hardy back to baseball, Betsey and Ginny continued to grumble at Batavia's uncharacteristic offensive silence. Perhaps frustrated by the Muckdogs' inability to generate any offense, or maybe just tired after a long day, they soon said goodbye and took off back to Buffalo.

Not long after they had made their exit, the Muckdogs would score a run in the bottom of the seventh and again threaten in the eighth, when Jerry Reinhart came to bat poised to be the hometown hero with two outs and men on second and third, but their potential rally would end when he flied out harmlessly to third base to end the inning. The Muckdogs would be retired in order in the ninth and fall to the visiting Tarp Skunks 3–2.

After the game, Robbie, general manager Marc Witt, and the team's interns gathered in the team's cinder-block office adjacent to the Dwyer Stadium entrance, trading jokes and taking a short breather before taking on the remaining tasks that needed to be completed before they could finally go home. One person who wasn't smiling was YouTube broadcaster John Carubba, who often seemed to take losses harder than anyone, save perhaps clubhouse manager Erik Moscicki. Carubba came shuffling into the front office with a frustrated mien. Gesticulating with the cane he carried, he lamented the team's batting slump and fretted about the following day's matchup against the Niagara Power, whom the Muckdogs had struggled with all summer, dropping three of their last four. "We can't turn Niagara into the 1998 Yankees," Carubba said, contrasting the lowly 14-28 Niagara Power with the late-nineties Yankees dynasty. Carubba's consternation seemed to sail over the heads of most everyone in the room, few of whom I suspect were even aware of how the Muckdogs had struggled against Niagara.

As the staff finally peeled themselves off their chairs armed with garbage bags to collect trash from the grandstands, the Tarp Skunks began to file out of their locker room to board the charter bus and begin their roughly two-hour drive back on Interstate 90 toward

Jamestown. It would mark another day in Barry Powell's forty-seven-year baseball career, one in which he'd spent thousands of hours on nights like this traversing lonely highways to and from small ball-parks tucked into towns like Batavia, Jamestown, Elmira, Auburn, Pulaski, Bristol, Danville, and countless more. He wouldn't have it any other way, though. "Knowing my destination is a baseball game, the journey itself is always amazing," he said, continuing, "I enjoy the back roads . . . You're able to travel at a slower pace and take in how people live in that part of the country." Like long-haul truckers, he had his favorite regions and routes, especially enjoying the Blue Ridge Parkway when it showcases the Appalachian Mountains with their "gorgeous leaves in the fall," preferable to the "traffic and speed-ing drivers" on Interstate 81.

Powell is a reflective man, seemingly more aware of baseball's place in the cosmic scheme of things than other lifers whose world-view sometimes doesn't appear to extend far beyond the foul lines. "When you get older you think a lot," he said; "you ride the bus and look out the window. When I do, I'm still grateful and thankful the good Lord allowed me to do this for so long," continuing, "I'm sixty-seven and the kids call me Grandpa. It's not all about who will make it to the majors, but about helping them become the best they can be and live a wholesome and good life. I'm not in it for wealth but for a good life with good people. In the news today there are a lot of negatives, but this sport reminds you there are still a lot of good people out there."

Still, he was a competitive man and harbored one final baseball dream. There were two more weeks in the Tarp Skunks' summer campaign before Powell would head home to his assigned region of Virginia and North Carolina to continue scouting for the Phillies. After nearly half a century in the game, he was still searching for the kid who, "when I am dead and gone, will be in Cooperstown, and they'll say, 'Barry signed him.'"

20

Auburn Doubledays at Batavia Muckdogs

July 28

I was sitting in the Eli Fish brewery as sunlight streamed through the windows from Main Street outside. The Muckdogs banner from the season ticket holder party remained where it had been on that spring evening months earlier. This small town, that had not so long ago felt foreign to me, now felt comfortable. I'd even made friends, something that isn't easy to do at age forty-six. At the same time, I was hit with the sobering realization that there were only a few weeks remaining in the season, and these pleasant evenings under the glow of the lights at Dwyer Stadium would soon be over. And then it would be nearly ten long months before the crack of the bat would again echo through the grandstands, as the regulars greeted each other and made their way to their usual seats, as if emerging from a winter's hibernation.

Perched at a high top, sipping on an Eli Fish IPA, I began to fully understand just how much, and why, some of these fans looked forward to Opening Day. I had discussed the approaching end of the season with Betsey a few days earlier. While she acknowledged that she and Ginny would "be in mourning and suffer from baseball withdrawal," she did try to console me—and herself—with the reminder that there would still be a couple of months of summer to enjoy after the last pitch was thrown at Dwyer. She planned to spend some of that time at a family cottage on the Canadian side of Lake Erie, hoping to get out on the water as much as possible.

On this night, most of those in attendance at Dwyer knew that a victory would clinch the PGCBL Western Division and ensure home field when the playoffs began. Tyler Prospero would be on the mound for the Muckdogs, looking to continue his strong season. The visiting Doubledays of Auburn were no pushover, though, entering the game with a solid 24-20 record.

It would be a special night for the Kauffman clan, as Joe and Sandra had celebrated their sixty-fourth wedding anniversary a few days ago with a dinner at Eli Fish, while Bill's only child, Gretel, was home visiting from Idaho. The daughter of a proud "localist," who in many ways shared her father's worldview, Gretel had nonetheless opted to move out west to pursue a career in journalism in the small town of Twin Falls. Gretel had inherited some of her father's flair for the written word and had displayed her narrative chops as an undergraduate at Notre Dame, where she penned a wonderful essay on her experience working at Dwyer Stadium's concession stand. In it, she captured, in observations at times lyrical and at times funny, the unchanging rituals of generations of children as they spent their summers growing up inside Dwyer Stadium's gates. Describing the concession stand, where she eventually worked and did "nothing that required skill, like working the grill or register," Gretel recalled:

> As I entered middle school and graduated to roaming the stadium with my friends each night, eating the same burnt hot dogs between bouts of tormenting the mascot, I came to view the employees with a sort of awe. The mass of red-visored teen elders emanated untouchable intrigue and the effortless coolness of being just a bit older, and this energy radiated through the park itself, tingeing the air with mystery and promise— as if anything could happen while "Who Let the Dogs Out" played on a warm summer night . . .
>
> One summer mid-college I, a concession-stand retiree, returned home and realized I had regained my taste for ballpark nachos. An electricity still filled the air, a sense of mystery and promise, though it wasn't mine to feel. I stood in line for food, eyeing the new faces who would inevitably bungle my order. *Kids*, I thought, but there was something timeless and familiar about them, and I smiled.

Gretel joined in the applause when the Muckdogs jumped out to a 1–0 lead in the bottom of the second on a Jerry Reinhart triple followed by a sacrifice fly, energizing the crowd, which always responded with extra enthusiasm when the former Batavia High School star made a valuable contribution on the field. Auburn, though, clawed back with two runs in the top of the third, taking advantage of what appeared to be a blown call by the umpires, before Prospero was finally able to escape the inning having surrendered two runs, and Batavia now trailing 2–1.

Curious to get public address announcer Paul Spiotta's take on the controversial call, I dipped into the press box to ask him about it. I discovered him more eager to discuss his recent Strat-O-Matic World Series victory over his friend John in Arizona, about which he was still ebullient. With the final out of their World Series, they had completed 690 games over the course of two years, four months, and four days. Each game had taken about an hour, though Paul's wife joked that it was longer when you factored in the time it took to log the stats and produce postgame narrative summaries.

Paul was good friends with Bill, and upon learning that Gretel was home visiting and at the game, he said, "Bill would give anything to have Gretel live here," which I'd already surmised, having witnessed how excited he and Lucine had been anticipating this visit. Bill had even retrieved their two baseball mitts and laid them out before she arrived so that they could keep alive their tradition of playing catch together whenever she came home to visit.

This sentimental talk of children made me think of Bates, and his experience about a month ago announcing the batters over the PA system. Recalling his initial nervousness followed by his surprisingly good delivery, and the pride that resulted from it, made me miss the little guy even more than usual, and left me saddened that I'd spent so much of the summer away from him, as well as Marcy and Shea. While not too many of the little episodes that I missed from Bates and Shea each day were especially noteworthy on their own, I knew that collectively they would make up a childhood, and that I might regret missing even bits of it. I'll always remember my father telling me how he'd never forgotten the last time I'd ever voluntarily raised my hand to grasp his when crossing a busy street. It had been outside Baltimore's Memorial Stadium when I was six years old as we approached the stadium for my first major league baseball game. Tears come to my eyes almost every time I recall that story now and imagine Bates, who would soon turn six, one day soon no longer reaching for my hand.

Exiting the press box, I saw Dr. Ross Fanara in his usual aisle seat a few rows behind the Muckdogs dugout. Neither Kartier nor Kamdyn was with him. I asked where his great-grandsons were, and he told me that they'd been left at home as a punishment for misbehaving. As was often the case, it had been Shirley who'd assumed the role of disciplinarian, with Ross confessing that if it had been up to him, he probably would've brought them. Still, the boys had not been shortchanged in the fun department, as Ross had already brought them to karate and to the Pok-A-Dot restaurant, where the western New York standby, Beef on Weck, was their favorite, before Shirley had imposed house arrest for the rest of the evening.

The heart of the Muckdogs order helped them to regain the lead in the bottom of the fourth when a double by center fielder Abner Benitez drove in two runs, pushing them ahead 3–2. This delighted Betsey and Ginny, who had adopted the stout Benitez as their favorite player. They were sitting near Bill Kauffman and his parents, Joe and Sandra. Even fiftysomething grad student and playwright Eric Zwieg was there, as his Mets were not playing. It always felt funny to see him somewhere besides his usual perch at the counter of the Pub Coffee Hub. I made the mistake of telling him how the major league baseball fan in me had been conflicted of late, encouraged by the Mets' free-agency spending yet frustrated by the contraction of the minor leagues and the overall direction MLB was going. I had intended it as an attempt to establish a rapport with him but, as with so many of the others, it had clearly come short.

"We'll get along okay as Mets fans without you," he said, stone-faced.

Thankfully the rest of the gang was more welcoming. Ginny kindly offered me some of the snacks she'd packed after she had prepared a chicken dinner for her family to enjoy while she was gone. I chatted with Betsey about her summer trips to Oxford to join other "nerds who love books" taking courses at Christ Church college. She loved the "Oxford dons" but, even more, the fact that everyone there was motivated by a genuine love of literature as opposed to the competition that drives many undergraduates. Betsey, who said she loved "studying three-hundred-year-old etymology," was proud to own the entire *Oxford English Dictionary* (*OED*), its twenty volumes carefully displayed and easily accessible on a cherry table in her living room. "I treat it like a plant, with lots of coddling," she would say. She likely inherited this love of words and language from her father, who, she said, "had the greatest vocabulary on the planet and read everything." She was in good company on this night, as fellow Muckdogs die-hard Bill Kauffman also possessed a prodigious vocabulary, explaining how he sometimes "played a game where I'll think of a word and then try to think of all the conceivable synonyms for it . . . Why say 'yellow' when you can say 'xanthous'?" His mother, Sandra, sitting nearby, remembered how, as a child, he would always read books with a dictionary nearby to look up unfamiliar words, resulting in no small amount of teasing from his brother.

Amazingly, it would not be the only reference to the *OED* during the night's game. In fact, not more than twenty minutes later, the dictionary would come up again when I said hello to Cathy Preston. She greeted me with yet another softball trivia question, asking me what NFL team's helmet featured a logo on only one side of it. She knew I lived near Pittsburgh and that all but the most sheltered Pittsburgh residents would know it was the Steelers. Always looking for ways to improve her trivia knowledge, she then told me she occasionally looked at the *OED* to prepare for competitions and that she loved the book *The Professor and the Madman* about its creation. Unfortunately, her cramming at Eli Fish had not yielded the result she was looking for at the recent regional team competition at Batavia Downs, where her team had again come up just short. "I guess we're just tragic like the other Buffalo sports teams," she said, referring to the Bills, and their epic four consecutive Super Bowl losses, and the Buffalo Sabres, who had the longest active NHL playoff appearance drought. This season's Muckdogs squad was showing the potential to change this narrative, though, as they had a chance to clinch a home playoff game tonight with a victory. Cathy told me that a good friend was visiting the following week, but that she'd had to explain to her, "I love you to pieces, but if the Muckdogs make the playoffs, I have to be there."

Skip Martinez pulled starter Tyler Prospero after he threw five innings and allowed three runs on six hits, turning to hard-throwing right-handed reliever Trey Bacon, who had proven to be one of the most reliable arms out of the bullpen. Bacon would again demonstrate impressive command to go with his sharp fastball, shutting down the Doubledays over the course of three innings of shutout ball. The Muckdogs offense, meanwhile, knocked around Auburn's relievers, punctuated by a wild bottom of the eighth where a base hit, three walks, a hit batsman, and an Auburn error resulted in two Muckdogs runs and a 6–3 lead. By now there was an energy coursing through the crowd that I hadn't felt before, as fans knew they were only three outs away from a postseason berth.

I spotted Nolan Sparks warming up in the bullpen, which suggested how much Skip wanted this win, as he had been the team's— and indeed the league's—most dominant starter all season but had never appeared in relief. In his eight starts Sparks had given up only one earned run to lead the league with an ERA of 0.22. With the playoffs so tantalizingly close, Skip's decision to turn to Sparks to close it out made it clear he wasn't leaving anything to chance.

Meanwhile in the grandstands, the evening's literary undercurrent continued when Ernie Lawrence introduced me to his son-in-law, who was a librarian and an English teacher, joking that "we have lots of librarians here tonight," as his wife was also one. Ernie, with a trace of deadpan humor, worried that a postseason game on Sunday would force him to decide between coming to the game and attending a "lecture on barns" that a friend was delivering as part of the 150th anniversary of the Wyoming County Historical Pioneer Association, of which Ernie was a trustee. His wry smile gave away the fact that his decision had already been made—an opportunity to learn more about regional barns would have to wait.

As the fans chatted all around me, Nolan Sparks was making quick work of the heart of the Auburn order. He quickly struck out the first two batters before a flurry of precision fastballs exploded into catcher Mitch Fleming's glove to strike out Auburn's cleanup hitter and end the game, sending the Muckdogs into the playoffs as the PGCBL's Western Division champions. As the players mobbed the pitcher's mound to celebrate and the remaining fans roared in approval, Ernie turned to me with a big smile and simply said, "Looks like you picked a good year to come to Batavia."

Several players dumped water on Skip and attempted to douse Robbie as well, who displayed some dexterity from his hockey days in dodging it before head groundskeeper Larry Hale finally got him from behind. The eighties rock ballad "Gloria" played as Skip gathered the team along the third-base line, congratulated them on making the playoffs, and told them their work wasn't done until they "brought a championship back to Batavia." The team then slowly made their way to the clubhouse, many of them stopping to sign some autographs for fans lining the fence along the left-field line on their way. As the players dug into large boxes of Ficarella's pizza, Olivia Rodrigo's "good 4 u" turned up as always after a win, Assistant Coach Tom Eaton was already at work in his office fine-tuning the pitching rotation for the playoffs. He knew it would be tough even with the best plan, as there would now be a game every day until the season ended, and there weren't enough top-end starters to go around. Skip, meanwhile, was savoring the moment with his players, dumping a can of Bud Light on the head of the team's catcher, and in many ways its inspirational leader, Mitch Fleming.

For Robbie and his front-office team, though, the confirmation of a playoff berth meant the day's work had just begun. It was approaching midnight on Thursday night, and they now had a Sunday afternoon home playoff game to sell tickets for. It would be a challenge, since advance group sales had constituted a large portion of regular-season ticket sales, and obviously there wouldn't be any of those for a playoff game that, until now, hadn't been on the schedule. It looked as if Robbie's other team, Elmira, would likely sneak into the playoffs as the bottom seed in the Western Division, meaning they would play on the road and, more importantly to Robbie, would be a money loser. This awareness made him even more determined to sell as many tickets in Batavia as possible.

As Robbie massaged his tortured feet by placing a baseball underneath them, one at a time, and shifting his weight back and forth, he spoke to his assembled interns and explained how important the next few days would be and that they would need to focus on getting the word out about Sunday's playoff game immediately, whether it was on the radio, in the newspaper, on social media, or literally holding signs at busy intersections in town. As the interns, clad in assorted Muckdogs T-shirts and ball caps, gobbled up leftover pizza and listened to Robbie, the gathering had the feel of a late-night dorm room assemblage of college kids planning to go canvass for a political leader who had captured their imagination, their youthful adrenaline overriding the fatigue that might otherwise have set in.

Robbie was not always the warmest guy to work for. His humor sometimes had a biting quality, more typical of the hockey locker rooms where he'd spent much of his life than the meetings composed mostly of college kids he was now running. And his parsimonious ways had become more obvious as the summer went on. That said, Nellie's frequent observation that he was the "hardest-working man she ever met" seemed accurate. He almost never tired, and on the few occasions when he did seem to be wearing down, and when his bum foot bothered him more than usual, he would usually just grimace and soldier on. Nellie told me that they were planning a trip to Cancun after the season because "Robbie deserves it." He clearly occupied an exalted place in her estimation, likely due in part to the fact that reliable and devoted men had been in short supply during her childhood as she bounced from one foster family to the next. I remembered when she told me how scared she had been when COVID first hit, and I had incorrectly assumed her primary fear was of its impact on their professional livelihood. She had corrected me, though, and told me that she'd been most afraid of losing Robbie, who she said had a heart condition, leading her to wonder, "What if he gets it, what would I do without him? He's my best friend."

Meanwhile in the locker room, I figured Erik Moscicki would be methodically working his way through his postgame tasks alone, the players having returned to their dorms to unwind for a few hours before bed. I was right, except for one noteworthy exception. He was joined by Caleb Rodriguez, the five-foot-ten middle infielder from Kean University in New Jersey. On the field he didn't have much power at the plate but was sure-handed defensively. Off the field he was soft-spoken and relatively unassuming. Tonight, though, he'd stayed behind to help Erik—whom he would sometimes gently encourage not to work so hard—and was busy returning the locker room chairs to their designated spots, putting jerseys in their lockers after Erik had finished cleaning them, and ferrying garbage bags filled with the discarded remnants of the night's regular-season Western Division championship celebration out to the dumpster.

Caleb carried himself with a quiet dignity, proud to help and a touch annoyed that it hadn't occurred to any of his teammates to lend a similar helping hand. Erik would later tell me that this wasn't the first time Caleb had remained behind and helped to lighten his load of responsibilities. It was clear that while Erik didn't expect any help—and would certainly never ask for it—he did appreciate it. And so I said good night to them, the young man from Batavia who was overcoming cerebral palsy to contribute to the local ball club and his new friend, a smooth fielder from North Brunswick, New Jersey, quietly laboring together late into the night to make sure the locker room was squared away. Players would begin arriving for early batting practice in little more than twelve hours.

21

Elmira Pioneers at Batavia Muckdogs

July 30

On the afternoon before the regular-season finale, I stopped at Betsey's home in Buffalo's Elmwood Village. I'd been lured there as much by her pleasant company as by the opportunity to explore her remarkable book collection more carefully. As my wife, Marcy, will attest, I'm drawn to libraries, bookstores, and book-lined homes such as Betsey's like moth to flame, and Marcy generally winced when she saw me emerge from such places carrying yet more books to try to squeeze into our home, which is of modest size and already jammed with about as many books (probably more in her estimation) as it can comfortably contain. Marcy likely had nightmares of her once tidy house suddenly going the way of Bill Kauffman's attic office, with books overflowing their shelves and piled up on every available inch of floor space.

Elmwood Village was only forty-three miles from Batavia, but culturally it felt a world apart. Beautiful homes, many, like Betsey's, dating back to the early years of the twentieth century, overlooked streets lined with mature trees. Betsey had called the neighborhood home for most of her life. Despite having traveled widely and experienced an itch every decade or so since she was a young girl to move to a more exotic locale—at various times being seduced by the allure of Rome, Paris, and even smaller Kinsale, Ireland—and going so far as to research overseas properties, she never pulled the trigger. "What would I do there?" she'd find herself wondering. "I love my surroundings and my life here, and it makes me mentally and spiritually happy . . . I love travel, but whenever I get home and see Elmwood Village and pull up to my house, once again close to my friends and family, I can't imagine leaving."

As I slowly navigated the neighborhood's stately boulevards, I couldn't help but notice the number of rainbow, BLM, and Ukraine signs and flags adorning houses, a stark difference from the Trump signs more common to Batavia. Living outside Pittsburgh, in what has emerged as one of the epicenters of a hotly contested political "battleground state," had turned me off to the ubiquitous signage communicating one's political allegiances. "Hate Has No Home Here" signs were less convincing after seeing, too often, such tolerance being extended only to those who shared the owner's ideological convictions, while on the other side, "Fuck Biden" and "Let's Go Brandon" signs were even more obvious symbols of societal corrosion.

Political signaling aside, I nonetheless found myself falling for this delightful neighborhood of open-air cafés (for the few months Buffalo's weather would allow it), farmer's markets, and independent bookstores and record shops. Whereas Batavia had been devoured by roadside chains, except for a handful of local institutions like the Northside Deli and a few trailblazing businesses like the Pub Coffee Hub and the Eli Fish Brewing Company, here one could still find the sorts of independently owned businesses that gave a neighborhood character.

Betsey greeted me at the door with a LEGO book for Bates in hand, having remembered how much he'd enjoyed the LEGO Club she ran at her library. I commented on the number of people strolling through the neighborhood, and she told me that it was a "garden walk" day, where proud residents could show off their gardens— some of which Betsey said were "as nice as those in England"—to passersby.

As had been the case on previous visits, a sense of tranquility soon enveloped me in Betsey's charming living room, its books staring down at me seductively. Some were rare and especially treasured, such as a signed copy of *The Red Badge of Courage* from her late father's collection. The extent to which I enjoyed this little oasis of calm again reminded me of the perpetual chaos that comes with raising young kids, something that is accompanied by sublime rewards of its own, but is also characterized by the general absence of even a few minutes of this sort of peacefulness. At the same time, I couldn't help but imagine that Betsey may have welcomed some of the disorder kids introduced to a home. I noticed how proudly she displayed a handwritten note on her refrigerator from a young girl she was friends with from Rochester, and how she always commented on how much she enjoyed Ginny's boys, who, though they were young men now, she boasted, "still hug me and say 'I love you.'"

Showing me around, Betsey happily told me that if she needed space she could sit on her back deck and "appreciate the silence," broken up intermittently by the pleasant singing of birds. "I know it sounds hokey, but I love St. Francis, and it's nice to wind down outside, alone in solitude, after talking all day at the library."

Betsey delighted in the diversity of both her neighborhood and greater Buffalo, which she said was a "refugee city," welcoming those fleeing oppression from all over the world. She derived a quiet satisfaction from volunteer work, something she didn't advertise but was happy to discuss if asked. Betsey worked through her parish, Our Lady of Hope, as well as with Jewish Family Services, to tutor refugee children in English and math, and found herself impressed by how "quickly they can suck up what I am teaching." The most recent arrivals she hoped to work with were from Venezuela and Congo. As with Ernie Lawrence and his volunteer work at a local hospice, and Dr. Ross Fanara, who, along with his wife, Shirley, was selflessly raising two young great-grandchildren, there seemed to be a correlation between helping others and personal happiness. As it did for Ernie and Dr. Fanara, religious faith occupied an important place in Betsey's life, though, like them, she didn't wear it on her sleeve. In fact, I wouldn't have even known about it aside from her casually mentioning having "biked to mass" before a Saturday evening Muckdogs game. And, of course, to the occasional smiling reference to a prayer for a Muckdogs victory.

Also like Ernie's and Dr. Fanara's, her faith was not of the facile, unchallenged and unchallenging, variety. Ernie was acutely aware of life's fragility, and occasional tragedy, with his work at the hospice, not to mention his own kidney failure and dialysis. Dr. Fanara, meanwhile, had been struck with polio as a young boy, and later in life had to confront the physical and psychological challenges associated with having to raise two young boys while in his late seventies and early eighties. Betsey, for her part, had seen her younger brother's life "shattered physically and mentally in a nanosecond" when he was rendered a quadriplegic after a diving accident as a young man, before passing at the age of thirty-eight. She would say, "I was angry he became a quadriplegic. I questioned how this loving god could allow this. There can't be a god. As a kid I was very aware of poor kids throughout the world, long-lasting wars, but in a removed, abstract way. But when you see your little brother with a halo screwed into his skull and hear heartless doctors announce to your parents he will not walk or move again, faith seems ridiculous. In time, though, I found myself praying when things would go awry, and my faith started to slowly grow."

Betsey's voracious reading also demonstrated that hers was not a faith insulated from the doubts introduced by great thinkers. Her favorite, Thomas Hardy, was a professed agnostic and famously skeptical of organized religion, authoring works that featured human tragedy without offering a psychological lifeline in the form of spiritual salvation. Betsey would say that she still loved and appreciated his writing, and that "it didn't faze me with my religion . . . Sure, I've had my doubts, but so did Mother Teresa." All of this resonated with me, as I too tried to be a regular churchgoer (though, admittedly, with a rather blemished attendance record), and wanted to believe but, like most of us, had experienced the sorts of things in life that make unquestioning belief difficult. Witnessing the deaths of close friends in Iraq had struck at the core of my faith. Like Betsey, I had also devoured books of all kinds, many of which powerfully expressed worldviews challenging organized religion. Dostoevsky's *The Brothers Karamazov* was my favorite novel due in part to the battle between a mystical faith and a reason-based unbelief powerfully presented in its pages. All of which helps to explain, I think, why I found myself drawn to her peaceful home, pleasant company, and stimulating conversation. And a bit amazed that a brief introduction in the Dwyer Stadium grandstands had produced this friendship.

It was soon time to make my way to Batavia for the regular season's final game, against the visiting Elmira Pioneers. Both teams were headed for the playoffs—possibly to face off against each other in the opening round. It was hard for me to believe this special season—beginning with my white-knuckle winter drives up through the snow from Pittsburgh to start meeting Muckdogs fans—was about to end.

Before heading to the ballpark, there was one stop I needed to make: Kelly's Holland Inn. I'd driven past this local Batavia dive bar on many occasions, and each time had resolved to drop in when I had the time but had somehow never managed to make it happen. The season almost over, I was determined to check it out before it was too late.

I'll admit that I've long been drawn to dive bars nearly as powerfully as musty bookstores and libraries, for the cheap beer, of course, but also the people watching. When living in New York's East Village, I was always curious to learn more about the patrons of the local dives who could be seen shuffling into them when most of the neighborhood was grabbing a breakfast sandwich on the way to work, the kind of dispossessed eccentrics profiled in books like Joseph Mitchell's *McSorley's Wonderful Saloon*.

Kelly's was one of the few remaining bars in a downtown that had once been packed with them. Ruth McEvoy, in her book *The History of the City of Batavia*, describes Joe Gaczewski's Saloon, not far from where the Pok-A-Dot restaurant now stands, as being dubbed the "Bowl of Blood" by local cops in rowdy pre-Prohibition days. Joe Kauffman recalled that when he was growing up in the 1940s, there must have been nearly ten bars on Main Street alone, with even more spilling onto State Street. He and his buddies would see it all as they darted through town as young kids—Joe atop his prized Schwinn bike—from "bums fighting behind the gin mills" to the cops walking the beat who maintained order in part by "just as soon taking a billy club to your head as look at you."

With a half-gray, half-green aluminum fake clapboard exterior perched unsteadily on an exposed concrete foundation, only one small window allowing any light in, Kelly's looked like the kind of place one went more to drown one's sorrows than to celebrate successes. Its potholed parking lot was usually populated by a few beat-up cars. The bar's online presence was, well, nearly nonexistent—very few Yelp reviews and zero Instagram posts, its patrons not the sort of people who visit bars to take cute photos in front of exotic, overpriced cocktails. One of the few reviews that did exist, posted by

Clark on Tripadvisor eight years ago, reads, "I feel like I stepped into a time warp. Junky old posters hanging on the wall from the 80's. Dirty walls and floor. Sketchy crowd. Only good thing was that the beer was cold, and cheap. Don't know if they offer food but I am certain I would not trust ordering if they did." Clark was not all wrong, though it was perhaps a tad unfair, based on the few visits I would eventually make, to label the crowd, such as it was, "sketchy." Then again, seeing as how I was one of them, perhaps I am a touch biased.

On this late afternoon, my first as a Kelly's patron, I ran into a man whose experience was painfully emblematic of the sort of sad tale one might expect to encounter in such a place. He'd worked at Batavia's *Daily News* for thirty-five years, an expert at the production side of the paper, which, until 2019, was published six days a week. He told me, over bottles of beer (Kelly's didn't serve draft beer), how he'd "learned everything there was to know about putting a paper out," something they did by hand for years before newspapers turned to high-tech graphic technology. He suspected layoffs were coming, though, when he began to notice that there were fewer and fewer paid advertisements in the paper. Sure enough, his premonition was proven correct. Advances in technology, and the merciless imperatives of cost savings and efficiency, led to the paper letting go of dozens of employees whose skills were no longer considered to be of value. He was one of them.

Sunlight barely penetrated through the one bay window facing the hockey rink across the street as he sat nursing his beer in the shadowy bar. He barely glanced at the pinup posters of scantily clad women from twenty to thirty years ago plastering the walls alongside old Bills schedules around him as he told me his story, still upset at the memories being dredged up as he recalled the end of his long career, returning again and again to how he'd been good at his job. I wondered how many people like him could be found this afternoon hunched over cheap beers inside darkened bars like this across the Rust Belt and beyond, sharing similar stories with anyone who might stop and listen.

I eventually made my excuses, telling him that I needed to make my way to the ballpark, and walked out the door, squinting to adjust to the bright sunlight. As I approached Dwyer, I passed the small sign Russ Salway put on his front lawn a few blocks from the sta-

dium the morning of every Batavia home game—and just as dutifully put away before bed each night—announcing "Muckdogs
Home Tonight" to passersby.

Arriving early, I met a photographer friend I was going to show
around the ballpark, which was still empty of fans. We saw Muckdogs YouTube announcer John Carubba emerge from his car, clad in
his usual red Muckdogs golf shirt, black pants, and unstylish black
sneakers. He'd likely been listening to podcasts of his favorite sports
broadcasters to "get in the groove," as he generally did during his
pregame drives from Buffalo.

Carubba didn't linger, eager as he was to settle into the press
box, where he would busy himself preparing for the game, carefully
reviewing the color-coded notes he'd typed up and printed out the
day before. As the season was winding down, he was now closer to
his hope that he could leverage—with Robbie's help—this summer's
unpaid broadcasting work into a paid gig the following summer,
somewhere in the landscape of minor league sports. To this end, he'd
spent the morning polishing up his resume in the hope that Robbie
and Marc could review it and provide some helpful suggestions on
improving it. Unfailingly optimistic and happy to be doing what he
loved, Carubba told me that he was trying to "enjoy every moment
left of this before it's over," when he would have to turn his attention
to announcing high school football games.

Sitting near Carubba in the press box was public address
announcer Paul Spiotta. Spiotta was another member of the Muckdogs game day staff whose professional devotion to doing a good job
far eclipsed the modest stipend he received for working the games. A
longtime Muckdogs fan, Spiotta was heavily invested, on a personal
level, in the team's success, and as this evening's game approached, he
was ruminating about possible playoff scenarios. He said that of the
playoff opponents Batavia could possibly face, Elmira—whom they
would meet in the playoffs if they beat them tonight—presented
the most favorable matchup, as they'd beaten the Pioneers six of
the seven times they'd played during the regular season. Therefore,
despite having already earned a playoff berth, Batavia would be playing to win. Tonight, though, Spiotta's attention would also be on the
field for another reason, as his grandson, Gabe, would be helping
Erik Moscicki as honorary batboy. He knew how much it meant to

the five-year-old Gabe to be on the field with the players he idolized, Jerry Reinhart chief among them. Seeing the earnestness with which young Gabe approached his task, the boy's face flush with excitement as he darted out to retrieve discarded bats, would put a warm smile on Spiotta's face.

Trivia guru Cathy Preston would display another skill tonight as she sang the national anthem before the game, something she was sometimes called on to do on the rare occasion when general manager Marc Witt hadn't arranged for someone to handle the pregame festivities. She rarely got anxious anymore, having done it so many times. She once even managed to get through "O Canada" for Canada Day, something she said she was able to do only because she'd watched so many Buffalo Sabres hockey games on TV over the years. On this night she belted out the anthem with aplomb before returning to her seat above the third-base dugout to retrieve her notebook, ready to keep score of the night's game.

Her usual spot was not far from Dr. Ross Fanara, who had an aisle seat one section nearer to home plate, also along the third-base line. He proudly told me that "thirty-five women hugged me at the last game," perhaps a slight exaggeration, but not by as much as one might think. He routinely received well wishes from passersby throughout the game, his seat located alongside the main concourse helping to facilitate such visits. It was obvious that the eighty-one-year-old thrived on the kind attention he received from friends of all ages. In this, he was a lot like Herb Tipton down in Elmira, the Korean War veteran who was over a decade his senior but who, like Fanara, went to every game and reveled in having people drop by his seat to say hello.

Perhaps feeling self-conscious about his boast at the number of hugs he'd gotten from women during the previous game, Dr. Fanara then told me how happy he was to have been married to Shirley for fifty-five years. Though a Batavia native who spent a long career practicing podiatry in his hometown, after having graduated from the town's Notre Dame High School and then nearby Niagara University outside Buffalo, Fanara was not a small town doctor with a provincial worldview. As a twenty-four-year-old student at the New York College of Podiatric Medicine, he had performed rotations at Bellevue Hospital in New York City, which exposed him to the dark underbelly of the metropolis, as the hospital had a long history of serving the indigent, mentally disturbed, and addicted. He had shadowed doctors in the psychiatric unit and never forgot the gross anatomy sessions in the morgue, where he would dissect the bodies of alcoholics whose corpses had washed up along the East River, the sight of their "perforated and diseased livers" and "black lungs from smoking" reinforcing to him the dangers of drink and tobacco. This recollection reminded me that Herb Tipton had also told me he didn't drink. Maybe there was a lesson, I wondered, that these two men, who seemed to be in remarkable health for their combined 170-plus years of age, didn't drink, a sobering thought, pun intended, as I nursed one of the Eli Fish craft beers I always enjoyed at Muckdogs games.

For me, this marked yet another weekend away from home, days I knew were particularly hard on Marcy, as she had the little ones from sunup to sundown with no break. Today I'd received an encouraging report from her regarding Bates's and Shea's behavior, though, which relieved the usual anxiety I felt, wondering whether they were wreaking havoc at home and making my absence more difficult for Marcy. She sent me some photos an amateur photographer friend had taken of them, which, predictably, made me wish I was home to hold four-month-old Shea and battle Bates in a Nerf gun war in the backyard. I went to show Joe and Sandra Kauffman the pictures, as they always asked about the kids. As they fawned over the photos, I relayed my reflection that maybe Dr. Fanara was on to something with his clean, alcohol-free living and longevity. Bill Kauffman, with whom I liked to enjoy the occasional pre- or postgame beer overlooking the farmland behind his house, was seated nearby and reassured me that he knew an old man who drank a martini every day and lived to 105. This knowledge made my IPA taste just a little better.

Bill told me they'd brought their daughter, Gretel, to Betsey's neighborhood of Elmwood Village in Buffalo that afternoon, in their continued efforts to "lure her" and her boyfriend on a move closer to home. As much as I'd been charmed by Elmwood Village, I had to be honest with Bill, and told him that Buffalo might be a hard sell for a couple accustomed to living at the base of a ski resort in Idaho. His enthusiasm for a possible return seemed undiminished by my observation, evidence perhaps of his "localist's" inflated view of Buffalo as a place to live, as well as of just how much they missed Gretel and wanted to keep the dream of future summers with her back in the fold at Dwyer Stadium alive. Bill, his mind now clearly on family, said that the approaching end of the season always made him think about how many more he had left to enjoy with his parents at his side in the bleachers, a ritual they'd enjoyed for decades, though their departure time had grown earlier as his mom's sensitivity to the evening chill seemed to become more pronounced each summer.

Ernie Lawrence sat nearby, carefully working on a rosary. Betsey told me about how much it had meant to her when he'd made one for her a few years back at a time that she "needed one." She had offered to pay for it, but he reassured her that he took satisfaction in simply knowing it had found a home, as many times he felt as if he just "sent them into the ether" when he donated them to various overseas missions. The rosary would continue to play a role in her life, as Betsey would later write to me from a hotel in downtown Buffalo, to which she'd fled during an especially dangerous blizzard, telling me, "Hi Will, I'm at the Westin in downtown Buffalo. As I hurriedly packed a bag, I grabbed Ernie's rosary. We almost didn't make it to the hotel because the driving was horrific. My rosary got me safely to the warm hotel. Can you give me Ernie's address so I can tell him? Merry Christmas, Betsey."

Meanwhile on the field, Batavia's Blue Pearl Yoga led the crowd in yoga demonstrations between innings. The sight of some of the larger male Muckdogs fans putting down their twenty-four-ounce Labatt's beers to show off their flexibility (or lack thereof) and chant "Namaste" in the bleachers as the instructors spoke of "growing big, beautiful branches" provided just the sort of comical incongruity that I'm sure Marc Witt had in mind when he'd arranged for the special promotion.

The offensive hero of this game for the Muckdogs would be Columbia University's Kyle Corso, who continued his hot hitting—he was batting .320 on the summer—with a three-run double in the third that put Batavia on top 3–2. Though the Pioneers would scratch their way back to tie it in the top of the fourth, the Muckdogs pulled away in the bottom of the fourth, plating two more runs and establishing a lead they wouldn't surrender, going on to win 9–6 and finishing the regular season with an impressive 30-15 record.

The usual postgame huddle at home plate during which the team would congratulate each other and then recognize the home crowd was punctuated by a surprise ceremony for Skip Martinez. The players had learned earlier in the season that the Martinez family's pet dog had been struck by a car and killed, leaving his young kids heartbroken. So, led by pitcher Tyler Prospero, they'd set up a GoFundMe account to raise money for them to buy a new dog. Tonight they presented Skip with a check for $2,300, raised from the team as well as some fans, to purchase a new puppy for his kids. Dallas Young, the outfielder from Detroit who'd taken to carrying the "Just Vibes" poster onto the field after every victory, cited this as another example that what this team possessed went "beyond great chemistry . . . I'd never played on a team that was so close, and it happened over the course of a few months in western New York no less."

I was impressed by the display of affection between players and coach, as my relationships with baseball coaches in both high school and college had been tolerable at best and acrimonious at worst. I chuckled at the contrast between what was taking place at home plate and one time when my coach at Princeton—an impossibly angry man with a legendary temper—got struck with a hard drive in the third-base coaching box and collapsed, and for a brief moment, before he struggled back to his feet, some later admitted having entertained a guilty fantasy that perhaps he was done for.

With their win, the Muckdogs had won the PGCBL Western Division and earned a home playoff game—and repeat showdown with Elmira—as the top seed of the division's four playoff contenders. The four Western Division playoff teams would face each other in a single-elimination bracket beginning the following afternoon and continuing Monday, the winner facing the team to emerge victorious from the league's Eastern Division in a best-of-three series for the PGCBL Championship beginning Tuesday.

The players then congregated along the third-base line so fans could bid for the jerseys they were wearing. This was a surprisingly big moneymaker for Robbie, in which the jerseys he may have bulk purchased for $20 each were resold at a handsome profit. Robbie stood alongside the players, microphone in hand, working the crowd like a seasoned auctioneer, driving prices way higher than I would have ever expected. For example, the mother of relief pitcher

A. J. Winger, an ICU nurse from Houston, who had spent much of her summer in Batavia to watch his games and whose other son, Chance, had often served as a batboy, offered $400 for her son's jersey.

Myles Wahr, the fifteen-year-old who had sweated inside the Dewey the Muckdog mascot uniform all summer, had grown especially close to outfielder Dallas Young. The two had enjoyed breakfasts together at Settler's Family Restaurant and had fun messing around before games. Myles's mother, Sherri, was impressed by how Dallas always went out of his way to make Myles feel included, and how he passed along the kind of encouragement about working hard in the classroom and in sports that kids often ignore when coming from their parents but will internalize when coming from "cool" older role models. Unfortunately for Myles, the charismatic outfielder from Detroit had become a fan favorite, and Robbie leveraged this enthusiasm to drive up the price of his jersey. As the bids crept into the triple digits, Myles was undeterred, eventually offering as much as $133—"my paycheck," he would say—for Young's jersey. Robbie barely even slowed down as he continued to push up the bidding far beyond Myles's capacity to pay, eventually selling the jersey for at least another $100. Myles was visibly saddened to lose out, but this was vintage Robbie. He wasn't going to take a financial hit, however small, just to make his hardworking mascot happy. As a dejected Myles headed home with his mom, Sherri, the auction wound down, and the players eventually retreated to the clubhouse after receiving some final well wishes from their most devoted fans, some of whom proudly showed off the game-worn jerseys they'd just procured.

I made my way to the front office, where, rather than popping champagne, the staff was hard at work planning how to maximize attendance for the next day's playoff game. Marc Witt was thinking aloud about the financial implications of Batavia having earned a home playoff game while Elmira would now be on the road visiting them once again. Marc worried that there was a chance that with record-high gas prices driving up Elmira's travel costs—the Pioneers would be returning to Elmira for the night, as the two-hour drive home and return to Batavia the next morning was still cheaper than overnight hotel rooms for the team—they may not do much better than break even between the two clubs, unless ticket sales in Batavia were extraordinarily strong. He feared that would be difficult, given the short notice, the fact there had already been home games on three consecutive days, and the lack of advance group sales. Nonetheless, he'd been working the phone aggressively, reaching out to sponsors and season ticket holders; by the following afternoon, he and his hustling interns had sold over eight hundred tickets to the first-round playoff game (as well as nearly one hundred season tickets for the following season).

As I watched them work the phones, I debated whether to grab a nightcap in town. If I had, I might have run into Foxprowl Collectables owner and part-time rocker Bill Hume playing at Copperhead Creek, the local honky-tonk where his band, Red Creek, often performed songs like "Blister in the Sun" and "Machinehead" to crowds of men with ample bellies filling out their Grunt Style T-shirts nodding to the music along the perimeter of the dance floor, sticky from spilled Miller Lite, sneaking peeks at *SportsCenter* highlights on nearby TVs while their wives and girlfriends danced together. Bill loved performing, shouting to me once from the stage—with a big smile between songs—"This is what I do when I'm not selling comic books."

As much as part of me craved a Labatt's and some fun music, it had been a long day, and so I decided to head back to the La Quinta to get some sleep and rest up for the Muckdog playoff run that was about to begin.

22

Playoffs—Elmira Pioneers
at Batavia Muckdogs

July 31

S unday, July 31, would mark the return of playoff baseball to Batavia for the first time since the city had been stripped of its minor league affiliate. The Muckdogs entered the game having won six of their last seven games, including the previous night against these same Pioneers from Elmira. The winner of this single-elimination game would go on to face the winner of the Auburn and Utica playoff game, while the loser's season would come to an abrupt end. As I prepared to head to the ballpark for the 4:00 p.m. start, I was thrown a bit of a curveball. Dr. Fanara had let me know that his friend Guy Allegretto, the decorated Vietnam combat veteran, really wanted to come but wasn't able to drive, as he was recovering from a recent operation. Recalling Allegretto's kindness toward my family, I volunteered to pick him up at his home outside Buffalo and drive him to the game. I figured it was the least I could do for such a nice man and passionate Muckdogs fan.

Pulling into a group of townhomes near the campus of the University of Buffalo, I quickly spotted Allegretto, clad, as always, in a red USMC shirt, waiting near an American flag flying next to the front door. I knew Allegretto was a talker, but I still found myself unprepared for the wild detours our conversation would take over the course of the next forty-five minutes during our drive to Batavia.

Shortly after we set sail eastbound on the New York State Thruway, his iPhone rang—the "Marines' Hymn" was his ring tone, of course—and he dove into an animated conversation with his son, who I learned was a bartender in his hometown of Elmira. This discussion complete, he propped his iPhone, which he'd tuned in to the afternoon's Mets game, on the console of my Kia so we could listen. Raising his voice to speak over the announcers' broadcast, he would go on to tell me about his complicated relationships with various family members, all while occasionally interrupting his reflections to cheer or curse the Mets. Pivoting to his childhood, Allegretto shared that his father had struggled mightily with PTSD and alcoholism after coming home from World War II, where he'd served on the USS *Yorktown* during the Battle of Midway. He said he always loved his father, even after his demons had led him to leave Guy and his mom.

In previous conversations Allegretto had alluded to intense combat he saw in Vietnam, though he had yet to provide detail on it, and so I wasn't surprised when he described his own difficulties returning home from war. Having been deposited in San Francisco following his deployment, he was told by the military doctors he was suffering from "shell shock," as he'd been jumping at loud noises and suffering from panic attacks, sometimes feeling as if walls were closing in on him when out in public. It was surreal to be transported from the pleasant countryside we were driving through to these dark recesses of Allegretto's psyche, but at the same time it was obvious that he wanted to unburden himself of some of these thoughts, and perhaps felt more comfortable doing so to me, a fellow veteran, than someone else.

I was glad to listen and have someone I could confide in about some of the bumps in my own road that I'd encountered over the years as I readjusted to American life after my time in the Army. On the surface, Allegretto would have struck some as an almost cartoonish caricature of a Marine veteran, fiercely patriotic, with views that sometimes seemed distilled from Rush Limbaugh's greatest hits. But, below that sometimes rough exterior, there was a decent man, a loving man, and a hurting man.

While I'd been spared the sort of acute PTSD Allegretto described, I still suffered from bouts of alienation from, and demoralization with, the society to which I had returned. There was, of course, the obvious challenge of adjusting from the dangers of life in a place where some people were pretty much constantly trying to kill you to the relative safety of life back home. The occasional absurdity of the Iraq mission compounded this disconnect. I will never forget earnestly asking my younger brother to raise money at his high school to purchase soccer jerseys and balls for us to distribute to local Iraqi schoolchildren, in the hope that it might generate some goodwill in the community. He did, and our efforts appeared successful, our visit to a local elementary school thrilling the kids and pleasing the teachers ... until our convoy of four Humvees got hit with a roadside bomb as we returned to our camp. Fortunately, the bomb exploded between two of the Humvees and no one was injured. Still, it was one of many "What the hell are we doing here?" moments we had. I couldn't help but wonder, if someone had been killed, how in the world I would have explained the loss to their loved ones.

Memories like that one aside, for me any difficulty assimilating back into American society stemmed not so much from being haunted by recollections of combat as sometimes feeling adrift in a place that could feel so discouragingly divided after experiencing such a powerful sense of unity with my Army brothers (the infantry world was all male at the time) overseas.

Though our wartime service impacted us in different ways, I suspect that it helped explain why Allegretto and I both so enjoyed Dwyer Stadium, and the welcoming embrace of our Muckdogs friends.

It was a humid, overcast day with almost no breeze as we pulled up to Dwyer, where fans were already milling outside, clad in Muckdogs gear, waiting for the gates to open. Our arrival happened to correspond with Betsey and Ginny's, so moments later we all filed into the ballpark together when Dave Fisher, the security guard, pulled the chain-link fence open and began welcoming fans. Betsey and Ginny stopped, as always, to hug him, as this summer he'd become one of their newer Dwyer Stadium friends. Betsey asked me for the contact info for clubhouse manager Erik Moscicki and Caleb Rodriguez, the middle infielder who sometimes helped him out in the locker room. I'd shared with her the fact that they'd worked into the wee hours of the morning cleaning jerseys and straightening up the locker room, and she'd decided she wanted to write them a card and enclose a small check.

After dropping Guy Allegretto off at his seat next to Ross and Shirley Fanara, hoping that he wouldn't grow too animated and begin shouting at the umpires and various coaches during the game, as he sometimes did to their chagrin, I made my way to the clubhouse. I wanted to ask Assistant Coach Tom Eaton what his pitching strategy was going to be, with the possibility of up to five playoff games in four days on the horizon. The Muckdogs simply didn't have enough quality arms to meet that sort of demand. He told me he adhered to the philosophy of "win now and worry about the next game later," and therefore would be starting their ace, Nolan Sparks, in this first playoff game. Eaton produced a stack of handwritten reports derived from the pitchers he had assigned to take turns charting every pitch of every game. From these he could produce a scouting report on how to pitch each batter, explaining that he planned on having the hard-throwing Sparks "pound them middle and in." Eaton's methodical preparation showed that neither he nor Skip Martinez was making impulsive decisions by the seat of his pants. But, at the same time, by both necessity and choice, they weren't slaves to analytics. It was a refreshing throwback to when the game enjoyed a healthier balance between data and human knowledge.

While Eaton put together the finishing touches on his pitching plan for the week, Skip Martinez spent his final moments before the game seated on a folding chair in the bullpen getting his dark hair dyed blond by one of the players, alongside a few others who awaited the same treatment. The contrast between the "players' manager" Martinez and the authoritarian martinets I had played for was striking. If a player on my Princeton team had arrived to a game—the most important one of the season no less—with his hair dyed blond, my coach would have let loose a string of rage-fueled epithets that would've been audible halfway to the Jersey Shore.

Not long before the opening pitch, Skip Martinez, with his newly dyed hair, gathered his troops and delivered a short pep talk from the top step of the dugout. "No matter what happens, I'm proud of you fucking guys. I'm more proud of you than any team I've ever coached. We only need four more wins, and we'll get them one at a time. You're the better team, now let's fucking go."

Elmira immediately launched a two-out double off the wall in the top half of the first, marking one of the hardest-hit balls off Batavia ace Nolan Sparks all season. When Sparks walked the next batter, resulting in men on first and second, the visiting Pioneers began talking a lot of trash from the top step of their dugout, surprising for a team that had been manhandled by the Muckdogs all season. Sparks, meanwhile, composed himself and escaped the inning.

Skip, no doubt having noticed the animated Elmira bench, shouted, "Get some runs and shut their fucking mouths" to the players due up. Returning to the dugout after his first at bat, leadoff hitter Josh Leadem reported that the Elmira pitcher was throwing a very hittable 86 or so miles an hour. It wouldn't take long for the Muckdogs to connect, with Levis Aguila Jr. putting them on the board with a line drive two-run home run that just cleared the left-field fence in the bottom of the second. Amazingly, it was the first home run for the Muckdogs all season at Dwyer, and it triggered a wild celebration in which even the pitchers in the bullpen raced to home plate to greet Aguila as he rounded the bases.

*   *   *

As I sat with Bill Kauffman and his parents, Joe and Sandra, Sandra provided some more insight into how exactly Bill had ended up back home in Batavia. She told me that Bill had always been interested in politics but that she could detect it had lost some of its luster after he spent time in DC working on Capitol Hill. And she knew he'd always harbored a deep affection for home. This didn't surprise me, as Bill had served as an unabashed apologist for Batavia—and, by extension, for all hometowns that are often left behind by natives and ignored by non-natives—with the evangelical zeal of someone born again to a faith. He was well aware of this, writing in his book *Dispatches from the Muckdog Gazette*, "No regional patriotism can match that of the returning prodigal."

"This is such an unlovely place, yet I love it with all my heart," Bill wrote. "To visitors, it is a charmless Thruway stop on the Rust Belt's fringe; to me, it is the stuff of myth and poetry, and of life weighed on the human scale—the only measurement that counts."

Joe mentioned Bill's bookish childhood, and how they used to warn him, "You're gonna go blind if you read all those books." He was picking up seamlessly from the last game, when Sandra had described Bill's omnivorous reading habits. While of course it was always fun to enjoy a few chuckles at Bill's expense, there was something else that struck me about Joe's observations. They were a wonderful example of how the regular nature of these games—the fact that the same people would congregate in the same place with predictable regularity—was conducive to the deepening of relationships, as conversations could linger and develop over multiple games, allowing people to gradually reveal themselves. There was a sense of unhurriedness, with days and weeks to digest and reflect on what was being discussed, that felt so refreshing.

*   *   *

Batavia would score four more runs in the bottom of the third, extending their lead to 6–0. With Sparks finding his groove on the mound, Batavia appeared to be in firm control. I saw Guy Allegretto, easily recognizable in his oversized red USMC jersey a few rows behind the on-deck circle, and was relieved to discover that he seemed reasonably composed and wasn't shouting at the umpires and players. Shirley Fanara was keeping Kartier and Kamdyn under closer wraps than her more lenient husband usually did, leading Ross to joke, "Sergeant Shirley is here tonight to make sure the boys behave." They were indeed on their best behavior, with Kartier proudly sharing with me his exploits at a recent karate exhibition. They were good boys despite, or perhaps because of, their unorthodox upbringing. If someone was sick, Kartier would reassuringly tell them, "I'll pray for you." Ross's pride in them was never far from the surface, at one point later telling me how glad he was that they were "respectful," since, "at eighty-two, most of my life is devoted to these boys and my wife."

The Elmira bench, which had been jawing almost nonstop since the game began, was finally quieted by another Batavia offensive salvo that put them ahead 11–1. While much of the crowd had been worked into a prolonged celebratory frenzy at the Muckdogs' offensive explosion, Ernie Lawrence was calmly threading his rosary beads, with his goddaughter, now a softball player at Clarkson University, studiously keeping score by his side, as she always did when she joined him at games. The better I got to know Ernie, the more

I envied the serenity he seemed to have been blessed with, a sensation that washed over me when in his company. Right now there was a small smile visible across Ernie's placid countenance, an indication that he, too, was enjoying the home team's dominant performance.

Ernie asked me about Bates and Shea, and I told him how extraordinary Bates's pre-kindergarten teacher had been, and how I was anxious about whether he would be equally lucky in kindergarten. I marveled at how much energy Bates's teacher put into her job—routinely putting in extra hours to make the classroom a place the kids loved rather than dreaded. As I spent the summer toggling between an exploration of the business of baseball and the challenges of ordinary Americans in an uncertain economy, I just couldn't cleanse my mind of the nearly constant nagging reminders that guys like Rob Manfred were earning upwards of $20 million a year—while fighting to prevent minor leaguers from making minimum wage during spring training, no less—while teachers like Bates's might have made $45,000.

I knew that Ernie had been a teacher, though I wasn't trying to curry favor with him so much as voice my frustration at how a society that liked to think of itself as fair-minded could get so far off track. He agreed, though his steady demeanor seemed to reflect a stoic resignation as opposed to my righteous indignation. And rather than take any credit for the good he did over the course of his own long teaching career, he used my venting as an opportunity to tell me about Mrs. Peretta, his eighth- and eleventh-grade English teacher, "the best teacher I ever had, who made a reader out of me." Ernie recalled how she would read a passage from a book in class, and when the bell rang he would run to the library to check it out, often discovering that another student had already beat him to it. Mrs. Peretta introduced Ernie to *The Yearling*, which made such an impact that when he was forty and brought his family on a vacation near Ocala, Florida, he insisted on visiting the cabin where the book was supposedly set. Fifty years later Ernie would pen a tribute to Mrs. Peretta in the *Buffalo News*, writing:

> With the beginning of the school year, I will begin to see children and young adults walk by my front window on their way to school. On the bookshelf behind me will be copies of *The

Human Comedy, The Yearling, and other books that have been important to me.

I will be mindful of the modest taxes I am permitted to pay in support of these learners. I will say a little prayer for them hoping they are taught skills and values that will help them to live useful and happy lives.

I will also hope they can find their own Mrs. Peretta in the face of one of their teachers.

I have no doubt that Ernie was one such teacher, and can only hope that Bates and Shea will be fortunate enough to have even a few like him. Before I said goodbye to Ernie, I made sure to deliver him the cookie that Betsey had made for him, which he accepted with a smile.

For some reason Skip Martinez left Sparks in until he recorded the first out of the seventh inning, finally pulling him after he allowed only one earned run on four hits in another stellar performance. He would be replaced by groundskeeper Larry Hale's son, Alex, who quickly retired the next two batters. Elmira would score a meaningless run in the top of the ninth before Batavia closed the door on the Pioneers' season with a resounding 12–3 victory. More important in the Muckdogs universe, Batavia had just won their first playoff game convincingly, and the stadium crackled with jubilant optimism.

Outside Skip's office was a dry erase board on which there were four dashes, each one representing one of the four wins that were necessary to secure the PGCBL Championship. Clubhouse manager Erik Moscicki was enlisted to update the team's status on the board and took pleasure in marking off the first win on it as the players enjoyed a somewhat muted celebration in the locker room, keeping in perspective that this win represented only the first step toward a championship. Though things were looking good for the Muckdogs as they advanced deeper into the playoffs, their already overtaxed pitching staff suffered a huge loss as ace Nolan Sparks told Skip that he'd be leaving the Muckdogs to finish out the summer with the Cape Cod League's Bourne Braves. Players and coaches seemed to take the news in stride, though. While they knew his departure would make their playoff run more difficult, they all recognized what an opportunity it was to be invited to play in the most prestigious collegiate summer league in the country and couldn't really fault Sparks for taking advantage of it. And they believed they were a special team that could still win it all, with or without their ace.

I ducked out early to pick up Guy Allegretto from Denny's, where he was enjoying dinner with Ross Fanara, and drive him back to his townhome outside Buffalo. The burly Allegretto and diminutive Fanara emerged from the restaurant with smiles on their faces, announcing to me that they'd just finished off some ice cream sundaes. I was impressed by how a simple meal at an anonymous Denny's off the New York State Thruway could deliver them so much happiness. I'd noticed a similar ability to enjoy life's simple pleasures in Ernie Lawrence, who one afternoon confided in me—as if sharing a guilty, extravagant pleasure—that he was going to treat himself to a Burger King veggie burger and side of onion rings on the drive home to Perry. I'd always believed deeply in the value of this quality—I'd developed something like it in the military myself, and observing them reinforced the importance of preserving it. One of the enduring benefits of infantry life was how the frequent "suck" of it—the cold, heat, fatigue, hunger, and general discomfort—endowed most who went through the experience with a lasting appreciation for basic comforts. To this day, more than fifteen years after my Army service ended, there is rarely an overnight rainstorm that doesn't lead me to be grateful that I'm indoors and dry, resting in a warm bed with a roof over my head.

As I drove Allegretto back to Buffalo, chasing the western sunset along Interstate 90, he returned to the conversation we had begun on our drive to the game, opening up more about his combat experience. I was humbled to discover just how intense his days as a Marine in Vietnam had been. He recalled July 17, 1968, "the worst day of my life." His unit, part of the 1st Battalion, 9th Marines, the "Walking Dead," were four miles west of Con Thien, near the DMZ and only a few miles from North Vietnam. They'd been ordered to remain on a hill and serve as a blocking force for an adjacent Marine element, when a ferocious and seemingly unending salvo of incoming North Vietnamese artillery rounds began to crash into them. Allegretto and others began using their "E-tools," basically small portable shovels, in desperate efforts to claw their way into the earth for some shelter from the explosions. The ground was hard and Allegretto recalled it was like "chipping concrete." About ten of them eventually jumped into a smoking crater that had just been blown out by an incoming round. They would huddle there for hours—Allegretto alternating between Our Fathers and Hail Marys—"begging for life." He would survive, but four of the men burrowing into the dirt near him would not. After one nearby blast, he would discover his best friend, a small but tough-as-nails kid from Tennessee, "white as a sheet, already dead," and another Marine "with his guts spilling out, shaking," who would die in Allegretto's arms a few minutes later.

As it has throughout his life, baseball would help Allegretto heal. He remembers an evening at the Oakland-Alameda County Coliseum during its inaugural season hosting the A's—the same ballpark that fifty years later is quickly becoming an abandoned husk as the team's billionaire owner prepares to move the team to Las Vegas—almost as distinctly as he remembers that horrible afternoon clinging to life on a Vietnamese hillside. It was only a little over a month later, but a world away, when he was in San Francisco out-processing from the Marine Corps on August 15, 1968. He was with a buddy from Elmira with whom he'd been sworn in and was soon to be discharged. They'd learned that Guy's beloved Yankees were in town playing the Oakland A's across the bay and decided to go. There were only about nine thousand fans there at game time, and as the game went on the crowd would shrink, allowing Allegretto and his buddy to snag choice seats behind the Yankee dugout. Only twenty, they befriended some older men sitting nearby who bought them some beers. Happily ensconced within earshot of their pinstriped idols, the young Marines began shouting, "Hey, Mickey, we're Marines back from Khe Sahn, hit us a homer!" when they saw Mickey Mantle stride into the on-deck circle in what would be his final season. Mantle turned and made eye contact. With two men on, he proceeded to hit a "440-foot line shot over the right-field wall," tipping his cap to the young Marines as he returned to the dugout. Allegretto was overcome with emotion.

"I had tears running down my cheeks . . . Sometimes true stories are the best ones," he said, tears again welling in his eyes—half a century later—at the memory.

23

Playoffs—Utica Blue Sox
at Batavia Muckdogs

August 1

Monday afternoon was bright and warm, but the mood in the Muckdog locker room was anything but sunny. It was hours before the evening's 7:00 p.m. game against the Utica Blue Sox, and Skip Martinez was as fired up as I'd ever seen him. "Fuck 'em, fuck 'em, fuck 'em," he said of the team he had coached in 2018 before—according to Skip's account—disagreements over the details of a contract extension led to a nasty divorce. Once the players had assembled, Skip shouted "Close the doors!" to Erik Moscicki before holding a rare closed-door meeting with the team.

"Skip told us a little bit about the history he had with that team and how this game was personal to him . . . That's the first time I'd ever heard him say that a game was personal to him," recalled Jerry Reinhart. In fact, despite both being in the league's Western Division, they hadn't faced each other all season—rumors circulated that this was a result of the bad blood between them—which served to magnify the evening's drama. For today, this was not the avuncular Skip Martinez who enjoyed joking around with Muckdogs fans near the third-base dugout before the game, but the Skip Martinez who'd scrapped his way through a tough childhood and fiercely competitive baseball world to escape the unforgiving streets of East New York, Brooklyn.

Even the ordinarily relaxed meeting at home plate between the coaches and the umpires before the game was tense. The awkward encounter—more showdown than pleasant greetings—made the stakes for everyone involved crystal clear. "We knew right there that we had to do whatever it took to win the game for Skip," Reinhart told me.

General manager Marc Witt was unaware of the on-field drama; he was more focused on how many fans showed up for the game. There were about 1,500, which he was pleased, but not overjoyed, with. He was mostly worrying about what he could do to maximize attendance for a possible championship series should Batavia win. "I live for filling seats," Marc said. He was outspoken and happy, in his element trying to sell tickets while under the gun, no doubt also energized by the fact that the finish line of the season was finally in sight. It seemed like a long time ago that he'd felt exhausted in late June when facing consecutive homestands in Elmira and Batavia that would require late nights and no days off for a few weeks. He'd briefly thought, *I can't do this anymore,* before shaking off the self-doubt and getting back to work.

Utica entered the game with a strong 27-19 record, including a blistering 18-3 start to the season highlighted by a fourteen-game win streak. They'd cooled off recently, the result of losing some players, but were still no pushover. Batavia, for its part, had finished the season having won thirty games to go with just fifteen losses, including seven wins in its last eight games, and its offense was clicking. But they had already used their ace, Nolan Sparks, who at any rate had left for his new team, so they would be starting right-hander Jackson Murphy, a relatively untested sophomore from Roanoke College who had started only three games all summer. On top of that, their bullpen was thin, having played six games in the last six days, and with the prospect of a best-of-three series beginning the next day for the title, they'd have to be careful how much they would tax it.

After walking the leadoff man, Murphy collected himself and retired the next three Utica batters to get out of the first inning with no damage. The Utica starter, meanwhile, was a portly junkballer with an unorthodox three-quarter delivery. "This guy is throwing fucking BP," Skip shouted to his players, meaning he wasn't throwing any faster than what they would warm up to during batting practice. Still, despite his unimposing appearance, Utica's hurler had pitched to an impressive 1.32 ERA over the course of ten games during the regular season and would cruise through the bottom of the first without giving up a hit.

The Muckdogs loaded the bases in the bottom of the second, though, with two singles and Jerry Reinhart getting hit by a pitch. Catcher Mitch Fleming came to the plate with two outs and a chance to give the Muckdogs an early lead. The mustachioed Fleming was a big kid—six-foot-three and 235 pounds—and a fan favorite. He'd immediately felt at home in Batavia, saying it reminded him of Alpharetta, Georgia, the town he grew up in. "I love to sign balls for the kids and watch their faces light up," he said. "We've all been in their shoes. There is no next step in baseball for most of us, this is it." He was equally popular in the clubhouse, as he was a fun guy and fiery leader, but he'd struggled mightily at the plate all season. Seeing him approach the plate, my heart sank a bit, as I'd seen him come up short in similar situations, and I feared the worst. I took one look at Bill Kauffman, sitting near me, and knew from his expression that he shared my doubts. Our pessimism was well founded, as Mitch struck out on a sloppy curveball, extinguishing the potential rally.

Betsey and Ginny introduced me to a friend of theirs, who they joked was the "third musketeer." Their friend was eager to discover more about this place she'd heard so much about. She wondered what made it so special in the eyes of her friends who were otherwise largely uninterested in sports. It was fun to welcome a new member to the little tribe, but I couldn't help but feel something was off. The usual Dwyer Stadium vibe of relaxed conversation and frolicking kids had been replaced by an atmosphere that was perhaps not better or worse, but certainly different. It more closely resembled the tense, emotionally charged atmosphere of major professional sports. There was an electricity coursing through the grandstands, the crowd invested in each pitch, but something about the undercurrent of competitive aggression seemed at odds with the peaceful ambiance that had attracted me—and fans like Betsey and Ginny—to Dwyer in the first place. The two longtime friends seemed to pick up on this at almost the same time I did, with Ginny explaining to their new compatriot that "it's not usually like this" following some loud complaints about the umpiring.

Maybe we were just all old curmudgeons, I thought, thinking

back to my rowdy visits to Shea Stadium as a young college grad reveling in the social life of New York City, pounding pregame beers with my friends on the ferry that used to shuttle fans from Manhattan's east side to the stadium. Almost on cue, Bill again complained to me—as he did during most games—about the decibel level of the walk-up music at Dwyer. Especially grating were the goofy children's songs they played when opponents approached the plate—like the theme songs from *Barney & Friends* and *Sesame Street*—in a hamhanded attempt to tease visiting players that quickly got old. (Bill would concede, "The kids do seem to like the 'Baby Shark' song, and so, in the spirit of compromise, I don't object to it being played once or twice a night.")

Despite this persistent annoyance, Bill reveled in how baseball in this latest incarnation in Batavia had a "defiant quality, a do-it-yourself spirit" that stood in welcome contrast to MLB's increasingly corporate feel, with any rough edges smoothed over in favor of a more streamlined product. Bill used the analogy that the minor league team in Batavia had been like a windmill that would generate energy destined to go elsewhere, and explained how he was now pleased to "no longer be providing power [in the form of players] to illuminate the big city." I nodded, as I was in general agreement, but countered with one of the hesitations I had with welcoming this new form of baseball too wholeheartedly, in that there was a special pride that had stemmed from the relationships the minor league system fostered between a select number of smaller towns and bigger cities. There was something special about watching a player roam the outfield grass at Dwyer and tracking his progress until, a few short years later, one could see him under the shadow of the Green Monster in Boston or alongside the ivy-covered walls of Wrigley Field. Bill brushed aside my critique, though, more proud that Batavia is "powering its own lights now ... Sure, they're not as bright, but that's okay."

Jackson Murphy, the six-foot-one Roanoke College sophomore who had grown up outside Washington, DC, continued to make short work of the Blue Sox, making me wonder why he hadn't been used more during the regular season. Despite his limited innings, he had been unwaveringly positive all summer, always with a quick smile, and it seemed like his easygoing and optimistic demeanor was perfect for this big moment. Each inning he was able to escape without giving up a run was another inning that Skip wouldn't be required to turn to his already overtaxed bullpen. Kyle Corso finally put the evening's first run on the board with an RBI triple in the bottom of the third, bringing the Dwyer crowd to its feet. They were joined by owners Robbie and Nellie, who, for one of the few times all season, had taken a portion of the night off to watch the game from behind the first-base dugout. If one thing was for certain, though, it was that a one-run lead in the PGCBL was not safe, as pitching staffs were thin and defenses unreliable. And so when Levis Aguila Jr. and Abner Benitez led off the fourth for Batavia with back-to-back singles, and advanced to second and third following a nice bunt by Jerry Reinhart (another example of a baseball art form that faces extinction in the major leagues), up strode Mitch Fleming, yet again with an opportunity to break the game open. This time Bill and I didn't even bother to disguise our frustration that our fortunes were again in the hands of the light-hitting Fleming, who had collected only ten hits during the entire regular season. We traded a few jokes of the gallows humor variety, both of us conditioned to expect the worst after lifetimes spent following teams that always seemed to find a way to come up short.

And then, to our thrilled astonishment, Fleming crushed an opposite-field home run over the right-field fence, pushing the Muckdogs in front 4–0. His teammates, and the crowd, were sent into a frenzy by the sight of the burly Fleming lumbering around the bases after finally harnessing the power everyone had long awaited at the most opportune time imaginable. Bill and I immediately felt guilty about the unkind thoughts we'd just been entertaining about Fleming's impotence at the plate and jumped to our feet to join in the celebration. Fleming would later tell play-by-play man John Carubba, "It was a surreal feeling. Hitting had been messing with my head all season, and Jerry Reinhart helped simplify it for me. 'See ball and hit ball,' he told me. So I swung hard in case I hit it ... and I did, and it went far."

The bottom of the sixth would bring more drama when the umpire called Muckdog Levis Aguila Jr. out at home on a force-out with the bases loaded on a play where the Utica catcher appeared to drop the ball. It was the first out of the inning and killed the momentum in what looked to be an opportunity for Batavia to shut the door on any remaining chance the Blue Sox may have had. Skip Martinez was irate, and the crowd equally incensed. "This is why you're in an independent league, Blue," shouted one fan. The man whom Betsey and Ginny had dubbed "the shouter" for his incessant shouting that grew louder with each tallboy beer he guzzled was justifying his nickname. After this play, he outdid himself with drunken exhortations, making me feel bad for his young son, who stood beside him, helplessly, baseball mitt in hand. Despite the shoddy umpiring, the Muckdogs would put two more runs on the board, pulling in front 6–0 before the Utica pitcher appeared to barely pick Jerry Reinhart off third base to end the sixth inning.

For some reason I still couldn't shake the sense that the atmosphere didn't feel right. On the one hand, I was thrilled to see the Muckdogs enjoying a large lead with only nine outs now separating them from a trip east to Amsterdam, New York, to begin a championship series with the Amsterdam Mohawks. But I didn't love how this evening—either my last or next-to-last visit to Dwyer—had taken on such an intense and almost belligerent vibe. That's not to say I didn't appreciate raucous playoff atmospheres. Some of my best memories as a sports fan were of wild Washington Capitals NHL playoff games, for example, where the Caps faithful "Rocked the Red" and the arena remained in a state of almost constant delirium. But that wasn't what made Muckdogs games special for me or most of the fans I'd grown to know. Absent tonight were the relaxed conversations that had accompanied so many brilliant Genesee County sunsets, and I couldn't help but wish to savor a few more before the summer came to an end.

Skip Martinez finally pulled starter Jackson Murphy in the top of the eighth after the right-hander had thrown seven stellar innings of shutout ball. Skip would hand the ball over to Trey Bacon, who'd been dominant in relief all season, earning three wins and three saves while pitching to a 1.58 ERA. Confident that Bacon could navigate his way to the final six outs with a six-run lead, Robbie ducked into the press box with a handwritten note for public address announcer Paul Spiotta, asking him to let the fans know a best-of-three championship series would begin tomorrow in Amsterdam and would be followed by a doubleheader (if necessary) the following day at Dwyer

Stadium beginning at 4:30 p.m. I knew the superstitious Spiotta would have misgivings about making the announcement before the Muckdogs had sealed their victory, but he nonetheless took the mic and delivered the message in his typically mellifluous diction. One sensed that he too was trying to soak in these final games behind the microphone in Dwyer's cozy press box before the leaves changed color. Soon enough, he knew he'd find himself serving as the public address announcer for Batavia High School football games and calling Canisius University soccer games, a sport he approached with noticeably less enthusiasm than his beloved baseball.

Spiotta was probably relieved that he hadn't jinxed the outcome when Trey Bacon smoothly navigated his way through the final two innings. The game ended when a Utica fly ball landed harmlessly in left fielder Daniel Burroway's glove, ending their season and sending Batavia to the championship series.

The crowd erupted and the players swarmed the pitcher's mound to celebrate. Clubhouse manager Erik Moscicki embraced hometown favorite and longtime friend Jerry Reinhart. Skip Martinez shouted, "This was my Super Bowl," referring to the bad blood between him and Utica, as the rock anthem "Gloria" played. Jackson Murphy was swarmed with teammates congratulating him on his clutch performance, his parents and grandma sharing in his excitement from home, where they tuned in to John Carubba's YouTube broadcast.

The players eventually made their way back to the clubhouse as the delighted fans streamed toward the exit. Erik Moscicki notched another win on the whiteboard playoff tracker, leaving only two more for a championship. Robbie even made a rare appearance in the locker room, pumping up the team with words of encouragement, telling them, "The Blue Sox are good but hadn't met the Dawgs. If you win the championship, I'll host the biggest fucking parade ever and we'll get the biggest fucking rings you've ever seen, they'll make Skip's look like a pimple on his ass. This town is so proud of you. We had one day to get the word out and had almost two thousand people here tonight." The players embraced the message from the owner, though I couldn't help but wonder how the parsimonious Robbie was going to go about financing those rings for the players should they win the championship.

Skip then stepped to the front of the locker room and delivered a simple message—"The plan is to win one game away at Amsterdam tomorrow and then come home Wednesday and finish this fucking thing." Then the team again broke into celebration, Skip punctuating it by spraying a Bud Light toward the mouth of his shirtless home run hitter Mitch Fleming, most of the beer spilling onto the catcher's exposed chest as the players roared in approval. As things began to settle down, John Carubba made his way into the locker room and politely asked Fleming if he would do a postgame interview for the podcast he'd taken it upon himself to produce following each home game. Despite being soaked in beer and high on adrenaline, Fleming was gracious enough to agree. In search of a place quiet enough to talk, they retreated to the darkened bullpen outside the locker room, and Fleming, still shirtless, recalled a phone call with Skip before the season. The manager had told him that, after coming up just short of the playoffs the previous summer, the goal for this season had been thirty wins and a Western Division title. Fleming was proud that they had just accomplished both. On a personal level, Fleming said he hadn't just returned for a second summer to play for the Muckdogs "for reps," but rather because he "wanted something special for Batavia. Playing here is the most fun I've ever had playing ball, the atmosphere is nuts, the fans love us, and I wanted to give something back to them."

After the locker room celebration had begun to quiet down, Skip retired to his nearby office. There was a plush blanket and pillow on the leather couch across from his large desk, giving the cinder-block-walled room a lived-in feel. Skip and Coach Eaton were baseball guys, used to being on the road and good at maximizing the comfort of no-frills environments. Skip, with a fresh can of Bud Light in hand and tin of Grizzly tobacco at the ready on his desk, described how he had real affection for his catcher, who had performed so well tonight. "Mitch is the epitome of a teammate. The team loves him and feeds off him. Mitch is the guy anyone would choose for such a big moment, and I'm blessed and honored to be his coach." It was the mark of a good manager who was in touch with his players that Skip recognized and appreciated Mitch's value to the team even when his performance on the field had been underwhelming for much of the season.

As the players made their way back to their dorms to catch some sleep before their fast-approaching three-and-a-half-hour bus ride to Amsterdam the following morning, Robbie, Marc, and the interns were in the front office—which was always disorientingly bright at night when one stepped inside from the darkened stadium and was greeted with its fluorescent overhead lights—brainstorming how to get word out about the home game (or doubleheader, depending on how things went) they'd be hosting in two days. Skip Martinez had ducked into the office to check in as well, as he usually did before heading back to his hotel room for the night. In addition to planning the usual social media blitz, the staff decided to have Dave Fisher, the Desert Storm veteran and volunteer security guard, drive Dewey the mascot around in his Jeep the next day holding a sign publicizing the championship series. Marc volunteered to make flyers to drop off early the next morning at the cash registers at McDonald's and Dunkin' to catch the morning rush.

Robbie tried his best to rally his young interns to exert themselves in a final push to the season's finish line, telling them, "This chance may never come again . . . We're close to a ring, and it's not often you can be chasing a championship. No matter what, all of this will be over in two and a half days, and you'll be thinking, *Fuck, I have a boring life now.*" As Robbie described it, you'd think the PGCBL title had a majesty akin to the World Series or the Stanley Cup, but it seemed to work, as the interns were enthusiastically nodding in agreement. Marc tried to seize on the enthusiasm Robbie's words were generating, saying they would need "boots on the ground" as early as possible the next morning to help get the word out. To sweeten the deal, Robbie said he'd be there at 7:00 a.m. with coffee and donuts. For hungry college kids with depleted bank accounts, offers like this went surprisingly far. Skip Martinez, while no doubt appreciative of everyone's efforts to pack the stadium for the last leg of his championship run, had other things on his mind for now, though. His Muckdogs had just driven a stake through the heart of the team he'd grown to hate more than any other.

"The casino stops serving drinks at eleven-thirty," he announced. "Let's go!"

24

Best-of-Three Championship Series
Game One—Batavia Muckdogs
at Amsterdam Mohawks

August 2

The next morning, by the time he arrived at the stadium, Robbie had already made a 6:00 a.m. visit to Walmart to buy poster-board and markers for signs to advertise tomorrow's home playoff game. His young charges arrived at the office shortly after he did, somehow still energized despite the late night. One of the interns, Dylan Potemri, who had been the YouTube broadcaster for away games and in-game "DJ" for home games, volunteered to don the Muckdog mascot outfit and head to Main Street for the morning. He'd already produced several "hype videos" for the team's Insta-gram and Facebook pages. All of these efforts would bear fruit, as a woman told Marc that by noon she'd already seen a flyer publicizing the game at Dunkin', Dewey the Muckdog waving a sign on Main Street, and received an email advertising the game from the Cham-ber of Commerce.

I noticed some cars parked in the lot adjacent to the right-field line and was curious as to why they were there on a cloudy and blustery day when the first game of the three-game series against Amsterdam would be on the road. I discovered they were visiting a community garden located just beyond the right-field fence that Richard Beatty, the hippie-ish Muckdogs fan I'd met who volun-teered with the local Landmark Society, assisted with. The garden had opened in 2012, taking the place of what had been an abandoned municipal swimming pool, where trees had begun to sprout through the crumbling concrete. What had once been a depressing symbol of decay was now a sign of community rebirth, with forty-five flower beds available for purchase.

On this afternoon there was a mother and her daughter quietly tending to their small patch of land. While self-effacing and modest about his efforts, Richard was clearly fueled by a real pride in Batavia and a corresponding desire to continue nudging it in a better direction. "Sure it's a small community between Rochester and Buffalo," he began, almost apologetically. "But we have decent artists and musicians, not to mention writers like Bill Kauffman." He was excited that Shake on the Lake from Buffalo would soon be bringing Shakespeare to nearby Pavilion, New York. While Shakespeare performances in Genesee County would likely never be as popular as the summer concert series at Batavia Downs featuring acts like the Marshall Tucker Band, or stock car racing at nearby Lancaster Motorplex, for a subsection of the community, events like these were a source of pride and deeply valued.

After a short stroll through the garden, I made my way to the Pub Coffee Hub for some caffeine and one of their tasty sandwiches for lunch. It was always more satisfying knowing that my dollars were supporting the business of someone I'd grown to know—the Pub's young owner, Rob Credi—than distant corporations like Dunkin' and its $1.4 billion annual revenue. Not long after my arrival, Eric Zwieg walked in. He was busy with his graduate course and said he hadn't been able to go to any of the Muckdogs playoff games so far, though he had, of course, remained faithful to his Mets. I knew better than to share my latest thoughts on the team, recalling his recent admonishment, "Please don't root for the Mets . . . We don't want fans like you in the parade if and when we win it all."

Eric seemed surprisingly chipper, though of course when I told him I'd elected to remain in Batavia for the evening and hoped to get together for a "playoff watch party," he immediately told me I should have accompanied the team to Amsterdam. I began to have flashbacks to his critiques of my first book, which for some reason made me feel as if I was back in a college English seminar being grilled by a tenured professor on a reading assignment I hadn't finished. This time he threw me off balance, though, by telling me how much he'd liked the epigraphs I'd selected for my first book. This was

Eric, always pushing me to the brink of walking away from him, then extending an olive branch. It was a bizarre dance and I'm sure said as much about my own idiosyncrasies as his. When I later confided to the Pub's owner, Rob Credi, how these interactions often went, curious as to his thoughts as someone who dealt with Eric every day, he chuckled and said, "That's the Eric we know and love." Still, despite our shared bewilderment with Eric's unique personality, I think we also shared an affection for him that not even his often curmudgeonly demeanor could extinguish.

Cathy Preston had suggested that Eli Fish would be the best spot to get the crew together to watch the night's games and volunteered to help work with the staff there to see if they could air the YouTube broadcast at the bar. Though it took the intercession of Matt Gray, the Eli Fish owner, who was camping in the Adirondacks, Cathy was able to have the staff make the necessary audio-visual preparations to show the game later. Proud of our handiwork, we sent out text messages to Muckdogs fans we knew (save Bill Kauffman, whom I had to call on his landline, given his lack of a cell phone) letting them know the brewery would be showing the game.

Despite Eric Zwieg's admonishment that I should have accompanied the team to Amsterdam, when I arrived at Eli Fish and discovered Muckdogs security guard Dave Fisher and his family eating at a table near the bar, I was reassured that I'd made the right decision. He enthusiastically recommended the brewery's Scotch Ale and mushroom burger. Cathy Preston was at the bar, in her "regular seat." I felt enveloped in a warm cocoon of like-minded souls. Cathy had no interest in the MLB game that was on before the bartender switched over to the Muckdogs YouTube channel, which they'd somehow jerry-rigged to play on one of the bar's televisions. "If MLB can pay those crazy contracts, they should be able to pay for a team in Batavia," she said dismissively. Still, she took solace in the fact that there was competitive baseball in Batavia again, a far cry from 2020, when the minor league season had been wiped out due to COVID fears and Cathy was left with "no idea what to do with myself all summer."

It looked like a delightful night in Amsterdam, a former manufacturing hub on the banks of the Mohawk River, once known as "Carpet City" for Mohawk Carpet Mills, which employed thousands of locals from the early 1900s until 1968, when the company pulled up stakes and moved to Georgia. It left behind the enormous 184,000-square-foot, six-story mill and associated power plant to rot, which they do to this day. The struggling city can't locate the current owner, an "anonymous LLC," and, already running a large budget deficit, can't afford to demolish the crumbling eyesore, which could cost up to $15 million. As for the company that fled to warmer climes, it went public in 1992 and is now an enormous conglomerate known as Mohawk Industries, with manufacturing facilities in fifteen countries. And so the carcass of the old mill remains, a hulking reminder of the town's former industrial might and present-day challenges, like so many of the postindustrial Rust Belt communities of the PGCBL, in which baseball remains one of the only connections to a more prosperous past.

Shuttleworth Park, named for the former president of Mohawk Mills Herb Shuttleworth, was bathed in sunlight save for shadows cast by the grandstands of the ballpark that dated back to 1914. The stadium's rich history included a wild sequence of events in July 1942, when part of it burned down just eight days before the New York Yankees were scheduled to take on the minor league Amsterdam Rugmakers in an exhibition game. Somehow the community rallied to repair the damaged ballpark in a week, and four thousand gathered to watch the Rugmakers fall to the Bronx Bombers 9–5 in ten innings, kids scampering after foul balls they would trade back for a dime.

There was an energetic crowd on hand supporting the Mohawks, who had become a powerhouse in the PGCBL, with a roster loaded with talent from Division I colleges and championship titles in 2016 and 2019. Batavia's Tyler Prospero would get the nod to try to keep the powerful Amsterdam lineup at bay, as good an option as any now that ace Nolan Sparks had departed to the elite Cape Cod League. Over the course of eight summer appearances, Prospero had posted a solid 4-1 record with a 4.01 ERA. On offense, the Muckdogs would capitalize quickly on an Amsterdam error to jump out to a 1–0 lead in the top of the first, but it wouldn't last long, as Mohawks right fielder Zach Gardiner from Marshall University would blast a home run over a short right-field fence to even the game in the bottom of the first.

Meanwhile, back in the comfortable confines of Eli Fish, Cathy Preston sipped on wine—though she enjoyed the camaraderie of the brewpub, she didn't actually like beer—and settled into her happy place. Her husband hadn't joined her this evening, as he didn't share her enthusiasm for the Muckdogs, nor, for that matter, for the Bills, which was borderline sacrilege in these parts. She'd explained to him from early in their relationship that Sundays were for Bills games, and even bought him Bills paraphernalia for Christmas, but nothing had succeeded in sparking his interest. She did, though, have her Muckdogs family, who began to trickle in. Bill Kauffman and Russ Salway soon joined the group assembled at the bar, cheering on Skip Martinez and the boys as they tried to steal a win over the favored Mohawks on the road.

Russ Salway, who was almost always in good spirits when I found him posted up with his buddies at Dwyer, tallboy of Eli Fish Muckdog Ale in hand at his usual high top, was noticeably subdued as he settled in beside us. He'd been at home, running an online auction for some of his father's belongings. His dad was now in the dementia unit of a nearby nursing home, and visiting him had grown extremely depressing, his floor resembling a gathering of "walking zombies." Russ felt bad that his father was there, but at the same time he knew his father needed the professional care. It was no longer safe for him to be home alone, as neighbors had been calling Russ and reporting that his dad was out "wandering." Bill Kauffman listened empathetically and assured him that this wouldn't be the way he'd remember his father. Russ said that the entire sad situation had reinforced in him the age-old lesson that we need to live every day to the fullest. Muckdogs games, holding court with his posse in the fading sunlight of Dwyer, delivered him—at least temporarily—from the stresses that none of us can fully escape in our lives.

Meanwhile in Amsterdam, things didn't look good for the Muckdogs. The Mohawks were demonstrating how they had ended the season with a 39-6 record, their pitcher, a six-foot-three, 195-pound right-hander from the University of Texas at Arlington, continuing the dominance he'd displayed all season en route to a 4-0 record and 0.91 ERA in eight appearances. He would end up surrendering only one earned run over seven innings to go with ten strikeouts before being pulled, with the Mohawks enjoying a comfortable

8–2 lead. They benefited in part from four home runs they launched over the short 279-foot left-field wall. The Muckdogs would show a little fight in the top of the eighth, pushing three runs across the plate to narrow the Amsterdam lead to 9–5, but that would be the final score. The Muckdogs no longer had any margin of error as they boarded the bus for the late-night ride west on the New York State Thruway, knowing they would need to somehow sweep the powerful Mohawks at home in Batavia the next day to win the championship. And they knew they needed to do it over the course of potentially eighteen innings in one day with a bullpen that was already running on fumes. "No one hung their heads, though," said Dallas Young, with players talking and listening to music, proud to have made the playoffs, proud to have defeated Elmira and Utica, and now still only two wins from a championship.

They may have been in better spirits than I, as my congenital pessimism when it came to sports fandom left me expecting the worst. While I was naturally bummed out by the loss, I at least felt vindicated in my decision not to make the eight-hour round-trip to Amsterdam to watch the game, as the outcome had never seemed in much doubt. It would've simply resulted in two long bus rides and a short night's sleep.

As we nursed our final beers at Eli Fish, dejected at the loss but still hopeful that the Muckdogs could pull off an improbable sweep tomorrow, the talk turned to one of the small pleasures that came from my life as a road warrior all summer; namely, the fact that I could actually sleep in until eight a.m., as opposed to the ungodly five-something a.m. wake-ups that were a feature of life at home with baby Shea. I told the remaining imbibers—Bill, Russ, and Cathy— that I had grown fond of the La Quinta, as it was generally affordable (though weekend prices in the summer did spike considerably), clean, and comfortable. This triggered Bill Kauffman, unsurprisingly, to lament the loss of Batavia's stately old "downtown" hotels, which had all but disappeared by the time he'd grown up, but that he was nonetheless familiar with from stories his parents and other older relatives had shared with him.

His dad, Joe, would recall the elegance of the Hotel Richmond, with its celebrated coffee shop and bar, serving as gathering places for visitors and locals alike. Joe remembered hearing stories of the big-band music on Friday nights at the Richmond, his dental hygienist sometimes playing the piano. Like so many things, those nights hadn't seemed so special at the time, when the Friday night music seemed destined to play forever, but now that they were consigned only to memory, they took on an outsized significance. I suspect that one of the by-products of MLB's contraction of the minor leagues was that it led residents of these communities—people accustomed to losing things that had once occupied an important part of their lives—to realize that baseball too was now endangered, and to a corresponding resolve not to let it go without a fight.

The Kauffmans' memories of the Hotel Richmond echoed those Ernie Lawrence had for the Hotel Oneida, constructed in 1925 and once a bedrock of his hometown in central New York. "The greatest experience in my father's life was when he spent two hours talking to Nat King Cole at the hotel bar one night," Ernie said. The musician had been passing through town while on tour, and, amazingly, as Ernie recalls, "One of the most famous people in the world was sitting and talking to my father, a local grocery store owner. We were poor, didn't even own a car, and my dad scratched out a living. And yet there they were. Enjoying a drink together."

Just as professional baseball players were once closer to regular people, often working ordinary jobs in the offseason and following their baseball retirement, so too were musicians like Cole. Why does it matter? one might ask. Times change, and we shouldn't begrudge supremely talented people from profiting from their ability. As Eric Zwieg had once tried to convince me in justifying the ever-widening chasm between the major league "haves" and minor league "have-nots" in baseball and, more broadly, in society, "It's not any different than most other starting gigs—such as literary professions, music and visual arts, politics, and acting—and the long odds of making it to the 'bigs.' It's the nature of the game to start at the bottom and suffer the indignities that come from pursuing what is imagined to be 'success' in America."

I agreed with this, in part. But I couldn't help but worry that when the gap between the celebrity class and those who labor anonymously doing the thankless work that holds society together—like our teachers, cops, and nurses—gets too out of whack, nothing good can come of it. Gaps turn into chasms—and ever-growing chasms like the ones we are facing now may rupture if not addressed.

The Hotel Oneida, which Ernie had described with such affection, had fallen into disrepair by the early 2000s and was shuttered for good in 2009. It still stands, abandoned, what was once a community treasure now an eyesore. As of the summer of 2023, there were redevelopment plans, but they had yet to be actualized.

As for me, tonight it would be back to the La Quinta after I swallowed the last of my beer. There was little chance I would encounter any world-famous celebrities in its lobby, or anyone at all, for that matter, as they were proud to be moving toward an ever-more "frictionless" guest experience, meaning, in layman's terms, fewer encounters with real people and an increased reliance on technology. The lively cross section of people I might have once encountered in the lobby and bar of the Hotel Richmond was being replaced by automated check-ins upon arrival, and self-service waffle machines in breakfast rooms, where a few guests would sometimes fidget uncomfortably in awkward queues, occasionally looking up from scrolling on their iPhones to check the two-minute timer, waiting for the buzzer to go off, informing them that the machine was again available for use and relieving them of the mounting pressure to make small talk with a stranger. It wasn't an existence anyone voted for, but rather one that distant tech titans and corporate overlords—the same people whose wealth insulates them from even participating in such experiences—seem to have ordained for us.

For now, though, there was something more pressing to worry about; namely, whether the Muckdogs could somehow sweep a doubleheader tomorrow from the powerful visiting Amsterdam Mohawks and deliver a championship to Batavia. And, before that, even if there was no lively hotel bar to retire to as in years gone by, there was still the simple pleasure of a good night's sleep in a comfortable bed with a roof over my head to enjoy.

25

Championship Series Doubleheader Game One—Amsterdam Mohawks at Batavia Muckdogs

August 3

Wednesday dawned, and with it the certainty that—win or lose—the day would mark the end of the Muckdogs' season. It would also be the last opportunity for us all to enjoy the "crepuscular hour," to use Betsey's term for Dwyer sunsets, together. As I dug into my omelet at the Miss Batavia Diner, scanning a pamphlet advertising the nearby Wyoming County Fair, I grew a little melancholy reflecting on how fast the summer had passed by. That said, I was also excited to know I would soon be home and able to spend more time with Marcy, Bates, and Shea, something that had assumed even more significance in light of the SOS-type call I'd gotten from Marcy the night before. She was near tears, telling me that Bates's behavior had taken a downward turn, punctuated by a visit to the playground, where he had been mean to a younger child, and later in the day taken something and lied about it. I couldn't help but blame myself, at least in part, for Bates's regression, as I knew it had been tough on him to have his dad gone for so much of the summer, the same summer that an infant sister had arrived and ended his privileged status as an only child.

The afternoon was pleasant but featured a sky that was more gray than some of the stunningly blue ones we'd been spoiled with for much of the summer. It was a reminder that fall was around the corner and, with it, a return to the gloomier weather that defines much of the year in western New York. As they took part in pregame warm-ups, the Muckdogs players seemed loose and confident. When they retired to the locker room to make their final preparations before the scheduled 4:30 p.m. opening pitch, I was able to get my first look at the Mohawks in person as they took the field to warm up. As soon as they began, I had a sinking realization that this team was for real and would be tough to beat. They ran through a series of infield drills with military precision, two coaches alternating hitting ground balls to waiting infielders who scooped them up smoothly and fired to first with strong arms. Unlike some of Batavia's other opponents over the summer, one of whom featured a few players fielding balls shirtless during pregame drills, these guys functioned with near-robotic discipline, with nary a booted ball or wild throw tarnishing their impressive display. It would be incumbent on Batavia's starting pitcher for the first game, Julian Pichardo, to keep the Mohawks' offense in check while hoping Batavia's bats could somehow break through Amsterdam's stout defense and strong pitching.

"Don't Stop Believin'" played on the PA system as the gates opened and fans began to stream into Dwyer. As he often did, Robbie posted up at the entrance to greet his fans in person. When one older one stopped to complain about the in-game music being too loud—echoing Bill Kauffman's perennial gripe—Robbie was friendly enough, but it was clear he had no intention of changing. As Bill had joked to me, Robbie was "not exactly a suggestion box kind of guy."

Guy Allegretto soon arrived, having received a ride from a younger neighbor of his, a fellow combat veteran who had been a Marine master sergeant. Guy immediately reached into his pocket and produced some cash he insisted I use to buy a gift for Marcy and a treat for Bates. Despite my intense discomfort accepting money from him, I knew that protesting would get me nowhere. I told him I'd take Marcy out to a nice dinner to celebrate my return from the summer's travels, but that Bates would have to wait a bit for his gift owing to his recent poor behavior. Allegretto smiled, and the two Marines made their way to their seats behind the Muckdogs dugout near Allegretto's good friend Dr. Ross Fanara.

Skip Martinez delivered the lineup cards to the home plate umpire as "Start Me Up" played, and fans hurriedly grabbed beers and snacks before finding their usual seats. Skip then gathered the team on the dugout steps for his final pep talk of the summer. "This

season's been a tough grind, and I'm proud of how you've never gotten too far up or too far down," he said with real feeling. "One at bat,
one inning, one game at a time. The pressure's on them. Fight hard
like you've been doing all season. And have fun!"

Once the usual elaborate pregame ceremonies that marked every
Muckdogs home game—the kids playing catch with the players, the
Muckdogs dance team performing, the ceremonial first pitch, the
presentation of colors, and the national anthem—had finally wrapped
up, public address announcer Paul Spiotta asked the crowd to please
observe a moment of silence for famed sportscaster Vin Scully, who
had passed the day before at age ninety-four. The name alone evoked
powerful memories; his career represented one of the last unbroken
bridges to the romance of baseball in decades gone by. Scully didn't
overwhelm the viewer with disquisitions on launch angles and exit
velocities. He understood that it was human stories that appealed to
fans, not avalanches of data. He famously said, "If I can get a story
about a player, I would give you a shipload of numbers, batting averages, and all just for that one precious story." Batavia fan Rich Schauf
echoes this sentiment, attesting to how, for him, it was always the
"stories" of young minor leaguers, fighting long odds to advance their
careers, that sparked his interest, and how, sitting alongside the players' parents or girlfriends in the grandstands, he enjoyed "learning
their backstories and seeing them as humans."

The voice of the Muckdogs on YouTube, John Carubba, also
offered a heartfelt eulogy to Scully, explaining how so many broadcasters, himself included, may have never pursued the career had it
not been for Scully's influence. There was something touching about
Carubba's earnest encomium, trying to elevate his broadcast to a
higher plane, something few summer collegiate league announcers
would think to aspire to. He took his job seriously, investing all of
himself into his unpaid position, placing himself—albeit with trademark modesty—in the footsteps of this legendary announcer, even
though his broadcast of this game would result in only 2,236 views.
Still, whether Carubba was reaching two thousand fans or two million, there was something undeniably intimate about the experience
of regularly listening to the same announcer call a baseball game,
whether it was Scully transporting you to Chavez Ravine in Los
Angeles or Carubba to Dwyer Stadium. Carubba concluded his

introductory remarks with a nice homage to Scully, borrowing Scully's trademark opening by inviting listeners to "pull up a chair" and enjoy the broadcast.

The crowd at opening pitch skewed toward retirement age, as many younger adults were still at work on this Wednesday afternoon, and children were busy with summer camps and sports practices. Betsey and Ginny arrived a little late, with Betsey blaming Ginny for their tardiness, explaining how she'd been at home "looking out my window waiting for Ginny like a little kid." Still, they were both optimistic despite the one-game series deficit. Betsey confidently told me, "We're gonna win." Despite the loss the previous night, Betsey said she had enjoyed eating ice cream and watching the game on YouTube, adding, "Bates and I are friends for many reasons, including our affinity for ice cream dinners, and not just LEGOs."

It was fitting that the imposing six-foot-five, 235-pound Pichardo had gotten the nod for the Muckdogs, as it was his second season and he was one of the team's most popular players. Meanwhile, Aidan Kidd, a six-foot-three left-hander from Laguna Beach, California, with an impressive 3-1 record and 0.82 ERA over the course of the summer, was on the mound for the visiting Mohawks, a team with a seemingly inexhaustible supply of strong arms.

The sun had begun to break through a few remaining clouds as I took a seat next to Bill Kauffman and his parents, Joe and Sandra. Bill told me he had an upcoming trip to Indiana and, in keeping with a habit of trying to read a book associated with places he was visiting, had attempted to read Indiana native Theodore Dreiser's *An American Tragedy.* He was unsuccessful, though, finally giving up on the "ponderous" writer's "eight hundred pages of gloom."

Maybe it was the thought of Dreiser's writing, but Bill appeared to be in a contemplative mood, and something about observing him watch what could be our final game together reminded me of that stormy winter night enjoying Guinness at O'Lacy's back in February. He had told me—not before apologizing "if it sounds maudlin"—that after decades spent in the bleachers, "I can sense the people who used to sit here, these games connect the living and the dead," sharing the story of the "long-haired cafeteria worker from Rochester who used to make the journey to Muckdogs games, where he would pull out a copy of Thomas Aquinas's *Summa Theologica* to read." Though the man's theological knowledge was impressive, he did possess some odd ideas about baseball, including an oft-repeated desire to replace the best-of-seven World Series with a best-of-nine affair, and a suggestion that players from each position should leave their glove on the field for their opponent to use. Bill had last seen the man in 2019 and now worried that the lonely eccentric had vanished into the realm of "myth and memory and stories" that imbued otherwise nondescript corners of his hometown with a mystical aura in his mind.

Not all of Bill's reflections on life's deeper questions featured such melancholy, however. There was, for example, his account of visiting Jim Owen, the local legend he joked was "Batavia's cheapest man," near the end of his life.

"Billy," the old man had said, addressing him just as he had when he coached the young Bill in Little League, "there's one thing you realize when you get old."

Bill leaned forward expectantly, sensing that he might be only seconds away from "having the meaning of life explained to me."

And, with that, the old man fell asleep.

"I guess I need to figure it out on my own now," said Bill of his brush with the eternal.

Thankfully, our crew was still among the living. Betsey, seated nearby, said that she'd recently been concluding her morning prayers with "Go Muckdogs," adding that since they were now in the finals, "someone must be listening upstairs." Her unique blend of religious devotion and humor reminded me of my grandmother, Helen, and her sister, Marie—the O'Shea sisters (from whom my daughter, Shea, gets her name)—who had both played outsized roles in my childhood. Theirs, like Betsey's, had been a real, but somehow relaxed and nonjudgmental, faith, one that assumed a comfortable, and comforting, relationship with God as a friend, someone with whom you could navigate life's daily ups and downs. One Saturday evening Betsey had told me how the priest at her 4:00 p.m. mass had "been chatty, and so mass was running late . . . I didn't want to be late to the Muckdogs game, so I said a quick prayer, told God I gotta go, whispered 'Go Dawgs,' and left . . . The priest may not understand, but God will."

I smiled, as it was just the sort of thing the O'Shea sisters might have done.

As the game entered the bottom of the third, there was still no score. The pressure on the Muckdogs' bats was gradually mounting to take advantage of Pichardo's strong pitching through the early innings. They finally would, scoring three runs on consecutive two-out doubles by sluggers Tyler Cannoe and Daniel Burroway, bringing the Muckdogs out of their dugout to celebrate—led by Dallas Young waving his "Just Vibes" posterboard—and the crowd to its feet. It was especially incongruous to see Betsey cheering wildly moments after we'd been discussing Proust, whom she confessed to giving up on after reading "107 pages of him describing being sleepy."

The grandstands continued to fill up gradually as people got off work and children's practices let out. A bunch of kids sitting nearby were still in their football uniforms and pads. As I took in the scene, aware that I would soon be back home, and these pleasant evenings relegated to memory, I was surprised to hear my name announced over the PA system as the "Veteran of the Game." I was somewhat uncomfortable, as I've never particularly enjoyed public recognition for my military service and had no idea how it came about. I thought maybe Paul Spiotta had taken the initiative to make the announcement. When I saw Guy Allegretto stand up and salute from his seat behind the on-deck circle, though, I connected the dots and concluded that he'd been responsible. I felt humbled, knowing now what he'd seen and done during his Vietnam service.

On the mound, Muckdogs hurler Julian Pichardo continued to work his way out of trouble, including a narrow escape with the bases loaded in the top of the fifth, when he induced an inning-ending ground ball that was scooped up cleanly and thrown to first for the final out by Kenny Dodson. (Dodson was playing for Jerry Reinhart, who was serving a one-game suspension for cursing at an umpire during a recent game.) The Muckdogs would extend their lead over the dangerous Mohawks to 5–1 in the bottom of the fifth, and then add two more runs in the sixth when unlikely playoff hero Mitch Fleming struck again, hitting his second two-run home run in as many days—a line-drive shot to the opposite field—prompting a wild celebration as he crossed home plate, putting the Muckdogs on top 7–1.

The stadium was pulsing with energy at the prospect of impending victory. But, as was the case with the last playoff game, it didn't quite feel right. As if reading my mind, Ginny said, "This isn't what I fell in love with" about Muckdogs games. I couldn't have said it better myself. In a somewhat counterintuitive way, it was precisely the absence of raucous crowds that we found to be part of Dwyer's appeal. I was reminded of Guy Allegretto describing the feeling that washed over him during a quiet regular-season game at Yankee Stadium shortly after returning home from Vietnam, and the old Marine's words do as good a job as any of capturing the way I felt watching Muckdogs games: "When I was in Yankee Stadium in April 1969, watching the Yanks and Indians play, I had a unique feeling. I felt an inner peace that I hadn't experienced in years. I was so calm and happy. It was the most beautiful experience that I'd had in years. It was magical."

As I reflected on this, it wasn't that I begrudged Muckdogs fans the opportunity to celebrate their team's success and cheer in a championship series, but rather that I now recognized how much I valued the elusive sense of peace that I'd discovered in the Dwyer grandstands, a peace that was best personified by Ernie Lawrence's Zen-like presence. The particulars were of course unique to this well-cared-for diamond in Batavia, but the overall sensation could be experienced at small ballparks across the country. They served as a reminder that the idealized land of Fourth of July parades and summer nights at the ballpark that I'd used as psychological fuel for my wartime service had not yet been entirely lost, and provided a psychological ballast that seemed to help me, and others, navigate the tempestuous waters of contemporary American life.

I found Ernie sitting alone, a biography of Stalin resting next to him. Ernie pointed to the nearest speaker from the PA system and told me it was broken, which we agreed was actually a good thing, as it spared us the deafening walk-up music. Ernie joked he'd come perilously close to using the side-cutting pliers he used to make his rosaries to "take care of the speaker" before it had conked out on its own.

Growing more serious, Ernie told me that he was awaiting the results of blood work done to assess the condition of his failing kidney, expressing once again the hope that he'd be able to enjoy a nice fall before commencing dialysis treatments. I detected a trace of real worry in the even-keeled Ernie's words, though it was also clear that he didn't want these health concerns to detract from our ability to enjoy these final innings of the summer together. He said he'd be sad when the season ended, as he'd really enjoyed this year's team, observing that they'd had the "best chemistry I've seen here—and I've had season tickets since 1985." But, he added as he thought back to so many nights at Dwyer in summers gone by, it still wasn't quite the same. Remembering the drafted professionals who had for so long played on this field, he recalled how they "had hard bodies and were serious athletes . . . Every one of them would be better than the Muckdogs today, who are just kids."

The comment would stick in my mind when I would later hear defenders of MLB's contraction of the minor leagues argue that strong attendance at collegiate league games in some of the communities that were stripped of minor league affiliates proved that nothing had been lost, or, as a senior MLB official told me, "There is the perception that we're taking baseball away from communities when in reality we're trying to create the right form of baseball for each community." The statement was analogous to a restaurant group pulling a good steakhouse from a town and replacing it with a fast-food burger joint, and then, when people still came out in strong numbers to buy burgers (since they had no other choice), citing this as evidence that the customers were just as well off. The reality was that two things could be true at once: Batavia was fortunate to have had Robbie and Nellie Nichols arrive and provide a well-run place to gather and enjoy ballgames all summer, while at the same time it was a real loss to replace drafted professionals—and the related connection to big-league teams—with college kids unlikely to be drafted. While Ernie was too astute a fan not to notice this loss, he chose to appreciate the good and not dwell on what had been taken away.

Muckdogs starter Julian Pichardo, meanwhile, turned in a clutch performance when Batavia needed it most, exiting the game to a standing ovation in the seventh with the Muckdogs holding a commanding 7–1 lead. Ginny told me that Muckdog Nation had even grown by one today, as her son James was tuning in on YouTube at home for the first time all summer. My phone buzzed with an incoming text from Julian's grandfather Mike Baluja from his home in Tampa, where he and his wife, Cindy, had, as always, been anxiously watching. He wrote, "It was such a perfect way for Julian to say farewell to Batavia . . . God scripted this better than anything I could have imagined. It was such an emotional moment with Julian coming off that mound, the hug from Skip, the ovation . . . wow."

While most of the crowd was still basking in the afterglow of Julian's triumphant performance, a few of us grew concerned by Skip's bullpen choices, as he elected to go with right-hander Joe Tobia to finish the seventh before turning to arguably his strongest closer, Trey Bacon, to pitch the eighth and ninth innings. While the choice was consistent with the philosophy of doing whatever it takes to win and force a tiebreaking third game in the championship series, it further taxed two of the best arms he had left in reserve for the increasingly likely winner-take-all game that would follow less than an hour after the conclusion of this one. As was often the case at Dwyer, though, the beautiful crescent moon rising as the sun dipped below the outfield pines was enough to—at least temporarily—set our minds at ease.

Bacon would, in fact, make short work of the Mohawks in the eighth and ninth, pushing the series to a deciding game three. The Muckdogs had advanced to within a game of the title.

The mood in the dugout between games was exuberant, the scrappy underdogs grateful to have dodged a bullet and earned a shot at the championship. Skip exclaimed, "No one would have believed this when the season started, beating Utica to get here, then Julian pitching us into the final, it's too Hollywood." While I shared in his happiness, my native superstition, coupled with a pessimism forged from years of cheering on the Mets, left me with a lingering unease. In situations like this, I often found myself adhering to the old adage I'd first heard in the Army: expect the worst and hope for the best.

26

Championship Series Doubleheader Game Two—Amsterdam Mohawks at Batavia Muckdogs

August 3

Business was brisk at the concession stand during the roughly thirty-minute break between games, to the point that Robbie began to run out of some of the menu options. The day-by-day nature of the postseason and possible elimination at any moment had made it hard for him to calibrate how much supply to have on hand, as running out would result in lost sales opportunities, while having too many perishable items left over when the season ended would result in wasted money. Nonetheless, he was exuberant as he rang people up at the register, the process of selling seeming to energize him even as his foot pain continued to plague him. "We've got diet water," he joked to a customer asking for a diet soda. He told another fan who'd asked for a hot dog, "We'll have that for you in thirty minutes or your money back," before running to the back to thaw out the last ones he had.

Robbie must have been thrilled to see latecomers continuing to stream into Dwyer, joining the crowd of over two thousand from the first game who were allowed to stick around for the second. It was an impressive crowd for a late afternoon midweek start, and a testament to the staff's nearly around-the-clock work hustling to sell playoff tickets all week.

Guy Allegretto's friend Dr. Fanara approached me and quietly suggested that it would mean a lot to Guy for me to return his favor and submit his name to be recognized as Veteran of the Game for the doubleheader's nightcap. I felt bad that the gesture hadn't occurred to me and happily agreed, quickly drafting a short account of Allegretto's Vietnam service and delivering it to Paul Spiotta, asking if he would read it during the game. Paul said he would be glad to.

The lights were on for the start of the second game as twilight gradually gave way to darkness, the temperature beginning to dip. Playoff hero Mitch Fleming, who had accounted for two of the Muckdogs' three postseason home runs (to go with none during the regular season), chatted with some kids still in their football pants beside the dugout, one of his young fans asking, "Mitch, are you gonna hit another home run?" It was a remarkable turnaround for the catcher, who had struggled to even make contact for much of the season.

John Carubba was in the press box, examining the extensive notes he always typed up and printed out at home. We were surprised to see slender right-hander Joe Tobia, the University of Albany sophomore, take the mound to start for the Muckdogs as the second game began at 8:15 p.m., little more than an hour after he'd retired the side in the top of the seventh of the first game. He looked none the worse for wear in the first, though, giving up an infield single before retiring the Mohawks with no additional drama.

The Muckdogs, meanwhile, would be facing yet another of Amsterdam's seemingly bottomless reservoir of talented pitchers, burly right-hander Santhosh Gottam from Brown University. The six-foot-one pitcher looked heavier than the 190 pounds he was listed as, and had some zip on his fastball, which appeared to be in the high 80s. Like all of their pitchers, it seemed, he'd had a dominant regular season, throwing to a 0.94 ERA in fifteen appearances, while striking out 37 in 28.2 innings pitched. He too got through the first with relative ease. The visiting Mohawks had arrived with an impressive cheering section, fans who had been willing to make the three-and-a-half-hour trip west on the Thruway despite the late afternoon weekday start. Both the Mohawks and their fans were engaged and enthusiastic, but without some of the more amateurish hijinks displayed by other visiting teams and fans. There wasn't the bad blood that had been palpable during the Utica game, for example, or the trash-talking of the Elmira game. Even when one of the Amsterdam fans with face paint did a lap around the concourse waving a team flag, it seemed more in good fun than belligerent, and the chorus of boos that greeted him was more good-natured than hostile.

I rejoined Bill Kauffman and his parents, Joe and Sandra, as I wanted to be sure to say goodbye to them for the last time before they headed home early to escape the evening chill. Sandra had assumed an endearingly maternal attitude toward me and expressed dismay—as she often did—on my lack of a warm jacket. I confessed that I had, once again, forgotten one. My stomach sank, though, when Bill told her of my plan to drive home deep into the night after the game so that I could surprise the kids with my presence at breakfast the following morning. I knew from interactions with my own mom that unnecessary late-night drives were universally frowned upon by mothers everywhere. Sure enough, Sandra did not approve, gently scolding me that it wouldn't be safe, and suggesting that I stay in Batavia for the night and return home the following morning after a good night's sleep. Little exchanges like this were endearingly comforting, making me feel at home despite being 250 miles from Pittsburgh.

The game remained deadlocked until the top of the third, when the Mohawks scored three runs, taking advantage of a successful hit-and-run (something that one almost never sees in the major leagues anymore) followed by Batavia's second baseman and right fielder making errors on consecutive plays. The Mohawk rally included a close call at third base in which one of their runners was called safe even though the throw appeared to beat him, triggering what for Dwyer constituted a ferocious torrent of abuse toward the offending umpire.

Things had settled down a bit between innings, when Paul Spiotta read the short account of Guy Allegretto's service in the Marine Corps at Khe Sahn that I'd given him, asking the old Marine to stand and be recognized as "Proud to Be an American" played on the PA system. Even from a distance I could see Allegretto's smile as he stood and received a standing ovation.

Paul then invited his five-year-old grandson, Gabe, into the press box to announce the Muckdogs batters as they came to the plate in the bottom of the fourth, as he'd done a few times during the season. Gabe's mom explained that it was past his bedtime, but he'd convinced her to stay, since his favorite player, Jerry Reinhart, hadn't played in the first game and Gabe wanted to see him play one last time before the season—and, quite likely, Reinhart's baseball career—came to an end.

Joe Tobia put forth a valiant effort on the mound, completing five innings (to go along with the one he'd pitched in the previous game) and allowing only the three-run Amsterdam outburst in the third. He couldn't match Mohawk right-hander Santhosh Gottam, though, who displayed impressive poise in a hostile environment, keeping the Muckdogs off the bases and unable to mount a threat to the 3–0 lead he'd been spotted.

The kids chased Dewey the Muckdog across the outfield after the fifth inning, as they always did, but it felt different, like the "race" was a minor sideshow to the game as opposed to a critical component of the overall experience. As the sixth inning came and went with no Batavia offense, Ginny had seen enough, telling her friend, "Ready to go when you are, Higgins." Betsey couldn't bring herself to give up on the Muckdogs yet, however, asking for "one more inning" to keep the slim hope of a comeback alive. When the Mohawks extended their lead to 7–0 in the top of the seventh, though, while Batavia's bats remained silent, even the eternal optimist Betsey Higgins was forced to concede that a comeback wasn't in the cards. So the two ladies, who had spent so many pleasant hours together in the Dwyer grandstands over the course of the summer, carefully packed up their snacks and headed to the exit for the last time before the gates were locked for the winter.

Not everyone had abandoned hope, though. Ernie Lawrence had flipped his cap inside out and backward—the old "rally cap"—in an effort to summon assistance from any source, earthly or supernatural. Still, Ernie was enough of a fan to appreciate the difficulty of the task at hand, fatalistically joking, "It's gonna take a lot of rally." Between Ernie's rosary making, Betsey's daily prayers for the Muckdogs, and even Dr. Ross Fanara, who had watched mass on television that morning, it was hard to imagine that there was a collegiate summer team that would be more worthy of divine favor. And for a brief moment, it appeared as if there might be magic in the air, as none other than Jerry Reinhart drove home the team's first run with a base hit to left in the bottom of the eighth. It would be his last at bat on the field he'd grown up playing alongside in Little League; it would also likely be the final at bat of his baseball career. The Muckdogs continued to threaten, eventually loading the bases with speedy lead-off hitter Josh Leadem at the plate. Leadem had had a great summer, batting nearly .350, and was always a tough out. But it was not to be, as he struck out swinging, stranding the three baserunners and all but extinguishing any remaining hope of a miracle.

After an uneventful top of the ninth, the Muckdogs were down to their final at bats, the visiting Mohawks fans in full-on celebration mode, doing the "tomahawk chop" and counting down the three outs that stood between them and the PGCBL title. The remaining Batavia fans, meanwhile, seemed focused on quietly soaking in their final moments in the bleachers, as if stockpiling memories of the ballpark to psychologically sustain them through the long winter ahead. The players, too, were now forced to confront the reality that their season, and, in some cases, their baseball careers, would soon be over. Dallas Young said all of this hit him when he saw Kyle Corso, who "never showed emotion," slumped in the dugout, eyes red, wiping away tears. "It was heartbreaking," recalled Young of those final innings, "especially since I didn't know if I'd ever be back."

The Muckdogs didn't give up without one last push as slugger Tyler Cannoe homered to left with one out in the bottom of the ninth. But it wouldn't be enough, as the Amsterdam closer would strike out the final two batters he faced, securing a 7–2 victory for the Mohawks and earning them their sixth league championship since the PGCBL's establishment in 2010.

As the Mohawks threw their gloves in the air and converged near the pitcher's mound in wild jubilation, the Muckdogs players milled around their dugout in stunned disbelief, not really eager to stand by idly and watch Amsterdam celebrate, but also reluctant to head back to the locker room for the last time, as if lingering on the field would somehow negate the finality of what had just happened. Skip Martinez rounded up his young players and told them to hold their heads high. "Be proud to be this community's team," he said, his own voice choking up, tears visible under his eyes, "and of fighting till the fuckin' end . . . This season was one for the ages. I'm proud of you fuckin' guys."

Pitcher A. J. Winger and his twelve-year-old brother, Chance, who had helped as batboy for much of the season and "could break both arms and not cry," according to his mom, Evelyn, were both in tears. Soon Evelyn, who had served as an ICU nurse during the darkest days of COVID in Houston, was as well. Recalling the season and its bittersweet completion, she would write on Facebook: "As I see A.J. take the mound for what will likely be the last time before hanging up his cleats, I still see my kid with his baggy baseball pants and hat that was too big for his head when he was five. As a mother, I couldn't have been blessed with a better stage for A.J. to finish, and Chance to begin. Thank you truly, The Moms."

The depth of emotion displayed by the team surprised me. Over the course of the summer, I'd noticed how tightly they'd bonded, and how invested they'd become in success, but to see Dallas Young openly weeping as he embraced Dave Fisher, the security guard, was remarkable to me. There was a striking innocence to it.

As the Muckdogs continued to hover near the dugout in dazed sadness, some interns delivered a folding table to home plate for the trophy presentation to Amsterdam. Robbie rode up in a green John Deere Gator with a white tablecloth and the PGCBL Championship trophy. He put them on the table and then handed a microphone to the league vice president to deliver some congratulatory remarks. After politely recognizing the victors, the Batavia players slowly made their way to the clubhouse, some shaking hands and hugging loyal fans, Dallas Young despondently trudging down the left-field line toward the locker room in tears, clutching his "Just Vibes" handmade sign.

Part of his sadness stemmed from how close he'd grown to the Batavia community, and the Wahr family in particular. Sherri Wahr, the mother of Myles, who'd been Dewey the Muckdog all season and grown to look up to Dallas like a big brother, would comment on Facebook: "Wow . . . who knew baseball could be so emotional. Tonight was tough but knowing that Myles's new best friend will be leaving tomorrow makes it even tougher. The bond these two created is something a mom could only dream of for her son. Dallas Young, I can't thank you enough for being exactly what Myles Wahr needed this summer." For his part, Dallas told them he was "adopting myself" into their family. When Myles helped Dallas pack up to move out of his dorm room the following day, Dallas would give him one of his jerseys—just like the one Myles had been outbid on a few nights prior.

After most of the players had made their way back to the locker room, I ducked into the front office to say goodbye to Robbie, Nellie, and the other Muckdogs staffers I'd spent so much time with all summer. John Carubba followed me in. He thanked Robbie and Marc Witt profusely for the opportunity to call the Muckdogs home games all season, which was exceedingly gracious of him, as he hadn't even been paid for all his hard work. Marc offered him a sincere thank-you for his efforts, presenting John with a box of Cinnamon Toast Crunch for the road, an affectionate inside joke in recognition of the fact that John's pre- and postgame ritual all summer had included eating a box of the cereal.

I left shortly before midnight, as I had a long drive ahead of me so that I could be home by sunrise to hug Bates and Shea for the first time in too long when they woke up. As I walked to my car, the lights inside the stadium shut off for the final time of the summer, the few lingering fans huddled along the fence separating the grandstands from the third-base line now silhouetted by the crescent moon. I saw the glow of the Amsterdam team bus still idling in the far corner of the dark, now-empty parking lot as the Mohawks celebrated on board. Nearby crickets provided the familiar soundtrack for my walk to the car, their comforting chirping delivering me, as it always did, to the sweet evenings of my childhood playing baseball with my brother in my grandfather's backyard. And, just as they had for so many summers past, the Muckdogs fans I'd grown to know had made their final journeys home from the ballpark for the summer. A short walk for Joe and Sandra Kauffman, Cathy Preston, and Russ Salway. A quick two-mile drive for Ross and Shirley Fanara and their young great-grandsons. A much longer drive for Betsey Higgins, Ginny Wagner, Guy Allegretto, and Ernie Lawrence. As Bill Kauffman had written years before, "Players come and players go . . . but it is the fans, passing lifetimes in the bleachers, who give minor league baseball its sense of permanence."

And it was precisely these fans who had been reduced to impersonal numbers populating an Excel spreadsheet when MLB decided to wipe out minor league baseball in forty-two communities like Batavia, each populated by its own unique cast of characters to whom the games meant so much. The value of their happiness was impossible to quantify, but the "inefficiencies" of the system that delivered them professional baseball had constituted "stuff around the edges" that could be "cleaned up," in the words of MLB commissioner Rob Manfred, in order to create "some economic flexibility that we can use." In the wake of this so-called cleanup, Batavia had refused to surrender baseball, though, rallying behind the new Muckdogs led by Robbie and Nellie Nichols, ensuring that, for now at least, you could still hear the crack of the bat echoing in Dwyer Stadium on summer nights.

Though the last pitch inside Dwyer had been thrown hours before, a called third strike that had ended the Muckdogs' season, the rhythm of life outside the stadium beat on. The green trees of the neighborhood surrounding the ballpark would before long begin changing colors, and, not long after that, the nearby streets, so pleasant and inviting in summer, would become snow-swept and frigid. Winter storms thundering in from Lake Erie would drive the fraternity of Batavia baseball fans into the solitary warmth of their homes, longing for the days when they could again emerge into the brilliant sunlight, make their way to their familiar seats, and enjoy each other's company cheering on the Muckdogs.

This reassuring cycle had once seemed timeless, until the elimination of Batavia's professional team had revealed it to be, in fact, quite fragile. The collective near-death experience of Muckdogs fans, who had been forced to confront the possible loss of baseball, ingrained in them a determination to preserve what was now clearly endangered by forces beyond their control.

As I pulled away from Batavia and drove deep into the early morning hours, eagerly counting down the miles remaining between me and my sleeping family, I found myself in a reflective mood. I thought back to what had at the time seemed like an offhand, almost throwaway line Bill Kauffman had said. It had been during the late innings of a blowout at Dwyer. I couldn't even remember whether the Muckdogs had been winning or losing. I did recall, though, that the grandstands had been nearly empty, it had been really cold, and

I'd been desperate to get back to the comfort of the La Quinta. As I'd fantasized about the hot chocolate I was looking forward to grabbing in the hotel lobby, Bill had said, almost to himself, "I wish the game could go on forever."

At the time, the comment had baffled me, as the game already felt like it had been going on forever, and I certainly didn't share in his desire for it to continue to drag on, one sloppy full count and wild pitch after another as the temperature continued to drop.

But tonight Bill had said something else that helped me better understand what he'd meant during that lonely vigil in the bleachers earlier in the summer. He'd told me how he "loved the conceit of Bradbury's *Dandelion Wine*," and how the ball games were sometimes like that, with "time somehow standing still, the memories bottled up like wine, and in the winter months you can go to the cellar, sip it, and bring those memories back."

Now that the season had ended, the evenings at Dwyer receding in my rearview mirror, I finally got it. It wasn't so much what was happening on the field that made the experience special (though of course loyal season ticket holders all wanted the Muckdogs to win), and to some almost sacramental. The real magic was found in the bleachers, among the fans. And it wasn't in the raucous atmosphere that had defined these final playoff games, but rather in the shared food, drink, and intimate conversation of those seemingly meaningless regular-season games of midsummer, where gathering together on a regular basis to cheer on the Muckdogs made everyone's life just a little bit better. Those ephemeral moments, so hard to capture, are the ones that satisfy the hunger we all have for acceptance and friendship, a hunger made more acute in a lonelier and more fractious America.

I knew I'd miss Batavia, and the friends I'd made in the Dwyer grandstands. While it could be demoralizing for it to sometimes feel like the America I'd imagined I was defending in the military was more distant than ever, I was grateful to have discovered in Dwyer Stadium a place where—though endangered—it endured. And for getting to know a special group of people who helped keep it alive, one summer night at a time. While I told myself I'd return a few times each summer to preserve those relationships and rediscover the peace that came over me there, I knew how life worked, and how hard it could be to follow through on even the most well-intentioned plans.

I did take some solace from the words with which Bill concluded one of his books, though. He wrote:

> I fear death because it may remove me from Batavia. I cannot conceive of a heaven that is preferable to my town, no angels more companiable than my family and friends, no celestial vistas more pleasing to my eye than the wrought-iron gates of the Batavia Cemetery, the twilight-shadowed outfield fence at Dwyer, the scarlet and orange maples that overhang Hart Street in October ... I'd just as soon stay here. Batavia needs its ghosts.

Batavia is not my hometown, and my ardor for it will never match Bill's. But my imagined afterlife isn't so different. I would reunite with departed loved ones on my grandfather's back lawn during a summer twilight just as we'd done on so many evenings gone by, welcoming over time new generations to join our ranks, once again marking the baselines with flour and playing ball as crickets chirped and the fireflies slowly began their flickering dance. Only this time the sun wouldn't set on our happiness.

There would be one new wrinkle, though ...

Every so often I would briefly take leave from this ethereal home game and join Bill, Betsey, Ginny, Ernie, Dr. Fanara, and all the rest for an away game at Dwyer, once again savoring the crepuscular hour together, the evening shadows advancing toward the infield as that familiar feeling of serenity slowly swept over us.

Acknowledgments

This book is dedicated to my grandfather Herb Bates, grandmother Helen Bates, and her sister, Marie O'Shea. Their boundless love for me as a child provided me with so many of the memories that help form this book. My grandfather taught me to love baseball and is responsible for any skill I may have developed. More generally, his love for life, and appreciation of its simple pleasures, was contagious and for that I am especially grateful.

Thank you to Chris Beha, former editor of *Harper's*, who commissioned me to write the story of the death of minor league baseball's Appalachian League that helped provide the inspiration for this book. He recognized how this was a "big" story and about far more than baseball.

Thank you to Daniel Greenberg, my literary agent, for helping to find a home for this book at Doubleday, in the reliable hands of Jason Kaufman, my wonderful editor. Thank you to Jason for hopefully helping the book realize the potential he identified in my proposal, and, just as importantly, I am grateful to them both for their unfailing optimism and encouragement during the ups and downs that are inevitable in the writing process. Thank you also to Jason's editorial assistant, Lily Dondoshansky, for her valuable editorial insights and for helping shepherd the book through the production pipeline in a timely fashion.

Janie Fleming Fransson has been with me every step of the way since I walked away from a job at the Pentagon to take the plunge into a writing career. I cannot thank her enough for her wise counsel, editorial suggestions, encouragement, and friendship. Thank you also to fellow writers Michael Patrick F. Smith and Dave Zweig for reviewing early drafts of the book and providing valuable feedback.

I cannot thank the people of Batavia and the Muckdog family enough for welcoming the bearded stranger in the Mets cap, notebook in hand, into their fold. The kindness they showed toward me was remarkable and convinced me that the people of western New York are some of the best our country has to offer.

In particular, thank you to Muckdogs owners Robbie and Nellie Nichols, and their son-in-law and Muckdogs general manager Marc Witt, for allowing me unfettered access to the club. I obviously couldn't have written the book without it.

Thank you to the Muckdogs players, coaches, and staff for being open to my questions and being so generous with their time. In particular, thank you to public address announcer Paul Spiotta for his insights into the team, the history of baseball in Batavia, and for welcoming my son, Bates, into the press box for some memories he will never forget. Also, thanks to YouTube play-by-play announcer John Carubba are in order. No one knew more about the Muckdogs than he, and I benefited enormously from the insights and invaluable material from his broadcasts and podcast that he generously shared with me. He deserves a permanent broadcasting job in professional baseball and would be a tremendous asset to any team that hires him. I hope it happens soon.

Thank you to Bill Kauffman, talented writer in his own right, who provided the initial encouragement to consider writing about the Muckdogs. When I first spoke to him, he was a possible source for a good story. I am now proud and grateful to count him as a close friend.

Thank you to Betsey Higgins and Ginny Wagner for sharing their contagious love of the Muckdogs with me, and for their kindness toward Bates on our trips to Buffalo and Batavia. I will now always associate the "crepuscular" hour with their pleasant company and hope to share many more with them in summers to come.

I consider myself blessed to have been able to spend so many hours in the Dwyer grandstands with Ernie Lawrence, who passed away after the book had been completed and was in production. He was an extraordinary human being, and memories of his faith and the loving empathy for others he exhibited every day will always remain with me. I treasure the rosary he made for me and am confident he is now looking down on Muckdogs games from above, serene smile on his face.

Thank you to Batavia entrepreneurs Matt Gray of Eli Fish, whose brewpub could always be counted on to serve up great food and tasty beers; Rob Credi of the Pub Coffee Hub, who delivered needed caffeine and nourishment with a smile; and finally Bill Hume of Foxprowl Collectables, for patiently directing me to the latest additions to his *Star Wars* and Pokémon stock in my efforts to procure the right gifts to bring home to Bates.

Thank you also to two of the biggest and most knowledgeable minor league baseball fans I have ever met, David Horne and Mark Cryan, for the countless hours they spent on the phone with me commiserating about the future of baseball as I navigated the back roads of Appalachia and western New York on reporting trips to small town ballparks. Their insights were invaluable.

Thank you to my in-laws, Mark and Connie Maple, and sister-in-law, Amanda Maple, for the countless hours spent helping my wife, Marcy, care for Bates and baby Shea while I was on the road researching this book. We truly couldn't have done it without them.

Thank you to my parents, Walter and Patricia, brothers Tad and Buddy, and sisters Nelly and Annie, for taking time out from their busy lives to read initial drafts, provide valuable feedback, and help me maintain an emotional equilibrium amid the occasional triumphs (and more numerous setbacks) that come with this line of work.

Thank you, Marcy, for your unwavering support and encouragement as I pursue this unconventional and unpredictable career path, which can be as maddening as it is rewarding. You never doubted me—even when I doubted myself—which is a testament to your character. Being married to an itinerant writer is tough, and yet you have never complained. I am so grateful to have you in my life.

And finally, Bates and Shea, you are the greatest blessings one could ever ask for, and your smiles are what make life worth living.

I can only hope that one day you will look back on your childhoods and feel the same joyful nostalgia that hopefully came across in this book as I reflected on mine.

And I hope you both grow up to be better hitters than your old man!

Author's Note

I interviewed well over one hundred people for this book. Some of those working in the business of baseball requested that our discussions be on background and not attributed to them by name, so as to not potentially damage personal relationships or professional opportunities. This was not, in my estimation, an unfounded concern, and, grateful for their time and assistance, I agreed to this request.

I also spent countless hours getting to know people in the bleachers and small towns I write about, most notably, of course, Batavia. They knew I was writing a book and were, without exception, happy to talk without reservation.

Finally, I read hundreds of articles and dozens of books related—both directly and indirectly—to the subject matter I write about. While the rabbit holes I disappeared into sometimes seemed bottomless, most of them served to deepen my general understanding in ways that hopefully benefit the book (even if they did not always generate specific material that made it into the narrative). I did note the sources of specific quotes and content drawn from external sources where applicable.